RULERS OF THE SEC

JAMES R. CROCKETT

University Press of Mississippi / Jackson

The University Press of Mississippi is the scholarly publishing agency of the Mississippi Institutions of Higher Learning: Alcorn State University, Delta State University, Jackson State University, Mississippi State University, Mississippi University for Women, Mississippi Valley State University, University of Mississippi, and University of Southern Mississippi.

www.upress.state.ms.us

The University Press of Mississippi is a member of the Association of University Presses.

Manufactured in the United States of America
First printing 2021

∞

Library of Congress Control Number: 2021938298

Harback ISBN 978-1-4968-3555-0
Epub single ISBN 978-1-4968-3556-7
Epub institutional ISBN 978-1-4968-3557-4
PDF single ISBN 978-1-4968-3558-1
PDF institutional ISBN 978-1-4968-3559-8

British Library Cataloging-in-Publication Data available

This book is dedicated to my wife, Dorothy Crockett, and our son, Clint Crockett. Dorothy is always my first reader and an unexcelled life mate. Clint inspired me to write about Mississippi sports and provided much-needed editorial support.

CONTENTS

A Note to Readers ix

Southeastern Conference Champions 1959–1966 xi

Foreword xiii

Introduction 3

★ ★ ★

CHAPTER 1 The Coaches: Babe McCarthy, Paul Gregory, Tom Swayze, and Johnny Vaught 7

CHAPTER 2 1959: The Beginning of Great Things 29

CHAPTER 3 1960: Another Banner Year 55

CHAPTER 4 1961: Another Championship, Basketball Rising 73

CHAPTER 5 1962: Maybe the Best Year in Mississippi Sports History 93

CHAPTER 6 1963: Two out of Three Again and History Made in the NCAA Basketball Tournament 123

CHAPTER 7 1964: A Baseball Championship and Freedom to Play in the College World Series 153

CHAPTER 8 1965: Mississippi State Baseball Climbs the Mountain 167

CHAPTER 9 1966: Another SEC Championship and the End of an Era 185

CHAPTER 10 The Jimmies and Joes 205

★ ★ ★

Afterword 225

Sources 229

Index 239

A NOTE TO READERS

Potential readers deserve a fair warning. This book contains a lot of numbers. In sports they keep score and they record statistics of many types that provide insights as to how well teams and individuals performed. The story I attempt to tell simply could not be conveyed without using many scores and statistics. Besides, as an accountant I like numbers. But in an attempt to be merciful, I rounded most averages.

This book is about an eight-year period, 1959–1966, when two Mississippi universities, Ole Miss and Mississippi State, won a total of 12 Southeastern Conference championships in the big three sports: 4 in basketball, 5 in baseball, and 3 in football. That is impressive because 12 is half of the 24 championships that were awarded during the eight years. The other 10 schools in the SEC had to divvy up the other half among themselves.

Ole Miss and Mississippi State did rule the SEC during that eight-year period. But not all of the schools' teams were successful. Ole Miss basketball had only one winning season during the eight-year period. The 1959–60 Rebels went 15-9; in the other seven seasons the Rebels were losers, often big-time losers, in basketball.

Over the eight years Mississippi State football was almost as bad as Ole Miss basketball. MSU had only one winning season, 1963, during which the Bulldogs went 7-2-2. State also posted a break-even season, 5-5, in 1961. Those sad tales are told in this book also.

SOUTHEASTERN CONFERENCE CHAMPIONS 1959–1966

Year	Basketball	Baseball	Football
1959	Mississippi State	Ole Miss	Georgia
1960	Auburn	Ole Miss	Ole Miss
1961	Mississippi State	LSU	Alabama/LSU
1962	Mississippi State/Kentucky	Florida	Ole Miss
1963	Mississippi State	Auburn	Ole Miss
1964	Kentucky	Ole Miss	Alabama
1965	Vanderbilt	Mississippi State	Alabama
1966	Kentucky	Mississippi State	Alabama

Championships by Schools in the SEC 1959–1966

Mississippi State—6 (1 tie)

Ole Miss—6

Alabama—4 (1 tie)

Kentucky—3 (1 tie)

Auburn—2

LSU—2 (1 tie)

Florida—1

Georgia—1

Vanderbilt—1

Georgia Tech—0

Tennessee—0

Tulane—0

Championships by States Represented in the SEC 1959–1966

Mississippi (Mississippi State and Ole Miss)—12

Alabama (Alabama and Auburn)—6

Kentucky—3

Louisiana (LSU and Tulane)—2

Georgia (Georgia and Georgia Tech)—1

Florida—1

Tennessee (Tennessee and Vanderbilt)—0

FOREWORD

This book celebrates the basketball, baseball, and football teams that represented Ole Miss and Mississippi State and excelled in the Southeastern Conference (SEC) during the late 1950s and early 1960s. Mississippi and the South in general clung to segregation in those days. The SEC consisted of 12 schools from the states of Louisiana (2), Mississippi (2), Alabama (2), Tennessee (2), Kentucky (1), Georgia (2), and Florida (1). The civil rights movement was beginning to change things but during the period covered in this book all of the SEC teams were virtually lily white. In most cases the Jim Crow culture of the South still denied African Americans the opportunity to attend SEC schools and to compete in SEC sports. Discrimination against African American athletes disadvantaged Ole Miss and Mississippi State in two ways.

Ole Miss and Mississippi State's teams that won SEC championships in baseball and basketball were denied the opportunity to compete in tournaments that determined NCAA national champions. This happened to the 1959 and 1960 Ole Miss baseball teams and to the 1959, 1961, and 1962 Mississippi State basketball teams. This problem was remedied in 1963 when the Mississippi State SEC Champion basketball team defied state authorities and participated in the NCAA basketball playoffs. After MSU's courageous stand, Ole Miss's 1964 SEC Champion baseball team and Mississippi State's 1965 and 1966 baseball teams were allowed to compete in the NCAA tournaments. The 1964 Ole Miss baseball team advanced to the NCAA's College World Series (CWS). Unfortunately, because of misguided racial attitudes that existed in the South we will never know how far Mississippi State's great 1959, 1961, and 1962 SEC basketball champions would have advanced toward the NCAA national championships. The same is true for the 1959 and 1960 SEC Champion baseball teams fielded by Ole Miss.

It is even more unfortunate that African Americans were for so long barred from competing for Ole Miss and Mississippi State and for the other SEC schools. One can only speculate about how many championships each SEC school would have won during the period covered by this book had African American athletes been allowed to compete. Such speculation is not productive. But it is appropriate to honor the athletes who broke the SEC color barrier and the first African Americans who did so for Ole Miss and Mississippi State. These pioneers overcame prejudices and made SEC sports and the South itself better.

Perry Wallace and Godfrey Dillard were the first African Americans to play basketball in the SEC. Both Wallace and Dillard played on Vanderbilt's 1966–67 freshman team. Dillard departed Vanderbilt after his freshman year, but Wallace went on to play on the Commodores' 1967–68, 1968–69, and 1969–70 varsity and to graduate from Vanderbilt. Tulane's Stephen Martin was the first African American to play baseball in the SEC. After playing on the freshman team a year earlier, on March 7, 1966, Martin played in the Green Wave varsity's opening game against Spring Hill College. Kentucky's Nathaniel "Nate" Northington and Gene Page were the first African Americans to play football in the SEC. Both Northington and Page played on the Wildcats' 1966 freshman team. Northington's first varsity game was against Ole Miss, September 30, 1967. On the night before the game Page died from complications that arose from a spinal cord injury suffered in practice 38 days earlier. In a 26-13 loss to Ole Miss, Northington suffered a shoulder injury and played only three minutes. Five games into the 1967 season Northington transferred to Western Kentucky University.

In the fall of 1970 Coolidge Ball became the first African American to play for the Ole Miss basketball team. Ball promptly led Ole

Miss to three winning seasons for the first time since 1936–1938. Ball became an All-SEC player and he is now an Ole Miss icon. Roy Coleman, who was recruited as a football player and played varsity football, became the first African American to play baseball for Ole Miss in the spring of 1976.

In 1972 Ben Williams and James Reed became the first African Americans to play football for Ole Miss. Reed played on the freshman team and Williams played on the varsity. During his varsity years Reed rushed for 1,309 yards and earned SEC Honorable Mention all three years. Williams earned All-SEC honors three times and was an All-American his senior year. Williams went on to a 10-year NFL professional career. During his senior year Ben Williams was elected Colonel Rebel by his fellow students. The Williams-Reed Football Foyer at the Olivia and Archie Manning Center honors both players' contributions.

The outstanding person that Ole Miss fans often refer to as "Gentle Ben" died at 65 in May 2020. Tributes from the Rebel Nation poured in. Athletic director Keith Carter recognized Williams's achievements for breaking the football program's race barrier and for being the first black to be elected by the student body as Colonel Reb, a campus favorite honor now called Mr. Ole Miss. Carter also said, "Gentle Ben's impact on our university, the SEC and college football as a whole is immeasurable, he was a great person, player and ambassador for our university, and will forever be beloved by Rebel Nation."

Jerry Jenkins and Larry Fry were Mississippi State's first African American basketball players. They joined the freshman team during the 1971–72 season and played on the varsity the next three seasons. During their time on the varsity Jenkins averaged scoring 19.3 points per game and Fry averaged 13.8. Jenkins was the team's second-leading scorer during his sophomore season and led the team in his junior and senior years. After finishing third in scoring during his sophomore and junior years Fry finished second in his senior year.

Harold Myles and Glen Young were the first African Americans to play varsity baseball for Mississippi State University. They suited up for the 1981 team that went to the NCAA's College World Series and finished fifth. Young also played for the Bulldog football team.

In 1969 Frank Dowsing Jr. and Robert Bell were the first African Americans to play football for Mississippi State. Dowsing, a defensive back, was named All-SEC in 1971 and 1972 and All-American in 1972. Dowsing was named a National Football Foundation Scholar Athlete and was elected by his fellow students Mister Mississippi State during his senior year. Both Dowsing and Bell were defensive players with Bell being a lineman and Dowsing a defensive back. In November 2017 MSU dedicated the Dowsing-Bell Plaza on the north side of Davis Wade Stadium that honors the legacy of these two trailblazers.

Many excellent African American athletes would wear Ole Miss's red and blue and Mississippi State's maroon and white in the years after 1966. The universities, the SEC, Mississippi, and the South are better for it.

RULERS OF THE SEC

INTRODUCTION

After writing three books about corruption in Mississippi (*Operation Pretense*, *Hands in the Till*, and *Power, Greed, Hubris*, all published by University Press of Mississippi), my wife, Dorothy, suggested that I write something positive about my beloved state. Our son, Clint Crockett, suggested that I write my memories and wrap tales about my life around my lifelong passion for Ole Miss athletics. My first thoughts were that no one other than family would be interested in the life of a CPA and professor of accountancy, but Clint convinced me that I had led an interesting life that should be recounted in print. It turned out that as I was about to finish the memories others agreed with my original idea about the public appeal of such a book and plans to try to get the memories published were squelched.

While researching Ole Miss sports for the memories project I discovered something very interesting—for eight calendar years, 1959–1966, Mississippi State University and Ole Miss ruled the Southeastern Conference (SEC) in the big three sports, basketball, baseball, and football. Now that was something very positive about Mississippi and the domination occurred during a time when events associated with the civil rights movement were justly shining a negative light on the state. In the crisis surrounding the admission of James Meredith to Ole Miss, President John F. Kennedy in his September 30, 1962, televised speech referenced Ole Miss's success on the gridiron and recognized the fact that sports success had reflected well on the state. The negative aspects about Mississippi during those years have been chronicled in hundreds of books, articles, and films. The dominance of SEC sports by Mississippi State University and Ole Miss was a bright spot during those years that also merits documentation; hence, *Rulers of the SEC: Ole Miss and Mississippi State, 1959–1966.*

The writer can truthfully say that he is and has been for a long time a fan of the athletic teams of all colleges and universities in Mississippi. I support all of the teams that represent my home state—Ole Miss, Mississippi State, Southern Mississippi, Delta State, Mississippi University for Women, Alcorn State, Jackson State, Mississippi Valley State, Mississippi College, William Carey, Millsaps, Belhaven, and Blue Mountain.

But I was born and bred a Rebel. Having my dad, Gaylen Crockett, a Rebel fan long before I was born, I really didn't have a choice but to become an Ole Miss sports fan. Being a student at Ole Miss during what Johnny Vaught called the "Glory Years" only strengthened my love for Rebel sports. I earned two degrees from Ole Miss, a baccalaureate (BBA) and a master's (MBA), and I earned a doctor of business administration (DBA) from Mississippi State. Later in my career I spent a combined twenty years as professor of accounting and director of the School of Professional Accountancy at the University of Southern Mississippi.

I was a Mississippi State fan long before I went to that great university. I followed their excellent basketball teams that featured Bailey Howell, W. D. "Red" Stroud, Doug Hutton, and several others in the late 1950s and early 1960s. In 1963 the SEC basketball champions, Mississippi State Maroons under Coach Babe McCarthy, defied state officials and snuck off to the NCAA Basketball Tournament to face a Loyola of Chicago team that featured four black starters. I distinctly remember how several Ole Miss students including me gathered in a dorm room at Ole Miss and pulled hard for the Maroons through their 10-point loss to Loyola. For as long as I can remember I have rooted for Mississippi State in every athletic contest that did not involve either Ole Miss or Southern Miss.

During my time in Hattiesburg, USM played Ole Miss in basketball and baseball and played MSU in football and baseball. I went to several of those contests and every time I left feeling like a winner.

USM won the NIT Basketball Tournament the year I arrived and later I watched as Clarence Weatherspoon dominated in the Metro Conference. Bret Favre was a freshman my first year at USM and over four years I watched him quarterback the Golden Eagles to victories over the likes of Mississippi State, Alabama, Auburn, and Florida State. Other "football powers" that USM defeated while I was there were Georgia, LSU, Nebraska, Illinois, Indiana, Louisville, Virginia Tech, and Oklahoma State. After USM defeated Oklahoma State a friend on the accounting faculty there called me and said people in Oklahoma could not believe USM won that game. I politely told him that nobody in Mississippi was at all surprised that USM beat Oklahoma State in football. How could I not be a big fan of the Golden Eagles?

While this book is about MSU and Ole Miss ruling the SEC for eight years, readers will note several references along the way to Mississippi Southern College (now the University of Southern Mississippi). While Southern Mississippi has never been a member of the SEC, it produced some great athletic teams that were highly successful during that same era. The three Mississippi schools that are all now comprehensive universities were truly dominant from the late 1950s through the mid-1960s. The writer considers those days the Camelot of college sports in Mississippi.

Mississippi State and Ole Miss are charter members of the Southeastern Conference, which was formed in 1932. From 1932 until the end of 1958 Ole Miss and Mississippi State had won a combined total of six SEC championships in the big three sports, basketball, baseball, and football. That was about to change.

Before 1959 Mississippi State had won no Southeastern Conference championships in basketball. The Maroons had won SEC baseball championships in 1948 and 1949. In 1941 State had won its only SEC football championship. That is, before 1959, Mississippi State had won a combined total of 3 SEC championships. During the 8-year period that is the focus of this book State won 6 SEC championships, 4 in basketball and 2 in baseball. Before 1959 Ole Miss had won no SEC championships in basketball or baseball. The Rebels had captured

SEC football championships in 1947, 1955, and 1956. Thus, Ole Miss, like Mississippi State, had won only 3 SEC championships. During calendar years 1959–1966 Ole Miss won 6 SEC championships, 3 in baseball and 3 in football. That is, during the period 1959–1966 Mississippi State and Ole Miss combined to win 12 SEC championships, which was twice as many as they had combined to win over the previous 26-year period.

Over an eight-year period the SEC's big three sports—basketball, baseball, and football—produced a total of 24 champions. During calendar years 1959–1966 Mississippi universities combined to win 12 of the available 24 championships, exactly half. That left 12 championships for the other 10 members of the conference to divide among themselves. During those years the SEC included universities in Florida, Georgia, Alabama, Louisiana, Tennessee, and Kentucky. Mississippi State and Ole Miss simply dominated the SEC from 1959 to 1966. This book documents that extraordinary feat and how it was accomplished.

THE COACHES

Babe McCarthy, Paul Gregory, Tom Swayze, and Johnny Vaught

"It's not about the X's and O's, it's about the Jimmies and Joes." This saying, which has been around sports a long time, may be considered a cliché, a truism, or a proverb. It is taken to mean that the quality of the players participating in a sports contest is more important than the quality of the coaching those players receive in determining who wins and who loses. X's and O's have long been related to football and basketball because coaches use those symbols to diagram plays they teach to their athletes. But, over time the term "X's and O's" has come to represent coaching in general. Regarding college sports the saying is at best a half-truth. Good athletes and excellent coaching are required to consistently win championships in college sports.

Stability at the head coaching position is recognized as an important key to success in sports. During the entire period 1959–1966 in which Mississippi State and Ole Miss combined to win 12 SEC championships (5 in baseball, 4 in basketball, and 3 in football), there was indeed coaching stability. Three of the coaches who won those championships—Paul Gregory, Tom Swayze, and Johnny Vaught—were on board during the entire period. Babe McCarthy was Mississippi State's head basketball coach for seven of the eight years.

Successful coaches have to be able to recruit and they have to be extremely knowledgeable about their sport. In addition, they must be able to communicate well with their athletes and motivate them. Although their personalities differed greatly, Paul Gregory, Babe McCarthy, Tom Swayze, and Johnny Vaught all had the traits necessary to be great coaches in spades. The quality of the Jimmies and Joes who were recruited by and played for those coaches is reflected not only in won-loss records but also by recognition garnered by individual players, which will be discussed throughout this book. The greatness of the coaches is reflected in their teams' overall won-lost records and the championships they won. The coaches' expertise is also reflected in the many coaching honors they won and their memberships in halls of fame. It is more than appropriate that all four coaches have been inducted into the Mississippi Sports Hall of Fame.

Babe McCarthy—Mississippi State University

James Harrison "Babe" McCarthy coached Mississippi State University's basketball team from 1955 to 1965. The Babe's tenure at MSU was a high point in his relatively short but full and interesting life. McCarthy's life was a very successful roundtrip from Baldwyn, Mississippi, to the world and back. He was born October 31, 1923, in Baldwyn and died of cancer there March 17, 1975, at the age of 51.

In 1939 McCarthy quarterbacked Baldwyn High School to an 8-1 record and the following spring he played on the school's basketball team, which finished second in the state. McCarthy earned both the BS and MS degrees from Mississippi State University where he did not participate in varsity sports. He was a coach at Baldwyn High School from 1947 to 1950 and his 1948 basketball team won a state championship.

McCarthy served his country a total of five years in World War II and in the Korean War. He was a transport pilot in WW II and he coached two Air Force basketball teams with combined records of

Mississippi State Basketball Coach Babe McCarthy Record 1959–1965

Overall: W-120, L-60 (67%)
SEC Record: W-66, L-36 (65%)
Four SEC Championships: 1959, 1961, 1962, 1963
SEC Coach of the Year: 1959, 1961, 1962, 1963
One NCAA Tournament Appearance: 1963 (Sweet Sixteen). Photo courtesy of Mississippi State Athletics.

54-17 during the Korean conflict. His 1952 Memphis Air Force team finished third worldwide.

During 1953 and 1954 McCarthy refereed Southeastern Conference basketball while coaching junior high teams at Meridian and Tupelo. After briefly working for Standard Oil he accepted MSU's athletic director Dudy Noble's offer to become head basketball coach at Mississippi State University. When it was noted that McCarthy's last coaching job was at a junior high school in Tupelo, Noble has been quoted as saying, "Well these guys play like a junior high team so they should have a junior high coach." Ah, but the rest is history. Mississippi State had never won an SEC basketball championship before McCarthy arrived. Ten years later when the Babe departed, MSU had four SEC championships and he had been named SEC Coach of the Year four times. Under McCarthy's tutelage the round-ballers had an overall record of 169-85; he had won 67 percent of his games. How big of a turnaround was this? In the 10 years before McCarthy's arrival MSU's record was 73-125, a winning mark of 37 percent. In those 10 years the Maroons had only two winning seasons and during both of those years the team finished one game above .500. The Babe's body of work at MSU was almost miraculous.

In the decade before McCarthy became MSU's coach, Kentucky and their great coach, Adolph Rupp, won eight SEC championships outright and tied LSU for another. To say the least, the Babe proved to be a challenge to Rupp. Their teams faced each other 10 times, Kentucky won six and MSU won four. State's victories included wins over Kentucky teams ranked third (1957), second (1962), and first (1959). Six of the games were played at Kentucky and four at MSU. Interestingly, Kentucky won at MSU once and MSU won at Kentucky once. Those two games spawned quite a tale.

In 1961 Kentucky won at State 68-62. Coach Rupp had disparaged the Maroons before the game, saying, "Hell, we could do well in the conference if we warmed up against a bunch of teachers' colleges. We can't go around playing a bunch of patsies like Mississippi State does." Before the game some MSU students put a sack containing a dead skunk under Coach Rupp's seat. Smelling the stench Rupp opened the sack, threw it on the gym floor, and walked away waving his hands. After the game Rupp nailed a black wreath along with the words REST IN PEACE on State's locker room door. The Babe secured the wreath. In 1962 the rivals played in the Blue Grass State. The second-ranked Wildcats entered the game riding a 16-game win streak and the eighth-ranked Bulldogs entered with an 18-1 record. MSU frustrated Kentucky the whole game with a slowdown strategy and walked away with a 49-44 victory, State's first win in Lexington since 1924. MSU manager Jimmy Wise had smuggled the wreath into Memorial Gymnasium under his raincoat. Lifted by his players, the Babe placed the wreath on the Wildcats' goal and cut down the nets.

There was no love lost between the Wildcats and Maroons during a public feud that lasted from the mid-1950s to the mid-1960s. But Kentucky's coach Adolph Rupp had only good things to say about Babe McCarthy just before and after his death. MSU honored McCarthy when they played Kentucky at home in March 1975. The Babe was dying and too sick to be there but his old archrival was there. Coach Rupp participated in the ceremonies and afterward said, "I had some trouble getting transportation. . . . But now I'm so glad I went down there. I talked (via TV) for three of four minutes to Babe, and I hope he got to see it." After McCarthy died, Rupp was quoted as saying, "Babe was a great competitor." Coach Rupp died in 1977, two years after the Babe. Rupp's record was 876-190, which means he won 82 percent of his games over his career that lasted four decades. It is doubtful that any other coach who faced Rupp's teams 10 or more times won 40 percent of their games.

Babe McCarthy is remembered and honored today for his audacious and courageous actions to assure that his 1963 SEC champions played in the integrated NCAA Men's Division I Basketball Tournament. Jones Junior College had played California's Compton Junior College in the 1955 Junior Rose Bowl. The game, which decided the junior college national championship, was the first time a Mississippi school at any level played an integrated opponent. Jones lost 22-13 before a crowd of 58,132 at the Rose Bowl in Pasadena, California. Compton's squad included eight African American players, and many white Mississippians were not pleased. That same year Mississippi legislators and educational leaders reached a "gentlemen's agreement" that the state's schools would not play integrated teams. MSU's 1959, 1961, and 1962 SEC Champion teams had to decline invitations to the NCAA tournament.

At the risk of their jobs MSU president Dean Colvard and Coach McCarthy determined to do whatever it took to assure that the 1963 SEC champions played in the NCAA tournament. On March 2, 1963, President Colvard accepted the automatic bid to the tournament that had been earned by the Babe and his players. McCarthy went public in TV interviews and on the radio, saying that he would be heartsick if his team was denied for the fourth time an opportunity to compete in the NCAA tournament. Before State's last regular-season game President Colvard issued a statement that "unless hindered by a competent authority" the team would play in the tournament. Well, "competent authority" and Mississippi media tried.

The MSU Bulldogs were scheduled to play the Loyola of Chicago Ramblers in their first game in the tournament. On March 7 the *Jackson Daily News* ran a picture of the Loyola starters, four of whom were African Americans. Under the picture the editor wrote, "Readers may want to clip the photo of the Loyola team and mail it today to the board of trustees of the institutions of higher learning." On March 13, the day before the team was scheduled to travel to the tournament, a court became involved. Former state senator B. W. Lawson and state senator Billy Mitts filed a suit in a Hinds County Court that resulted in an injunction prohibiting the MSU team from leaving the state. After the recent riot at Ole Miss over the admission of its first black student, James Meredith, Governor Ross Barnett chose to sit this one out. Not by a long shot did all Mississippians oppose MSU playing in the NCAA tournament. The team participated in a pep rally on campus where effigies of the filers of the suit were hung.

Law enforcement officers who were dispatched to Starkville to serve the injunction were expected to arrive by 10 p.m. Wednesday, March 13, and the team was scheduled to depart Thursday at 8:30 a.m. The powers that be at MSU put a sophisticated plan in place to thwart efforts to stop the team from leaving the state. The athletic director, assistant athletic director, and head coach snuck off to Memphis during the night and flew to Nashville the next day. The varsity players hid in a dormitory that night. The next day the freshman team was sent to the airport posing as the varsity. They went early and were never intercepted by the law officers. The varsity soon arrived at the airport and boarded a private plane while the propellers were turning and flew to Nashville where they connected with McCarthy and the two administrators. The contingent flew commercial to East Lansing, Michigan, where the NCAA Mideast Regional Tournament was to be played.

Doug Hutton, a junior standout on the MSU team, told the writer that the people of East Lansing were great hosts and he thought they actually favored the Bulldogs. Hutton also told a funny story about landing in the city. A band met the plane as it arrived, but they didn't know whether the Mississippi State Bulldogs or the Georgia Tech Yellowjackets were on the plane. Georgia Tech, which finished second in the SEC, would have represented the conference had MSU again declined an invitation to play in the NCAA tournament. The band was prepared to play either team's fight song, "Rambling Wreck" for

Tech or "Hail State" for MSU. So as soon as the players started getting off the plane, a band representative came over to ask whether they from Mississippi State or Georgia Tech. I would love to have heard the "Hail State" that the band played!

On March 15, 1963, the Mississippi State University Bulldogs played the Loyola of Chicago Ramblers in their first game of the NCAA Mideast Regional. Loyola had already defeated Tennessee Tech 111-42 in a first-round game played in Evanston, Illinois. The game has become an important part of sports and civil rights history. In 2015 it was named one of the Top 25 defining moments in college sports history. The drama surrounding it and the game itself have been extensively documented by the media including two books and a documentary. There is an iconic picture of the two centers, one black and one white, shaking hands before the tipoff. Loyola started four black players against the all-white Bulldogs. Mississippi State was led by a trio of seniors, Leland Mitchell, Joe Dan Gold, and W. D. (Red) Stroud, who had won three SEC championships. Loyola won that contest 61-51 and went on to win the 25-team tournament, defeating Cincinnati 60-58 in overtime in the final game. The NCAA champions finished with a final record of 29-2. Led by All-American Jerry Harkness, the Ramblers outscored their opponents by an average of 24 points per game for the season. Harkness averaged 21 points per game and 7 rebounds. Five Loyola players averaged scoring in double figures.

State finished third in the NCAA Mideast Regional by defeating Bowling Green State of Ohio 65-60. Bowling Green, the Mid-American Conference champions, started three African Americans including the great 6'11" All-American Nate Thurmond. The MSU players made a good showing against the eventual national champions and proved they belonged in the upper echelon of college basketball. Coach McCarthy and his squad also helped change Mississippi for the better. This is being written in spring of 2019 and all of the starters on this year's MSU basketball team are African Americans.

McCarthy resigned from Mississippi State in 1965. He returned to coaching in 1966 as head basketball coach at George Washington

University. His record at GWU was 6-18 and he didn't stay for a second season. In 1967 he began coaching the New Orleans Buccaneers in the American Basketball Association. Over a seven-year period he coached four ABA teams and was named Coach of the Year in 1969 and 1974. He was the first ABA coach to win 200 games and ended his ABA career with a 480-484 record. Two great players, Artis Gilmore and Dan Issel, led McCarthy's 1973–74 Kentucky Colonels to a 53-31 record and a second-place finish. Following that season Babe McCarthy shared Coach of the Year honors with Coach Joe Mullaney of the Utah Stars but McCarthy was later fired by the Colonels. The Babe would be dead within a year.

This sketch of James Harrison McCarthy needs to close on a light note. The Babe was a funny guy and quite a character who had a way with words and was known as the Magnolia Mouth. Here is a sample of his many quips:

> "Boy, are you planning to play basketball this year?" The Babe was talking to Doug Hutton after finding out that Hutton had not gotten the flu shot McCarthy had told him to.
>
> "Boy, I gotta tell you, you gotta come out at 'em like a bitin' sow."
>
> "My old pappy used to tell me the sun don't shine on the same dog's butt every day."
>
> "Now, let's cloud up and rain all over 'em."
>
> "Why panic at five in the mornin' because it's still dark out?"
>
> "They can't score when we've got the ball."

Paul Gregory—Mississippi State University

Paul (Pop) Gregory was born in Tomnolen, Mississippi, in June 1908 and died in Southaven, Mississippi, in September 1999. His 91-year life centered around sports and he saw many successes. Gregory lettered in baseball, basketball, and football at Mississippi State from 1926 to 1930. He pitched for the class A minor league Atlanta Crackers in 1931 and for the Chicago White Sox in 1931 and 1932. Over his two-year

Mississippi State University Baseball Coach Paul Gregory

Overall: W-131, L-80 (62%)
SEC Record: W-72, L-47 (61%)
Two SEC Championships: 1965, 1966
SEC Western Division Champions: 1962
SEC Baseball Coach of the Year: 1965, 1966. Photo courtesy of Mississippi State Athletics.

major league career, he compiled a 9-14 record and a 4.74 earned run average. The highlight of his brief time in the majors was a 1933 victory over Red Ruffing and the New York Yankees. In that game Gregory gave up only one run in seven plus innings and retired Babe Ruth five consecutive times. In 1934 he was back in the minors where he spent nine years before joining the US Navy in 1943. Discharged from the navy at the end of World War II, he returned to minor league baseball for the 1946 and 1947 seasons.

Mississippi State athletic director Dudy Noble hired Gregory to coach the university's basketball team in 1947. Coaching basketball turned out not to be Gregory's strong suit. Over nine seasons his basketball teams won only 58 games and lost 100. He had only two winning seasons 1951–52 (12-11) and 1953–54 (11-10). His best record against SEC competition was 6-10, which were marks posted by both his 1947–48 and 1949–50 squads. Dudy Noble made a brilliant move in 1955 when he hired Babe McCarthy as head basketball coach and named Paul Gregory head baseball coach. Gregory's accomplishments as a baseball coach and McCarthy's as a basketball coach would put both men in the Mississippi Sports Hall of Fame.

Gregory was head baseball coach at Mississippi State for 17 years, 1957–1974. He won 62 percent of his games and compiled an overall record of 328-200-1. His 1962 team lost in the SEC championship series, but he went on to win four SEC championships (1965, 1966, 1970, 1971). During the time period focused on here, 1959–1966, his record was 131-80-1 overall and 72-47-1 in the SEC. Gregory was named SEC Baseball Coach of the Year four times. In 1977 he was inducted into the American Baseball Coaches Hall of Fame, and he was named to the Mississippi Sports Hall of Fame in 1982.

There is no-tried-and-true-correct template for how one should approach the job of being a head coach in any college sport. Some successful coaches are screamers, and they appear to be trying to intimidate their players into performing at the height of their potential. Others, such as Johnny Vaught, never raise their voice. Some are encouragers and like to praise good performances while pointing out and demonstrating in nonintimidating ways how weak facets of a player's performance can be improved. Some successful coaches are hyper and some are laid back. Some stress technical proficiency while others are more motivational.

How did Paul Gregory become such a successful baseball coach when he had been, to put it politely, an unsuccessful basketball coach? I suspected that it was the Jimmies and Joes, not the X's and O's. That is, he had coached good baseball players but not-so-good basketball players. Interviews with Frank Montgomery and Doug Hutton, who pitched for Gregory during the 1960–1964 time period, confirmed what I had suspected. The players nicknamed Gregory "Square Deal," often shortened to "Deal." As he would recruit a player to come to MSU to play baseball, he would always say something like this, "If you come to Mississippi State, I promise you a square deal."

Well, whether it was the square deal gambit or not, Gregory brought some outstanding baseball talent to Mississippi State. From 1959 to 1963 State signed four pitchers from Jackson, Guy Parker, Frank

Montgomery, Claude Reeder, and Frank Chambers, and a catcher, Charles Smith. He also secured the services of pitcher Doug Hutton from nearby Clinton, who went to State on a basketball scholarship. These six players were major contributors to State's baseball success. All of them had been well coached in high school. Reeder, Smith, and Chambers played for the great Robert "Cooter" Berry at Jackson Central. Parker and Montgomery had been coached at Jackson Murrah by Kermit "Rosey" Davis, and Hutton had been coached at Clinton High School by Roy Burkett. All six of them were coached in American Legion Baseball by Robert Berry. Billy Ray Lea, my best friend and roommate at Ole Miss for three years, played freshman baseball at MSU in 1961 and batted .500. He had played at Jackson Central and Legion ball under Coach Berry and, had he not decided to change his major to pharmacy and transfer to Ole Miss, he could have been a big part of MSU baseball.

Starting with good athletes who had usually been well coached in high school, Gregory did very little in the way of teaching fundamentals. His practices were informal as he would often ask his pitchers, "Who wants to pitch batting practice today?" Gregory would also say to his pitchers, "Tell me when you are ready to pitch or start," and he would put them in games when they said they were ready. This style worked for Paul Gregory when he coached baseball.

Tom Swayze—Ole Miss

Thomas King Swayze was born March 15, 1909, in Yazoo City, Mississippi, and died at the age of 93 in Oxford, Mississippi, February 1, 2003. He graduated from Raymondville, Texas, High School and attended Edinburg Junior College in south Texas. Young Tom Swayze returned to Mississippi and enrolled at Ole Miss in 1929. While an undergraduate at Ole Miss, Swayze played end on the football team and was a left-handed pitcher on the baseball team. He earned three letters in football and four in baseball. Swayze played for the South

Ole Miss Baseball Coach Tom Swayze Record 1959–1966

Overall: W-141, L-67 (68%)
SEC Record: W-80, L-37(68%)
Three SEC Championships: 1959, 1960, 1964
SEC Western Division Champion: 1963
SEC Baseball Coach of the Year: 1959, 1960
College World Series (1964). Ole Miss Athletics Photo.

team in the 1932 North-South All Star Football Game in Miami. After graduating from Ole Miss in 1933, Swayze played professional and semiprofessional baseball for several years in Tennessee, Mississippi, Georgia, North Carolina, and Canada.

When his baseball playing days ended, Swayze began his coaching career as a football coach at Benoit, Mississippi. He left coaching briefly and entered the insurance business and later worked for a tire recapping plant in Yazoo City. Moving to Moss Point, Mississippi, Swayze coached both basketball and football and became a high school principal. He soon returned to Ole Miss where he would leave his mark on athletics in Mississippi and the SEC like no other person ever has.

Ole Miss head football coach Johnny Vaught hired Swayze as an assistant in 1947. His newly created job was contact man and field representative. That meant Swayze was the South's first football recruiter. He would remain an assistant football coach and recruiter until 1971. His nose for talent and recruiting skills were instrumental in building and maintaining the football juggernaut that was Ole Miss football under Johnny Vaught. The NCAA Record Book shows that during the time Swayze served as recruiting coordinator Ole Miss won six

SEC football championships (1947, 1954, 1955, 1960, 1962, 1963) and a share of three national championships (1959, 1960, 1962). Ole Miss football never won an SEC or national football championship before 1947 nor has it after 1971. When his longtime colleague died, Coach Vaught had this to say about him, "Tom was a wonderful man and a great friend of mine. He meant so much to our football program and the University. He was a shrewd recruiter and had the ability to see the potential in a player better than any other coach I have known."

Tom Swayze was an assistant coach under Johnny Vaught, but he did not live in the great football coach's shadow. Swayze cast a long shadow himself as a highly successful head coach. He made his mark as the University of Mississippi's head baseball coach. Swayze served in that capacity for 21 seasons (1951–1971), and he posted a 361-201-2 overall record and a 195-120-1 SEC record. That is, he won 64 percent of all of his games and 62 percent of his SEC encounters. Eighteen of Swayze's teams had winning records. Under Swayze's coaching, Ole Miss baseball won four SEC championships (1959, 1960, 1964, and 1969). He was named SEC Coach of the Year for each of those championship years. The 1967 Rebels lost to Auburn in the SEC championship series. Swayze's teams posted a 10-1 record in three NCAA District III tournaments as they advanced to the College World Series in 1956, 1964, and 1969. He was named NCAA District III Coach of the Year all three years.

Coach Swayze developed 38 All-SEC players, 8 All-District players, and 4 All-Americans, Jake Gibbs, Don Kessinger, Bernie Schreiber, and Jimmy Yawn. Five of Swayze's players went on to play major league baseball, Jake Gibbs, Don Kessinger, Jack Reed, Joe Gibbon, and Steve Dillard. This was written in February 2019 and the great Joe Gibbon died this month. Gibbon pitched for Coach Swayze at Ole Miss and played basketball for Coach Bonnie Graham. In 1956 Gibbon led the Rebels to the College World Series. In 1957 Gibbon was the second highest scorer in college basketball, averaging 30 points a game. He went on to appear in 400 major league baseball games over a 13-year career.

Jake Gibbs

Football: 1959 and 1960
(All-American 1960)
Baseball: 1959, 1960, 1961
(All-American 1960, 1961).
Ole Miss Athletics Photo.

During his 16 major league seasons Don Kessinger was a National League All-Star six times. Kessinger told this writer that several major league coaches told him that he had the best fundamentals of any player they had ever coached. He attributed that to having played for Coach Swayze at Ole Miss. Don Kessinger was later Ole Miss's head baseball coach and his two sons, Keith and Kevin, and grandson Grae have all starred for the Rebels on the baseball field.

When Swayze was head coach, the baseball Rebels played in the shadow of Vaught-Hemmingway Stadium on All-American Drive. The writer has many pleasant memories of going to baseball games there in the 1960s. In 1976 the baseball diamond was named Swayze Field. When the new Oxford-University Stadium opened in 1989 its playing surface was named Swayze Field. These days Ole Miss baseball fans are said to go "Swayze Crazy" during the baseball season.

Robert Khayat, who was twice named All-SEC catcher, was the chancellor of the university when Tom Swayze died. Khayat had this to say about his former coach:

> Coach Tom Swayze devoted his life to young people and the University of Mississippi. An outstanding student-athlete and then later as

> a recruiting coordinator for football and head baseball coach, he was a major contributor to the extraordinary success of Ole Miss football and baseball. From 1947 to his retirement from coaching in 1971, the university enjoyed great success in athletics. Continuing his commitment to the University, he led the Loyalty Foundation in its infancy to a position of strength and a critical funding source for athletics. His values and competitive spirit inspired thousands of student-athletes and was the basis for naming the baseball field in his honor. The University community is profoundly grateful for his many years of service and we mourn his passing.

Two of Coach Swayze's best teams, the 1959 and the 1960 Rebels, were denied the opportunity to play in the NCAA District III tournament. The sad tale of how Mississippi's attitude about racial integration prevented those teams from playing in the district tournament and possibly advancing to the College World series is related in chapters 2 and 3.

Coach Tom Swayze's life and career are memorialized in three halls of fame. He was inducted into the Mississippi Sports Hall of Fame in 1978 and the American Association of College Baseball Coaches Hall of Fame in 1982. He was also named a charter member of the Ole Miss Sports Hall of Fame in 1986.

As has been noted, Coach Vaught indicated that Coach Swayze "had the ability to see the potential in a player better than any other coach I have known." It appears that as he was evaluating an athlete's football potential he noted baseball potential also. His baseball teams were jam packed with football players. Their numbers include Robert Khayat, Jake Gibbs, Doug Elmore, Freddie Roberts, Dave Jennings, and Rodney Mattina.

In the early 1970s Swayze was director of the Ole Miss Loyalty Foundation, which supports Ole Miss Sports. He returned to Ole Miss baseball as a volunteer coach for the 1986–1988 seasons. Coach Swayze's daughter Kay, an Ole Miss Beauty, married former Rebel football player Warner Alford, who would go on to serve several years as the university's athletic director.

Ole Miss Football Coach John Vaught Record 1959–1966

Overall: W-66, L-16, T-4 (80%)
Three SEC Championships: 1960, 1962, 1963
SEC Record: W-37, L-9, T-3
SEC Coach of the Year: 1960, 1962
Three National Championships recognized by the NCAA: 1959, 1960, 1962
Bowl Record: 4 Wins, 4 Losses (3 Sugar Bowls and 1 Liberty Bowl; 1 Sugar Bowl, 1 Cotton Bowl, and 2 Bluebonnet Bowls). Ole Miss Athletics Photo.

John (Johnny) Vaught—Ole Miss Football

> John Howard Vaught should inherit the copyright on the Boy Scout motto: Be Prepared.
>
> In his coaching days at Ole Miss Vaught studied football game film and scouting reports with the dedication of a 12th century monk putting together a religious tract. For Vaught it was a sin to field a Rebel team uncertain about the toughness and the tendencies of the enemy. He wanted all his scouts to be as observant as Mark Brumbelow, who in the words of team manager Bubba Blackwell, "could tell Vaught how many knots a player had in his shoelaces."
>
> **—William W. Sorrels and Charles Cavagnaro**

Ole Miss Rebels Mississippi Football, 1976

John Howard Vaught was born to Rufus and Sally Vaught May 6, 1909, on their 640-acre ranch just outside the little town of Ingleside, Texas. He was the middle child of a brood of 11 children. He went through the eighth grade at Ingleside and then went to Fort Worth to work and live with his grandmother Gertrude Harris. He got a job as a redcap at a train depot. Vaught appreciated his grandmother, who encouraged him to go back to school and taught him to do things right. "Grandmother wouldn't tolerate anything that was half done," Vaught said. "She was a disciplinarian and a tremendous influence on my life."

Vaught did well for himself at Polytechnic High School where he encountered another disciplinarian, football coach Rube Leissner. Young Johnny's first-ever football game was a disaster; Polytechnic lost big to the Masonic Home, an orphanage. That defeat stayed seared in Vaught's mind because it taught him to hate losing. Johnny's grandmother monitored his grades closely and he liked to study. He was elected president of his senior class and graduated as valedictorian. Vaught played several different positions on the football field and caught the eye of TCU's coach Francis Schmidt, who offered him a football-work scholarship. Texas A&M's Matty Bell made a similar offer. Vaught chose TCU, which was about five miles from his grandmother's house.

It seemed that Johnny was always under the influence of people who demanded a lot. Schmidt was said to be a perfectionist who once ran a play numbered 72 seventy-two times in practice because a player had not run it correctly. Vaught was a freshman in 1929 when Mark Brumbelow, the Horn Frogs' captain, led TCU to an undefeated season. Schmidt's five-year record at TCU was 46-5-3. Coach Schmidt made Vaught a guard where he was coached by Ray (Bear) Wolf. In his senior year of 1932 Vaught was captain of a TCU team that went undefeated and won the Southwest Conference championship. The 1932 SWC champs scored 256 points and gave up 24. After his senior season Vaught was named TCU's first All-American.

Coach Schmidt introduced Vaught to game films, and the student immediately recognized their value and he began to think of a coaching career. Vaught thought Schmidt was the best coach in the country and far ahead of everybody else offensively. After graduating from TCU Vaught coached high school ball at North Side High in Fort Worth for a year and then went to work for Graybar Electric in

Houston. But Vaught's old position coach Bear Wolf came calling in 1936. Wolf had been named head coach at the University of North Carolina and he hired Vaught to be his line coach. That job lasted six years during which UNC went 38-17-3, and the ever-learning Vaught picked up a master's degree. On a 1938 trip back to Fort Worth, Vaught got reacquainted with a family friend, Johnsie Stinson, and in 1939 the two got married in Broadway Baptist Church in Fort Worth. Johnsie became a football fan and stood by her man the rest of her life.

When the Japanese bombed Pearl Harbor and pulled a reluctant United States into World War II, Johnny Vaught volunteered to serve in the navy. He was sent to Annapolis for six weeks to train for the Pre-Flight and Physical Training Section, the V-5 program. Under the leadership of Lieutenant Commander Tom Hamilton, a former football player and coach at the Naval Academy, the navy had decided to use football to train fliers. Coach Vaught heard Hamilton say to the first indoctrination class, "There are certain qualities desirable in an aviator which can be developed through the medium of football."

V-5 programs were established at several universities and colleges across the country. Here is what Vaught wrote in his book *Rebel Coach* about the effect on college football:

> Modern football owes much of its popularity explosion to Hamilton and the men who became Cloudbusters and Seahawks. His idea created a cross-pollination of coaching skills unlike anything the country had ever seen. Day after day at the pre-flight schools—Georgia, North Carolina, Iowa, California, St. Mary's and many more—coaches from each great section of the nation worked together and picked each other's minds. Techniques and ideas learned from the V-5 program would bear fruit in peacetime at Ole Miss and other schools.

In 1943 Vaught was assigned to Rensselaer Polytechnic Institute (RPI) in Troy, New York, where he was put in charge of cadets just entering the program and did no coaching. There he met RPI's athletic trainer, Wesley I. (Doc) Knight, who volunteered to help without pay. In 1947 Doc Knight would follow Vaught to Ole Miss where he became a legendary and much-loved head trainer. In 1944 Vaught was promoted to the rank of lieutenant commander and was put in charge of the physical training program at Corpus Christi Naval Air Station. Vaught learned from the likes of Tom Hamilton; Jim Crowley, one of the four horsemen of Notre Dame and head coach at Michigan State and Fordham; and Larry (Moon) Mullins, who had played fullback for Knute Rockne at Notre Dame and would coach three different college football teams and serve as athletic director at two universities. Mullins had learned the split-T from Missouri's Don Faurot and Oklahoma's Bud Wilkinson at Iowa Pre-flight. Other coaches associated with the V-5 program included Paul Bryant, Harold Drew, Homer Jones, Buster Poole, and Parker Hill. When he returned to civilian life in 1946 Johnny Vaught, who soaked up football knowledge like a sponge, was well prepared to become a successful head coach. No doubt some of the coaches associated with the V-5 program also learned from a certain Mr. John Vaught.

Vaught departed the navy February 2, 1946, with job offers from Red Drew at Ole Miss; Ray Wolf, then at Florida; and Moon Mullins at St. Mary's. Within a month he had traveled to Oxford and accepted the position of line coach at Ole Miss. Even with the great Charlie Conerly playing tailback, Ole Miss suffered through a miserable 1946 season going 2-7 overall and 1-6 in the SEC. One of the victories was over Arkansas 9-7. Coach Red Drew gave Vaught much credit for that victory because of the excellent scouting report he had produced after watching the Hogs lose to Texas 20-0. When Coach Drew left for Alabama in 1947 he asked Vaught to go with him but Vaught decided to stay at Ole Miss. Several members of the football team including Conerly and several influential alumni soon vocally supported Vaught for the vacant head coaching position at Ole Miss. Athletic director Tad Smith, who was already talking to Vaught about the job, sealed a hand-shake agreement for Johnny Vaught to become the University of Mississippi's head football coach on January 14, 1947. Few if any better hires have been made in college sports.

The rest is history. When Vaught took over, Ole Miss had played in the SEC since its founding in 1933 and had never won more than three conference games in a season. In 1947 Coach Vaught would put a stop to that. Led by Charlie Conerly, Ole Miss's first Heisman Trophy candidate, Vaught's first Rebel team posted a 9-2 record and won the SEC championship with a 6-1 conference mark. That was just the beginning. From 1947 through 1973 Vaught's Ole Miss Rebels won 75 percent of their games, posting a 190-61-12 record. Coach Vaught's 1959, 1960, and 1962 teams were named national champions by one or more rating organizations. In his 24-year head coaching career, Vaught's Rebels had only one losing season. Vaught won six SEC championships, three of which were won during the 1959–1966 period focused on in this book. Johnny Vaught was named SEC Coach of the Year six times. No other Ole Miss coach has ever won an SEC football championship.

Coach Vaught introduced the split-T formation to the South and with the athletic quarterbacks he coached made the sprint-out pass popular. Vaught spent a lot of time with his quarterbacks and involved them in game planning. In fact, he might have been the original "quarterback whisperer." Think of some of the quarterbacks who prospered under his tutelage—Charlie Conerly, Eagle Day, Raymond Brown, Bobby Franklin, Jake Gibbs, Doug Elmore, Glynn Griffing, Perry Lee Dunn, Jim Weatherly, Archie Manning, and Norris Weese. In his book *Midnight Train*, famed songwriter and former Rebel quarterback Jim Weatherly wrote about how great a coach Vaught was. He emphasized the amount of time Vaught spent with his quarterbacks and noted one big difference between him and some other famous coaches—Vaught never raised his voice, probably because he didn't have to.

During the decade of the 1950s Vaught's Rebels won 78 percent of their games, going 80-21-5, a record surpassed only by Oklahoma. In the 1960s the Rebels won 76 percent of their games, posting a 72-20-6 mark, which was the fourth best in the country. Vaught's home field record is even more impressive. His teams compiled a 57-6-2 record on campus, a 90 percent mark. The Rebels were undefeated in Oxford during a 33-game win streak that lasted from 1952 to 1964. Vaught's teams were ranked dozens of times in the AP and UPI polls. From 1957 to 1971 his Rebels played in 15 straight bowl games, a national record at the time. Twenty-six first-team All-Americans played for Coach Vaught and four players finished in the top five in the Heisman Trophy voting: Charlie Conerly, Charlie Flowers, Jake Gibbs, and Archie Manning.

As has been noted Coach Vaught was a student and he was well educated. He taught his players the importance of a good education. Chancellor Porter Fortune said on Johnny Vaught Day in 1971, "Many coaches train their boys to become football players. John Vaught trained boys to become men, while imparting to them some of his important skills as an athlete." As will be emphasized in chapter 2, which deals with the 1959 football team, Vaught's players were successful in life as well as football.

In a 2016 article published by *Mississippi Today*, Rick Cleveland wrote about the rivalry between Coach Vaught and Paul (Bear) Bryant. Noting the closeness of the rivalry, Cleveland wrote, "Bryant was one of just a few coaches with a winning record against Vaught—and that, by the most narrow of margins. Bryant was 7-6-1 vs. Vaught. That included 2-4-1 when Bryant was at Kentucky and 5-2 at Alabama." Cleveland noted that Vaught and Bryant were close friends and he quoted Vaught as saying, "I always loved to coach against him [Bryant] because it was such a challenge. He was a good friend and as good a coach as there was. I miss him. He died way too soon." Bryant was quoted as having said of Vaught, "Johnny's teams were always ready to play. They were always well-prepared and Johnny was always a gentleman, in victory or defeat." Only one other SEC coach had a winning record against Vaught, Tennessee's Robert Neyland, who went 3-2 against Vaught's Rebels.

1959

The Beginning of Great Things

1959 SEC Basketball Champion—Mississippi State
1959 SEC Baseball Champion—Ole Miss
1959 SEC Football Champion—Georgia
Final score: Mississippi schools 2 SEC championships, all other SEC schools 1

The Champions

1959 SEC Basketball Champions—Mississippi State University

Mississippi's eight-year dominance of the Southeastern Conference in the big three sports of basketball, baseball, and football began with Mississippi State University winning the SEC basketball championship in 1959.

After a decade of winning only 37 percent of its basketball games, Mississippi State hired James Harrison (Babe) McCarthy as its head coach. The Babe went to work recruiting, and both MSU and SEC basketball were about to change dramatically. McCarthy's first recruiting

Bailey Howell

One of the greatest college basketball players of his generation, Bailey Howell led Mississippi State to an overall record of 24-1 during the 1958–59 season. He averaged 27.5 points and 15.2 rebounds while leading MSU to an SEC championship. As one of the top five players in the country he was named first-team All-American. Photo courtesy of Mississippi State Athletics.

class included Bailey Howell, who played his high school basketball in Tennessee. Playing at Middleton High School, Howell was all-conference three times, all-state twice, and All-American as a senior. During his senior year the 6'7" Howell averaged 31 points per game and was recruited by Mississippi State, Ole Miss, Kentucky, Memphis State, Vanderbilt, and Tennessee. By the end of the 1959 season Babe McCarthy and Bailey Howell had led Mississippi State basketball to new heights.

McCarthy's first MSU team finished the 1955–56 season12-12 overall and 6-8 in the conference. When Bailey Howell joined the varsity as a sophomore for the 1956–57 season the Maroons went 17-8 overall and 9-5 in the SEC. During the 1957–58 season the Maroons improved to 20-5 overall and 9-5 in the SEC. This steadily improving performance culminated in a 24-1 overall record and 13-1 SEC mark for the 1958–59 season when Howell was a senior.

By the time the 1958–59 season arrived, McCarthy had surrounded Howell with excellent teammates. The Associated Press Pre-Season Poll ranked State eighth in the nation. The starting five—Bailey Howell, Charles Hull, Jerry Graves, Jerry Keeton, and Ted Usher—were outstanding. Four of the five averaged scoring in double figures, Howell 28, Hull 11, Keaton and Graves 10. Usher, the other starter, averaged 9 points per game. Howell made 50 percent of his field-goal attempts, Hull 44, Graves 41, Keeton 46, and Usher 47. Their free-throw percentages were Howell 77, Hull 80, Graves 77, Keeton 77, and Usher 74. Few, if any, starting fives today generate comparable numbers.

State was still ranked eighth when they played their first SEC game against Auburn January 3, 1959. Going into the Auburn game the Maroons were 9-0. Mississippi State had won the Sugar Bowl Tournament and the pre-conference games included victories over Maryland 56-45 and Memphis State 73-55 in that tournament.

State lost its first SEC game to ninth-ranked Auburn by a lopsided score. The next day a headline in the sports section of the *Clarion-Ledger* read, "State Cagers Mauled by Auburn 97 to 66." State made only 27 percent of its field-goal attempts while the Tigers made 54 percent of their shots from their home floor. Although Bailey Howell scored 19 points, he did not shoot well. He made only 7 of 27 shots from the floor and 5 of 11 from the free-throw line. Howell was the only Maroon to score in double figures, while four of Auburn's players scored 10 or more points. Auburn's zone defense, which collapsed on Howell, was very effective. As the final score shows, State's defense left a lot to be desired. The Maroons' SEC prospects looked dim at this point. But the results of that game were far from an omen of things to come. That loss proved to be the only loss Mississippi State would suffer all season.

The Maroons made a return trip to Alabama on January 5 to play the Crimson Tide in Tuscaloosa. This time the results were significantly different as State left town with their tenth victory of the season and their SEC slate squared at 1-1. In the 60-47 win, four MSU players scored in double digits led by a rejuvenated Bailey Howell, who poured in 24 points. The Maroons' shooting touch returned as they shot 47 percent from the field compared to Alabama's 43 percent. State took 15 more free throws than Alabama (39 vs. 24) and made 11 more points from the line. No doubt the Babe had his chargers practicing shooting and defense before the game. After the loss to Auburn and the victory over Alabama MSU dropped to twelfth in the AP Poll.

State's next game was played in Starkville against Georgia Tech on January 10. MSU posted its twenty-fourth straight win at home dispatching the Yellowjackets 75-67. Bailey Howell scored 31 points and grabbed 15 rebounds. Charles Hull and Jerry Keeton chipped in with 11 and 14 points. Three Yellowjackets also scored in double digits but their high scorer, Bud Blemker, tallied only 14 points. The game was won at the free-throw line where State made 35 of 44 attempts, while the Yellowjackets connected on 21 of 29. The contest was not as close as the final score indicates; with 3 minutes and 33 seconds left, the Maroons led by 20 points, then came wholesale substitution by both teams.

The Vanderbilt Commodores, who had beaten number-one-ranked Kentucky the week before in Nashville, rolled into Starkville January 12. Led by Bailey Howell's 26 points the Maroons took the air out of the Commodores sails with an 83-65 victory. Howell scored 12 points in the first half despite not scoring during the first seven minutes and heading to the bench with three fouls with 1:40 left in the half. Vanderbilt's top scorer, Jim Henry, did not play because of an injury. Nevertheless, four of Vandy's players posted double figures with their high scorer Ben Rowan scoring 15 points. MSU also had four players in double figures, Howell 26, Keeton 20, Graves 17, and Hull 17. State's rebounding edge, 51-21, allowed the Maroons to dominate the game. With the victory, State ranked twelfth nationally in the AP poll and stood 12-1 overall and 3-1 in the conference.

In-state rival Ole Miss came to Starkville January 17, and the results were not pretty for the visitors. Before a full gym State simply dominated the Rebels by a score of 87 to 58. It was State's twenty-sixth consecutive home-court win. Once again Bailey Howell led State with 34 points, while three other Maroons scored in double figures. Howell simply dominated, canning 12 of 24 field goals and 10 of 12 from the free-throw line. Jack Waters, who fouled out with 4 minutes and 39 seconds left in the game, led the Rebels scoring with 22 points. The rebounding battle went to State 47-25. Playing without starters Ivan Richmann and Garnie Hatch, the Rebels, who were 0-4 in the SEC coming into the game, were simply no match for the Maroons. State's victory made them 4-1 in the conference behind only undefeated Auburn.

After the Ole Miss game the Maroons took a break from the SEC by playing two games against nonconference foes. MSU easily defeated Murray State at home 63-48 January 24 but struggled to beat Memphis State on the road 53-52 on January 29. Outstanding sophomore big man Jerry Graves did not play in the Memphis State game because of a concussion. When SEC play resumed, the Maroons stood 15-1 overall and 4-1 in the conference and were ranked eleventh by the AP.

LSU invaded Starkville January 31 and like the previous 27 opponents who played State in the Maroons' gym went away disappointed. LSU dropped a 78-71 decision to MSU. Bailey Howell led the way in what appeared to be a runaway victory until late in the contest. State led by 15 points with 2:48 left in the game. At that point the visiting Tigers went on a run that cut the final margin to 7 points. Led by Howell's 17 rebounds, State won the battle of the boards 43-25. Topped by Howell's 30 points, four Maroons scored in double digits. Lynn Moon scored 20 points for the Tigers, and three of his teammates also managed double-digit scoring. With a 16-1 overall record that included a 5-1 conference mark, State now faced a daunting February schedule of eight consecutive SEC games.

February 2 brought the Tulane Green Wave to Starkville. The visitors were again disappointed as the Maroons walked off their home court as victors for the twenty-ninth consecutive time. Final score, 55-46. Nobody would have ever dreamed of such a win streak before Coach Babe Murphy and Bailey Howell arrived in Starkville. Bailey Howell scored 24 points and was the only Maroon in double figures. Gary Stoll led the Green Wave with 15 points while Vic Klinker connected for 11 points. The game was played at a slower pace than usual. The slow pace is reflected not only in the final score but also in the rebounding and shooting statistics. State grabbed 34 rebounds and Tulane 28. Both teams shot well from the field, State 44 percent and Tulane 42 percent. Relatively few fouls were committed. State attempted 15 free throws and made 9, Tulane attempted 9 and made 8. State was now 17-1 overall, 6-1 in the SEC and ranked eleventh by the AP.

The Maroons had an opportunity to extend their 29-game home-court winning streak February 7 and they did not disappoint. Tennessee came to Starkville and left on the short end of a 52-45 score. Bailey Howell was matched against Tennessee's 6'8" big man Gene Tormohlen. Advantage Howell, who scored 22 points to Tormohlen's 13. But the Tennessee giant actually outrebounded Howell 11 to 10. But Howell had a lot of help on the boards from Jerry Graves, who grabbed 14 rebounds. Tormohlen had no such help as the Volunteers next leading rebounder secured only 5. Facing State's zone defense for most of the game Tennessee had to attempt long-range shots and hope to get rebounds and shorter shots. That didn't work as State outrebounded the Vols 35-24. Despite the Maroons' rebounding advantage Tennessee actually attempted 14 more shots from the floor than MSU. But State made 16 of 39 while the Vols connected on only 17 of 53. State stood 18-1 overall and 7-1 in the conference but Kentucky was coming to town.

Defending national champion Kentucky was ranked number one in the country February 9, 1959, when the surging Mississippi State team got its chance to topple a giant in Starkville. To the delight of 5,400 fans who packed into Maroon Gymnasium the home team took care of business 66-58. The Cats left with their tails between their legs. *Clarion-Ledger* sportswriter Robert Fulton hit the nail on the head, writing, "The stunning victory, undoubtedly the sweetest of all the Maroons' 31 straight home-court wins, lifted State into hot contention for the SEC lead with unbeaten Auburn." McCarthy's 1957 contingent had beaten the number-3 ranked Wildcats 89-81 at MSU. Was the Babe building a program that would consistently challenge Kentucky and Adolph (The Barron) Rupp's supremacy in the SEC?

Bailey Howell was again a difference-maker. The All-American grabbed 17 rebounds and scored 27 points. But Howell had a lot of help. Jerry Graves snatched 11 rebounds and scored 7 points and Charles Hull got 6 rebounds and scored 14 points. Thanks to Graves's defense, Kentucky's high scorer Johnny Cox managed only 14 points. None of the Wildcats got more than 6 rebounds. State made 53 percent of its field-goal attempts and its tenacious defense held the Wildcats to 35 percent from the floor. Two first-half statistics reflect the pace of the game. The score was 4-3 seven minutes into the game and the half-time score was State 25, Kentucky 16. Howell fouled out with 4 minutes 25 seconds left to play and State holding an 18-point advantage. The Maroons controlled the backboards outrebounding the Cats 38-25 with Howell grabbing 17 and Graves 11. State shot 34 free throws and converted 28 while Kentucky shot 25 and hit 15. Bailey Howell said after the game, "Coach McCarthy had it figured out just right. All we had to do was go out there and do what he said." The game ended as hundreds of State fans chanted, "We're number one." The AP boosted State to number 10 the next day.

Fresh from the victory over Kentucky the Maroons went on the road February 14 and proceeded to crush the Florida Gators 105-68. State never trailed and was never even threatened. Led by Howell's 43 points, a total of 10 Maroons scored and 4 posted double figures. State shot 65 percent from the floor, the Gators 35 percent. Howell's 43 points were the most ever scored by an individual in Florida's gym. The Maroons defense was stifling against all but one Gator, Bobby Sherwood. He had a great game and scored 32 points by going 12 for 21 from the floor and 8 of 11 from the foul line. With Howell grabbing 22 rebounds State again dominated the boards 66-44. Mississippi now stood 20-1 overall and 9-1 in the SEC.

The Maroons headed north to Athens, Georgia, to play the woeful Georgia Bulldogs, who stood 7-12 overall and 1-8 in the conference.

The February 16 game played in Woodruff Hall was not much of a contest; State won 76-56. Bailey Howell played like the All-American he was, grabbing 15 rebounds and scoring 33 points. While the Maroons did not put the game on ice until the 16-minute mark in the second half, Georgia led only once by a score of 5-2. Just like in the Florida game, State's defense stifled all but one of their opponent's scorers. The Dog's Gordon Darrah scored 30 points, hitting 9 of 18 shots from the floor and 12 of 13 from the free-throw line. No other Bulldog scored in double figures. It makes you think Babe McCarthy had emphasized stopping everyone else thinking Darrah could not beat State by himself. On the other hand, Howell had several teammates who were offensive threats, including Charles Hull, who scored 14 in this game, and Jerry Keeton, who sacked 10. As usual the Maroons won the battle of the boards, this time 35-25. With State sporting a 21-1 overall record and a 10-1 SEC mark the AP ranked the Maroons fifth in the country.

With three games left to play, Mississippi State was sitting in second place behind undefeated Auburn in the SEC. The SEC champion would get an automatic bid to the NCAA Basketball Tournament that would determine the national champion. Auburn was on NCAA probation and could not advance to the NCAA tournament even with an SEC championship. That left State and third-place Kentucky in contention for the conference bid. Mississippi State had a potential problem. Would MSU's president and the state's board of trustees of the institutions of higher learning allow its basketball team to compete in a racially integrated tournament? On February 17, 1959, the *Clarion-Ledger* ran AP and UPI stories indicating that MSU's funding might be reduced by the Mississippi legislature if its basketball team played in the NCAA tournament. Governor J. P. Coleman explained:

> I am beginning to get considerable mail concerning the possibility of Mississippi State University entering the NCAA basketball championship tournament. . . . For the information of all concerned I think it should be pointed out that in 1944 the constitution was

> amended by a vote of the people so as to place our institutions of higher learning under the sole and exclusive control of a 12-man board of trustees, each serving staggered terms of 12 years. Therefore, the decision in this matter will be up to the president of Mississippi State University and the Board of Trustees.
>
> However, in the final analysis these officials have to go to the legislature every two years for the money to support the institutions. It necessarily follows that if the NCAA problem arises, the legislature will likewise have to be consulted.

The road challenges continued as the Maroons next faced the Fighting Tigers of LSU at John Parker Memorial Coliseum in Baton Rouge on February 21. As expected, MSU prevailed, downing the Tigers, who were 1-11 in the conference, 75-67. Bailey Howell, who got into foul trouble and spent most of the second half on the bench, scored *only* 17 points and grabbed *only* 7 rebounds. Four other Maroons stepped up and scored in double figures, Charles Hull 13, Jerry Keeton 14, Jerry Graves 13, and Ted Usher 11. Two LSU players scored in double figures, Lynn Moon 20 and Tommy Raborn 11. MSU barely won the battle of the boards 36-33. A total of 50 fouls were called in the game as the second half became very physical. State made 21 of 36 free-throw attempts and LSU made 15 of 29.

The *Jackson Daily News*'s Lee Baker wrote that many more fouls could have been called and fairly well captured the game in one long and winding sentence: "Mississippi State hit for a .475 clip in the first half in building a 17 point lead, 52-35, but in the second half without Howell's guidance, the percentage fell off to a mere .296 by making 27 of 67 shots, the final average stood at .403."

The victory tied MSU with Auburn for the SEC lead as the Tigers fell to Kentucky that same day. Both teams stood 11-1 in the conference, but the Maroons had now won 22 games and 13 in a row. The Babe's Boys retained their number-5 rank in the AP poll.

Next up for the Bulldogs was Tulane on February 23 in the Fogelman Arena in New Orleans. The Green Wave entered the game 12-10 overall and 5-7 in the conference. State readily dispatched the overmatched Tulane team 65-51. The lead switched back and forth several times in the first half but by halftime State held a 13-point advantage. Two State players scored in double figures: Howell scored a game high 32 points and Jerry Graves chipped in 10. Tulane's Dick O'Brien scored 17 and Gary Stoll 13. With Howell grabbing 24 rebounds, the Maroons won the battle of the boards 46-31. Howell also made 14 of 17 free throws as State outscored Tulane from the line 25-17. The Maroons maintained their fifth-place rank in the AP poll.

With the victory, Mississippi State qualified for its first-ever NCAA tournament and Bailey Howell broke Bob Pettit's SEC scoring record. Former LSU great Pettit had held the SEC scoring record for a 3-year career with 2,002 points. Howell's 32 points against Tulane gave him a total of 2,024, and he still had a game to play. Those two accomplishments epitomized what Babe McCarthy and Howell had been able to do at Mississippi State University.

In the meantime, Tennessee had handed Auburn its second straight SEC loss. Now, even if the Maroons were to lose to Ole Miss in their last game and ended the season tied with Auburn at 12-2 in the conference, they would get the conference's automatic NCAA invitation because Auburn was on NCAA probation.

On February 25 State played Ole Miss in Oxford in a contest that would become legendary. The Maroons were 23-1 and 12-1 in the conference while the hapless Rebels were 7-16 and 1-12 in the conference. The game wasn't expected to be much of a contest, but it was very exciting. Ole Miss Coach Bonnie (Country) Graham decided to take advantage of existing rules and the lack of a shot clock. The Rebels stalled all game and the strategy basically worked. State led at the half by one point, 9-8. With a minute and a half left in the game the Maroons led 15-14, had possession of the ball and were holding it. At that point the Rebels had to foul to get the ball back. During the next 73 seconds the Rebels scored 2 points and the Maroons 4. With 17 seconds left in the game, MSU led 19-16. The Rebels had to continue fouling, resulting in a final score of 23-16 MSU. During one stretch in the second half Ole Miss held the ball 9 minutes and 22 seconds.

The Maroons' victory gave them a 24-1 overall record and a 13-1 SEC mark, by far the best in MSU history. According to College Basketball at Sports-Reference.com, of the 173 NCAA Division I teams Mississippi State had the best record for the 1958–59 season. Bailey Howell, who won the SEC scoring title, was a unanimous All-SEC pick and he was named All-American.

Mississippi State won the SEC championship outright with its 13-1 conference record. Kentucky and Auburn finished tied for second with 12-2 records. As conference champions the Maroons earned an invitation to the NCAA tournament that would decide the national championship. Mississippi State president Ben Hilbun and the Mississippi Board of Trustees of the Institutions of Higher Education caved to political pressure, and Hilbun refused to accept the NCAA's invitation. President Hilbun said he was not empowered to set aside or amend state policies against playing teams with Negro players. As noted in chapter 1, administrators of Mississippi-supported schools and state legislators had reached a "gentleman's agreement" in 1955 that the schools' sports teams would not play against racially integrated teams. What a disservice to maybe the greatest college basketball team in Mississippi State's history and to Bailey Howell, no doubt its greatest basketball player ever, and to Babe McCarthy, its greatest basketball coach ever.

SEC commissioner Bernie Moore named Kentucky the conference's representative in the NCAA tournament. Kentucky had won the NCAA tournament in 1958. But the 1958–59 Wildcats had posted an overall 23-2 record having lost to both Vanderbilt and Mississippi State in conference play. The AP ranked Kentucky number one and State was number five at the end of the season. Kentucky lost to Louisville in the first round of the NCAA tournament but went on to defeat Marquette to finish third overall. In the final AP rankings, Kentucky finished second and Mississippi State third.

1959 SEC Baseball Champions—Ole Miss

While Babe McCarthy's MSU basketball team was finishing off the Maroons' first SEC championship, Tom Swayze's Ole Miss team was working on its first overall SEC baseball championship. The 1960 Ole Miss yearbook had this to say about the 1959 Rebels magic season on the diamond.

> In baseball, there is an ancient adage which was reflected in full measure by Tom Swayze's 1959 Ole Miss team. It tells that "strength down the middle" is basic in the building of championship teams. For the record, the 1959 Rebels were (1) All-Southeastern from catcher to center fielder, and (2) they captured every Southeastern title in sight. It was Ole Miss' first overall SEC championship in baseball. Because Swayze, in his ninth season as Johnny Reb coach, was fielding rebuilt infield and outfield units, the title-taking came as a pleasant surprise. What happened was this: Ole Miss won 10 out of 13 Western Division games to cop divisional honors for the third time since 1954, leading defending champion Alabama to the wire by two full games. In the East-West playoffs with Eastern winner Georgia Tech, the Rebs lost the series opener—at home—to Tech in a 4-3, 10 inning decision, then stormed back in the two "blue chips" games staged in Atlanta, 8-5 and 11-7, to make the series win one of the year's big comeback stories. To make the second game triumph all the more remarkable, Tech went out front by 5-0 after an inning of play.

That's a great description of the season in a nutshell, but there is much more of interest about the 1959 baseball team and season. The X's and O's and the Jimmies and Joes aligned to produce a magical baseball season for Ole Miss in 1959.

Tom Swayze was a great coach. During his first eight seasons as head baseball coach, 1951–1958, his Rebels won 127 games and lost 63 for a winning percentage of 67. During that time the Rebels suffered no losing season and in 1956 tied Florida for the regular-season championship before losing 2 games to none in a playoff. There is a saying in baseball that goes something like this: Assuming teams are relatively evenly matched you can expect to win a third of your games and lose a third of your games; it's the third in the middle that count. During this eight-year period, Coach Swayze's teams won all of the third in the middle. That's comparable to going 11-1 in football. Coach Swayze would go on to win more SEC championships and develop more outstanding players but there is no doubt he was at the top of his game in 1959.

During the 1959 season five Rebels earned All-SEC honors, catcher Robert Khayat, shortstop Al Bullock, center fielder Don Jobe, third baseman Jake Gibbs, and pitcher Larry Williams.

In addition to Ole Miss, the Western Division of the SEC included Alabama, LSU, Mississippi State, and Tulane. The Rebels won the season series against each of these rivals and compiled a 10-3 record against the division. The three losses were to LSU, Tulane, and Alabama. In the middle of the season the Rebels reeled off a nine-game winning streak.

In early May the Rebels were scheduled to play a four-game series against defending champion Alabama in Tuscaloosa. Ole Miss sported a 6-2 conference record while the Crimson Tide clocked in at 5-3. Alabama captured the first game, leaving the two teams with identical 6-3 conference records. The Rebels won the second game and set up a third game matchup, which turned out to be crucial for Alabama's hopes of repeating as champions. Larry Williams tossed a gem of a four-hitter as Ole Miss won 1-0. The winning run was scored in the eighth inning when Al Bullock doubled and Jake Gibbs followed with an RBI single. The Rebels failed to score in the top of the ninth, and Williams needed three outs in the bottom of the inning to protect that slim one-run lead. Not to worry, following a leadoff triple by the Tide's Ken Chapman, Williams politely retired the next three batters, striking out the last two. The scheduled fourth game was rained out and the Rebels left Tuscaloosa with a two-game lead over the Tide. Alabama's only hope to repeat as Western Division and overall SEC champions was that Ole Miss would lose its last two regular-season games against Mississippi State and the Tide would win out. The Rebels took care of business by sweeping State 4-2 and 6-2.

Next up was Eastern Division champion Georgia Tech in the SEC championship series. As noted above the Rebels dropped the first game but won the final two games to clinch the championship. Future Ole Miss chancellor Robert Khayat, who had hit .350 for the season, hit a grand slam home run in the third game to seal the victory over Tech. The Rebels finished the season with an overall record of 18-6, having gone 12-4 against SEC teams and 6-2 against nonconference opponents.

The Rebels had not won an overall conference title since 1929 as a member of the old Southern Conference, which was the predecessor of the SEC. Ole Miss had claimed SEC Western Division crowns in 1954 and 1956. After losing to Florida in the 1956 SEC championship series the Rebels received a bid to the NCAA District III playoffs. Ole Miss went on to win the playoffs 3-1 and proceed to finish third in their first-ever College World Series. As SEC champions, Ole Miss received an automatic invitation to the NCAA district playoffs after the 1959 season. Unfortunately, the Rebel baseball team suffered the same fate as the Mississippi State basketball team. Ole Miss had to refuse its well-earned place in the NCAA tournament because of Mississippi's misguided policy against state-supported institutions' teams playing in racially integrated events.

How Did the Other Teams Fare?

1959 Ole Miss Basketball

The 1958–59 season was Bonnie (Country) Graham's ninth as the Rebels' head basketball coach. After finishing the 1957–58 season 12-12 overall and 6-8 in the conference, Ole Miss hit rock bottom in 1959. Graham had to replace four starters from the 1958 team. Unfortunately, he lost three promising sophomores before the season began, two to academic deficiencies and one who decided to transfer. Three Rebel starters (Ivan Richmann, Jack Waters, and Glynn Griffing) fouled out a total of 21 times. In five of their loses, the Rebels were outscored by five points or fewer. Plagued by lack of speed and constant foul trouble the Rebels posted a 7-17 overall record and a 1-13 SEC mark, last in the league. The conference record was the Rebels' worst showing since the Southeastern Conference was formed in 1932. There was one very bright spot, sophomore Jack Waters averaged 19 points and 7 rebounds per game. Over his three-year varsity career Waters would prove to be one of the best to ever wear the Rebel uniform.

1959 Mississippi State Baseball

Paul Gregory's Mississippi State baseball team had a disappointing season in 1959. But for a while it looked like the Maroons would be in contention for at least an SEC Western Division championship. State was 10-7 overall and 5-4 in the conference and in second place behind Ole Miss in the SEC West when they played defending overall SEC champion Alabama April 24. Unfortunately, the Maroons lost all of their last 6 conference games and finished with a 5-10 conference record and 12-13 overall. State finished last in the Western Division and tenth in the conference. Nevertheless, the future was bright. Coach Gregory would go on to build championship teams and not finish below .500 in the SEC again until 1968.

1959 Ole Miss Football

Ole Miss had never won an SEC football championship before the Johnny Vaught era. As a rookie head coach in 1947 Vaught guided a team that finished 2-7 the previous season to a 9-2 record and an SEC championship. In 1954 Ole Miss posted another 9-2 record and won another SEC championship. Coach Vaught's 1955 team was even better as they finished 10-1, won another SEC championship, and beat

Vaught's alma mater TCU 14-13 in the Cotton Bowl. Under Vaught's tutelage the Rebels went 7-3, 9-1-1, and 9-2 from 1956 to 1958 but did not win an SEC championship. However, by 1959 Vaught had built a juggernaut.

Ranked eighth in the country at the beginning of the 1959 season by the Associated Press, Ole Miss played its first game on September 19 against Houston in Rice Stadium in Houston, Texas. Before 45,000 fans the Rebels dispatched the Cougars 16-0. Scoring began in the second quarter when Robert Khayat intercepted a pass and took it 52 yards to the Houston 7. Four plays later quarterback Jake Gibbs scored on a short keeper around end. The third quarter saw quarterback Bobby Franklin score on a one-yard plunge after fullback Charlie Flowers had carried six times for 32 yards to set up the score. Khayat missed the extra point but on a later drive kicked a 32-yard field goal to close out the scoring.

On September 26 the fourth-ranked Rebels played Kentucky in Lexington and their visit to the Bluegrass State brightened their rising star. There was no score until the third quarter when Cowboy Woodruff broke the goal line on a 3-yard run set up by two Gibbs passes and a short run by Dewey Partridge. The extra-point attempt failed. Then a fourth-quarter Khayat field goal made it 9-0. Quarterback Doug Elmore finished the scoring with a 52-yard run. This time Khayat's extra-point attempt was good and the Rebels left Lexington with another 16-0 victory. Unfortunately, senior starting quarterback Bobby Franklin sustained an injury in the game that he did not fully recover from until near the end of the season.

After beginning the season with two road games, home cooking must have looked appetizing to the Rebel players. The third-ranked Rebels played Memphis State at Hemingway Stadium in Oxford on October 3 and administered 43-0 thrashing. The first quarter saw the Rebels take a 10-0 lead as Bobby Crespino ran for a touchdown and Khayat chipped in with an extra point and a field goal. Both Charlie Flowers and Doug Elmore scored on one-yard runs in the second quarter. In the third quarter Cowboy Woodruff took flight for a

56-yard gain that set up Crespino's second touchdown run, a 12-yarder. In the fourth quarter Flowers rushed for a 15-yard touchdown and George Blair ran from one yard out for another. Jake Gibbs threw to Johnny Brewer for the game's final score. Memphis State did not play major college football in 1959 and the blowout victory did not impress the pollsters.

After slipping to a number-five national ranking Ole Miss took it out on Vanderbilt in Nashville on October 10, winning 33-0. The point differential was the Rebels' largest margin of victory in the history of the series. Fullbacks Charlie Flowers and Hoss Anderson and quarterbacks Jake Gibbs and Doug Elmore each rushed for scores and Bobby Crespino caught a touchdown pass. The defense was its usual magnificent self, posting its fourth straight shutout. The outcome was never in doubt.

On October 25 Tulane showed up in Oxford to play the Rebels, who were still ranked fifth nationally. Ole Miss simply dominated the Green Wave 53-7 at Hemingway Stadium. However, in this fifth game of the season, the Rebel defense was finally scored on. But the defense did not give up a touchdown drive. Tulane recovered a fumble at the Ole Miss three-yard line and cashed that miscue in for a touchdown.

Fourth-ranked Ole Miss took on Arkansas October 24 in Memphis and whipped the Hogs to the tune of 28-0. Going into the game the Hogs had lost only a single game and that one by a score of 13-12 to undefeated and third-ranked Texas. According to the 1960 Ole Miss yearbook: "Thirty-two thousand people turned out at Crump Stadium to witness the wanton slaughter of eleven Arkansas hogs. The bloody business resulted in a fall in cracklings of 28 points while Rebel stock still sold at a premium." (Only a Mississippi writer could compose such wonderful sentences to describe a football game.) The encounter featured two touchdowns by Arkansas native Charlie Flowers, and one each by Jake Gibbs and Dewey Partridge. Khayat was good on all four extra-point attempts. The Rebel defense pitched a shutout that included stopping the Hogs four times after they started at the Rebels' one-yard line with a first and goal. On that magnificent goal-line stand the Rebels stopped Arkansas great and Mississippi native Lance Alworth for no gain on first down. Then All-American guard Marvin Terrell sacked quarterback George McKinney for a 6-yard loss. Alworth tried again and gained 3 yards. McKinney threw an incomplete pass on fourth down and the Rebels took over at their own four-yard line. Ole Miss nearly doubled the Hogs' total offense, gaining 299 yards to Arkansas's 159. The Rebels also exceeded the Hogs in first downs 21-13. Knowing he would face LSU the next week and leading 28-0 early in the second half, Coach Vaught used backups for the rest of the game except when Arkansas threatened to score.

Then came the never-to-be-forgotten Halloween debacle of October 31, 1959, in Baton Rouge, Louisiana. Third-ranked Ole Miss lost 7-3 to number-one ranked and defending national champion LSU in Tiger Stadium on Billy Cannon's 89-yard punt return. Robert Khayat's first-quarter field goal accounted for all of the Rebels' points. It was no surprise that the game was a titanic defensive struggle. Ole Miss had given up only seven points all season, and LSU had not had a touchdown scored on them in nine consecutive games.

LSU never mounted an offensive drive that came close to scoring. The Rebels kept the Tigers bottled up with fumble recoveries and excellent punting. Future Ole Miss head football coach Billy Brewer recovered three LSU fumbles. Jake Gibbs punted six times and averaged 51.5 yards. Bobby Franklin punted out of bounds twice, once on the LSU 5 and once on the Tigers' 1. LSU's star halfback Billy Cannon gained only 48 yards from scrimmage on 12 carries. The Rebels' star fullback Charlie Flowers gained only 35 yards on 10 carries. On the Rebels' last drive, fourth-string sophomore quarterback Doug Elmore almost stole Cannon's thunder and rescued the Rebels. Elmore, who played behind Bobby Franklin, Jake Gibbs, and Billy Brewer, took the Rebels on a drive that started at the Ole Miss 32-yard line and was finally stopped at the LSU 1-yard line. The *Clarion Ledger*'s Carl Walters wrote that it was the best college football he had seen in 32 years of sports reporting and the best two teams.

The game statistics show how the two defenses dominated:

First downs—OM 13, LSU 7

Yards rushing—OM 160, LSU 142

Yards passing—OM 19, LSU 29

Punts—OM 8 for 48 avg., LSU 6 for 39 avg.

Fumbles lost—OM 0, LSU -3

Penalties—OM 3 for 15 yards, LSU 3 for 32 yards

Immediately after Ole Miss's Halloween nightmare, Carl Walters wrote, "They [Ole Miss] lost very little in prestige, however, as they had the best of the brawling except for Cannon's electrifying gallop."

The Associated Press's Mercer Bailey wrote that the Sugar Bowl should invite OM and LSU for a rematch and that even in defeat Ole Miss had "bolstered its claim to greatness."

The next Saturday, November 7, the fifth-ranked Rebels took out their frustration on lowly Chattanooga in Oxford 58-0. Enough said about that game.

Still ranked number 5, Ole Miss next played number-9 ranked Tennessee in Memphis November 14 and came away with an impressive 37-7 victory. The Vols had lost only one game, 14-7 to Georgia Tech, and had given up only 47 points in the seven games. The Rebels overcame a blocked punt, two fumbles, and 143 yards in penalties while posting the impressive victory. Charlie Flowers gained 168 yards on 26 carries as the Rebels dominated both sides of the line of scrimmage. Carl Walters wrote, "Saturday in Memphis the Rebs could (and would) have beaten anybody who took the field against 'em, including Syracuse, Southern Cal, LSU Texas, Auburn, and Slippery Rock." First downs OM 22, Vols 8, total yards OM 436, Vols 143. For the first time in history, Ole Miss had beaten Arkansas (7-2) and Tennessee in the same season. The Volunteers scored their touchdown after they recovered a blocked punt on the Rebels' seven-yard line. That would end the scoring on Ole Miss for the entire season, total of 21 points.

The Rebels had jumped to a number-two ranking when they played their last regular-season game, the Egg Bowl, on November 28 against Mississippi State at Scott Field in Starkville. Ole Miss put an exclamation point on their brilliant regular season by shutting out their in-state rivals 42-0. State was determined to stop Flowers so Gibbs passed for 222 yards and two touchdowns and ran for 62 yards and another touchdown. Mississippi State did not mount a single scoring threat. Ole Miss gained a total of 432 yards and made 23 first downs; Mississippi State gained a total 115 yards and made 6 first downs. The Rebels finished the regular season with a 9-1 record and ranked second in the final AP poll.

Immediately after the victory over Mississippi State, Ole Miss accepted an invitation to play in the Sugar Bowl against LSU. It is no mystery why Ole Miss agreed to play the rematch with LSU. Although they had lost 7-3 to the Tigers in the regular season, most likely all the players and coaches believed they were better than LSU. The writer knows for a fact that Ole Miss fans thought so. Beating the Tigers in the Sugar Bowl could provide sweet revenge and ease the pain caused by the earlier loss. But why did LSU agree to play Ole Miss in the Sugar Bowl? It seems that LSU had nothing to gain and a lot to lose.

Before the bowl game, former Ole Miss head coach and sports columnist Harry Mehre opined that LSU's decision to accept a bid to the Sugar Bowl was the biggest upset of the year. (This writer agrees.) Mehre wrote:

> I don't know just where the pressure came from but SOMEBODY up there, who liked bowl bids must have suggested to the athletic officials at L.S.U. that it would be [in] the best interest of all concerned to play in New Orleans, New Year's Day. The Tigers slipped out of the noose the Rebels had tied around their neck Halloween Night when Billy Cannon raced 89 brilliant yards with a punt return to tarnish Ole Miss' perfect record. I did not think it was legal to place a man's life in jeopardy twice during the same football season. Personally, I am all for the game but if I were Coach Dietzel, I would not relish the double header. I was the unselfish type coach. I was satisfied with defeating a team once a season. I didn't want to be greedy about the thing. I must confess to some snootiness because there were teams I wish I had never played.

The Sugar Bowl was played New Year's Day 1960 before 81,141 fans in Tulane Stadium in New Orleans. Both teams had 9-1 records and the Rebels and Tigers were ranked second and third respectively in both the AP and UPI polls. Ole Miss won 21-0 and completely dominated the game while avenging their earlier loss to the Tigers. Just how dominant were the Rebels? After a scoreless first quarter, Ole Miss posted 7 points in each of the last three quarters. Jake Gibbs passed for a 43-yard touchdown to Cowboy Woodruff; Bobby Franklin threw two touchdown passes, 18 yards to Larry Grantham and 9 yards to George Blair. Bobby Franklin, who had finally completely recovered from his early season injury, was named Most Valuable Player. The Rebel defense was simply magnificent, giving up minus 15 yards rushing and only 74 yards of total offense. LSU never got past the Rebels' 38-yard line. LSU's Heisman Trophy winner Billy Cannon was held to 8 yards on six carries. After the bowl victory the Rebels' final worksheet looked like this: 10 wins and 1 loss, 350 points scored, 21 points given up.

The Sugar Bowl victory clearly demonstrated that Ole Miss was better than LSU. The Tigers having lost to Ole Miss and Tennessee ended 9-2. The earlier 7-3 LSU win had been extremely close as the score and statistics show. But in the Rebels' Sugar Bowl victory, Ole Miss manhandled the Bayou Bengals. During the season Ole Miss and LSU played four common opponents, Kentucky, Tennessee, Mississippi State, and Tulane. The Rebels won all of their games against those opponents and LSU won against three, falling only to Tennessee. Against those common opponents Ole Miss scored 148 points and LSU scored 63.

The 1959 Ole Miss football team did not win the SEC championship. Led by the great Fran Tarkenton, Georgia won the championship with a 7-0 SEC mark. Coach Wallace Butts's Georgia Bulldogs finished the season 10-1, the Dogs' only loss was to South Carolina, an ACC team, 30-14. During the season Georgia scored 228 points and gave up 89. Ole Miss and LSU with 5-1 marks tied for second. Georgia ended the season ranked fifth nationally. Ole Miss was clearly better than LSU and Georgia.

The Associated Press and United Press International both released the results of their final polls before the bowl games in the 1950s. Syracuse, with a 10-0 regular-season record that included a 20-18 victory over seventh-ranked Penn State, was named national champion by both the AP and UPI. Syracuse won the Cotton Bowl against fourth-ranked Texas and ended their season 11-0. Both the AP and UPI ranked Ole Miss second, LSU third, and Georgia fifth. But the Dunkel, Berryman, and Sagarin rating systems all rated Ole Miss as the best college football team of 1959. The Associated Press later named the 1959 Rebels the SEC Team of the Decade. Later, Sagarin rated the 1959 Rebels the third-best team in college football during the period 1956–1995 behind the Nebraska teams of 1971 and 1995.

Despite not winning the SEC or national championship the 1959 Rebels are rightfully recognized today as one of the best Ole Miss and college football teams ever. There are many reasons that the 1959 Ole Miss football is legendary.

The only setback in Ole Miss's fabulous 1959 season was the defeat by LSU 7-3 in a Halloween night horror. During the season the Rebels scored 350 points and gave up only 21. No team mounted a scoring drive against Ole Miss. In their 10 victories the Rebels scored 347 points (34.7 per game) and their opponents scored 14 (1.4 per game) resulting in an average margin of 33.3 points per game. Two touchdowns were scored after a fumble recovery on the Ole Miss 3-yard line and after a blocked punt was recovered on the Rebels' 7-yard line. The other touchdown was scored by Billy Cannon on an 89-yard punt return that earned him the Heisman Trophy.

A number of 1959 Ole Miss players earned postseason honors:

Two were named All-Americans: Charlie Flowers, FB (AP, UPI, Camp, NEA, CP, FWAA-Look, Coaches, NBC, SN, NY News, FB News)

Marvin Terrell, Guard (FWAA-Look)

Five were named to All-SEC teams.

Larry Grantham—1st AP

Johnny Brewer—2nd UPI

Marvin Terrell—1st AP & UPI
Richard Price—UPI 3rd
Jake Gibbs—2nd AP & UPI

Fourteen members of the team have been inducted into the Mississippi Sports Hall of Fame. Two players, Jake Gibbs and Charlie Flowers, are members of the national College Football Hall of Fame. Eight of the team's nine coaches are inductees of the Mississippi Sports Hall of Fame. In addition, head coach Johnny Vaught and assistant coach Bruiser Kinard are in the College Football Hall of Fame; Kinard is also in the Pro Football Hall of Fame.

Rick Cleveland had this to say in a December 2014 column after the death of Charlie Flowers, the team's All-American fullback and recognized leader.

> Years ago, Charlie Flowers was showing me a photo of the 1959 Ole Miss football team. He was pointing to each player, face by face, row by row.
>
> There were 43 players in the photo. Forty-two, Charlie said, graduated.
>
> "Bank president, CEO of his company, successful lawyer," Charlie said.
>
> "Athletic director, mayor, Chancellor," he continued.
>
> "Head football coach, Major League baseball player, insurance executive, another mayor," he kept going and going.
>
> Finally, he finished. "There will never be another team like it," Flowers said.

As this is being written it's safe to say that so far Charlie Flowers's statement about there never being another team like the 1959 Rebels has proven prophetic.

Charlie Flowers was a leader from the first day he set foot on campus. Rick Cleveland recorded how it started.

> In 1956 when Flowers came to Ole Miss from Mariana, Ark. broad-shouldered and bare-chested, hazing was the norm for fresh-

> men football players. Flowers, who could have gone anywhere to play football, couldn't see the point of it. Why recruit the best players in the South and then abuse them, he surmised. Nobody touches me he declared. And nobody did.

During his senior year Flowers probably saved the career of Larry Grantham, who contributed greatly to the success of the 1959 Rebels. Under conditions that had alienated his teammates, Grantham left the team after its victory in the 1958 Gator Bowl. Before the 1959 season began Grantham asked Coach Vaught to reinstate him. The wise Mr. Vaught asked the team to meet and vote on whether to take Grantham back. Flowers made a rousing speech that condemned some of Grantham's actions but said that he was one outstanding football player and the team needed him. Charlie knew as few others did just how good Grantham was. When the Rebels were on defense, Flowers played next to Grantham at linebacker. He has been quoted as saying that he did not get many tackles because Grantham got them all. Flowers asked the team to give Grantham another chance, which they voted to do. As they say, the rest is history. Grantham was a mainstay in the Rebels' great 1959 defense, and he simply dominated in the 1960 Sugar Bowl against LSU. Grantham went on to a 13-year NFL career with the New York Jets. He was named first-team All-Pro five times and played in five Pro Bowls. He was a mainstay for the Jets when they won the 1969 Super Bowl. Both Charlie Flowers and Larry Grantham are enshrined in the Mississippi Sports Hall of Fame.

Mississippi State Football

The 1959 Mississippi State football team coached by Wade Walker won two games and lost seven. The two games they won were against Arkansas State (49-14) and Memphis State (28-23), neither of which played major college football at the time. The Maroons' lost all seven of their SEC contests. MSU scored only 19 points and gave up 161 points in their SEC games and were shut out in five of the seven games. The Maroon offense was shut out in five of the SEC games. In short, 1959 was another in a growing list of "wait until next year" seasons for MSU football.

1960

Another Banner Year

1960 SEC Basketball Champion—Auburn
1960 SEC Baseball Champion—Ole Miss
1960 Football Champion—Ole Miss
Final score: Mississippi schools 2 SEC championships, all other SEC schools 1

The Champions

1960 SEC Baseball Champion—Ole Miss

With a 22-3 record the Ole Miss baseball team won the university's second consecutive SEC championship during the 1960 season. The Rebels also finished fifth nationally in the Associated Press poll. Along the way Coach Swayze's powerful team posted a 17-game winning streak and won all of their home games. Once again because of the silly "gentlemen's agreement" between the legislature and school officials that state schools would not play integrated teams, the Rebels turned down an opportunity to advance on the national stage by competing in the NCAA Regional Tournament.

Seventeen-game winning streaks are rare in baseball. The Rebels' streak is worth a serious examination. It went like this:

LSU—5-3
Illinois Wesleyan—8-7
Illinois Wesleyan—13-7
LSU—7-0
LSU—13-2
Mississippi State—8-0
Mississippi State—14-1
Alabama—3-0
Alabama—10-4
Tulane—13-2
Tulane—13-2
Alabama—8-2
Alabama—8-2
Memphis State—8-5
Vanderbilt—10-0
Vanderbilt—16-0
Memphis State—6-2

The Rebels' pitching was fantastic, and they outscored their opponents 163-33 during the streak. Rebel hurlers threw four shutouts and gave up 2 or fewer runs in 13 of the contests. Against SEC teams the Rebels scored 136 runs and gave up only 20.

In the summer of 2020 this 17-game win streak still stands as an Ole Miss record. However, it was threatened in the spring of 2020 when Mike Bianco's Rebels lost the first game of the season to number-one Louisville and then reeled off 16 straight victories. Unfortunately, the 2020 Rebs never got a chance to tie or break the record. The Rebels did not play another game after they defeated the University of Louisiana Monroe 18-7 on March 11. The COVID-19 pandemic caused all NCAA sports to be canceled for the rest of the spring. Ole Miss ended the season 16-1 having not played a single SEC game.

After being crowned 1960 Western Division champion, the Rebels met Eastern Division champion Florida in a two-game series that decided the overall SEC championship. One game was played in Gainesville and the other in Oxford. The Rebels prevailed in both games. After falling behind 7-0 in Gainesville, the Rebels stormed back to win 15-7. The Oxford contest resulted in a 6-1 Rebel victory.

While the Rebel team was denied the opportunity to play in the NCAA tournament, accolades poured in for individual players. Star third baseman Jake Gibbs led the SEC in batting average .424, hits 42, and RBIs 30. He was named All-SEC and All-American. Pitcher Larry Williams, who earned All-SEC honors for the second time, posted a 7-2 record, struck out 80 batters, and compiled a 1.80 earned run average. Pitchers Denny Bomquist and Don Porter posted 7-0 records to tie Williams for the SEC lead in wins. In addition to Gibbs and Williams, outfielders Billy Ray Jones (BA .281, 5 HRs) and Jamie Howell (BA .304) and catcher Robert Khayat (BA .326) were named first-team All-SEC by one or more media sources. Second-team All-SEC honors went to pitcher Denny Bomquist (7-0 as a pitcher, BA .406), shortstop Bobby Kilpatrick (BA .382), and first baseman Ken Netherland (BA .253). It is doubtful that any other school in a single baseball season has ever fielded five first-team All-SEC players and three second-team All-SEC players. Even with his .424 batting average, Jake Gibbs did not lead the team in hitting; that honor went to Chuck Tuohey, who edged him out by batting .425. However, Touhey did not have enough plate appearances to qualify for the SECS batting title.

1960 SEC Football Champion—Ole Miss

The writer matriculated as a freshman at Ole Miss in the fall of 1960. I grew up a Rebel fan, but I was especially a fan of Ole Miss football and I expected great football to continue during my years at Ole Miss.

I would not be disappointed as the Rebs won the SEC championship three of the four years I was an undergraduate.

My real fascination with Rebel football began when I was in the ninth grade. On October 6, 1956, the Rebels defeated the University of Houston in Jackson's old Hinds County War Memorial Stadium. That was the first Ole Miss football game that I actually attended. It made an indelible impression on this 14-year-old Enochs Junior High football player and provided me with my first favorite Rebel player, Paige Cothren. Several of my teammates accompanied me to the stadium, and we were treated to one of Cothren's best games. The Rebel fullback gained 144 yards on 15 carries, scored a touchdown, and kicked two extra points as Ole Miss won 14-0. Cothren, who suited up for the Rebels in the 1954, 1955, and 1956 seasons, rushed for a total of 1,390 yards over his career as Ole Miss compiled a 26-6 record. He played on two Rebel teams that won SEC championships, and he played in the 1955 Sugar Bowl and the 1956 Cotton Bowl. Later he had a three-year NFL career. After football, Cothren led a very interesting life, becoming a business owner, a preacher, a football coach, a counselor, and a published author.

Years after watching Cothren play against Houston I got to meet and talk to him on three occasions. When he was the marketing director of Grand Oaks as it was being built in Oxford, I was considering buying a lot there. Cothren drove me around the development in a golf cart. I told him about going to the Houston game and that really got him started; he remembered every detail. Later when I was living in Hattiesburg he came and spoke to a civic club I belonged to about his books and I got to talk to him again. Finally, I ran into him at a Rebel baseball game and we talked again. I remember two things vividly about my limited interactions with Cothren. He said over the years that he played high school, college, and professional football he never got one single drink of water on the practice field. I could identify with that because the coaches at Enochs would not let us have any water during practice even on hot Mississippi summers days. One of his books, *Walk Carefully around the Dead*, is mostly about J. W. "Wobble" Davidson, a legendary Ole Miss assistant coach who ran the athletic dorm and coached the freshman football team. His tales about Wobble are hilarious and emphasize the toughness of the man. I could identify with that too. I took a volleyball class under Davidson with a bunch of football players. Wobble had to be the toughest volleyball coach ever.

The 1960 Ole Miss football team got this green freshman's college experience off to a good start. Compiling an undefeated 10-0-1 record, Ole Miss won its fourth SEC football championship in the fall of 1960. Thus began a four-year period that saw the Rebels completely dominate the SEC in football.

Ole Miss began the season ranked second by the Associated Press and United Press International preseason polls. The Rebels went to Texas September 17 to play the Houston Cougars at Rice Stadium. After a slow start, the visitors led 7-0 at halftime. Coach Vaught must have had a good halftime chat with his chargers because they scored 35 unanswered points in the second half to win 42-0. Ole Miss's brilliant set of quarterbacks—senior Jake Gibbs, junior Doug Elmore, and sophomore Glynn Griffing—put on a show as all of the Rebels' touchdowns came on passes. Gibbs passed for three touchdowns, Elmore two, and Griffing one. Willis Dabbs caught two touchdown passes from Elmore and one from Griffing. Gibbs's touchdown passes went to Hoss Anderson, George Blair, and Johnny Brewer. Griffing's touchdown pass went to Wes Sullivan, and that score was followed by Sullivan catching a pass from Griffing for a two-point conversion. Allen Green was successful on four of five extra-point attempts. The Rebels gained 433 total yards, the Cougars 163. The Cougars managed 16 first downs but lost four fumbles while Ole Miss had 26 first downs and lost one fumble. After crushing Houston, Ole Miss moved to number one in the polls.

There used to be a saying that people in north Mississippi thought Memphis was the capital of Mississippi. Maybe that was because in the 1950s and early 1960s Ole Miss played some of its home games in Memphis. There were and still are a lot of Ole Miss alumni in the city, and in those days it was much more accessible and had many more accommodations than Oxford. Crump Stadium in Memphis hosted 30,187 fans for the Rebels' next game against the Kentucky Wildcats on September 24.

The Wildcats proved to be much more of a challenge than the Cougars. But the Rebel defense was too much for the Cats, who didn't register a first down until the third quarter. Although the powerful Ole Miss offense possessed the ball most of the first half, the score stood 7-0 Rebs at the half. The lone first-half touchdown was scored on a three-yard quarterback sneak by Jake Gibbs. In the third quarter Bob Benton recovered a Kentucky fumble at the Cats' 13-yard line. Three plays later, Gibbs ran a keeper around right end and scored from the 8-yard line. Late in the fourth quarter Doug Elmore scored the Rebels' final touchdown on a three-yard keeper over right tackle. Allen Greene converted the extra-point attempt after each of the Rebels' three touchdowns. Kentucky's six points came in the fourth quarter when Charles Sturgeon's running attempt from the Ole Miss one-yard line resulted in a fumble and Tom Hutchinson recovered the ball in the end zone. The Cats missed the extra point. The Rebels' passing acuteness of the prior week never materialized. Gibbs and Elmore both went 2 for 7 for a total of 56 yards. The 21-6 Ole Miss win is reflected in the game statistics. Kentucky garnered only 26 yards rushing, and the Rebels led the Cats in first downs 16-6 and in total yards 267-115. Ole Miss maintained its number-one national ranking.

For three quarters Memphis State went toe to toe with Ole Miss at Crump Stadium in Memphis on October 2. Five minutes into the game the Tigers led seven to nothing when John Griffin intercepted a Jake Gibbs pass and returned it 22 yards for a touchdown. Gibbs soon redeemed himself on a 64-yard drive that included a 29-yard pass to Bobby Crespino and a 6-yard rollout left for a touchdown. After a fumble by George Blair at the Rebels' 45-yard line the Tigers jumped ahead again on James Earl Wright's 15-yard pass to Charles Killett. Early in the second quarter Gibbs hit Crespino on a 14-yard touchdown pass, but Allen Green missed the extra point. Another

Gibbs to Crespino touchdown pass, this one a 24 yarder, and a missed two-point conversion attempt left the Rebels up 19-14. The Tigers registered the second half's first score on a 2-yard plunge by Killett. The two-point conversion attempt failed but the Tigers led 20-19 at the end of the third quarter. The Rebels were not used to trailing after three quarters, and they went to work remedying the situation. Treva Bolin blocked and recovered an attempted quick kick at the Tigers' 28-yard line. Four rushes took the Rebels to the 3-yard line and Hoss Anderson bulled his way into the end zone. Anderson's two-point conversion attempt failed, Rebels 25, Tigers 20. Ole Miss quickly stopped the Tigers on their next possession. Art Doty scored on a 2-yard run to complete a nine-play 64-yard drive for the game's last score. The Rebels' two-point conversion attempt failed, and the game ended Ole Miss 31, Memphis State 20. The Rebels punted only three times while the Tigers punted nine times. Ole Miss led in first downs 17-8 and total yards 380-197. From an Ole Miss perspective, the game was very sloppy; the Rebels lost a fumble and had four passes intercepted.

The 1959 Rebels had given up only 21 points all season and no team had scored 20 or more points on Ole Miss since Tennessee scored 27 in 1956. The pollsters found the Memphis State score shocking, and Ole Miss dropped to number two in the polls.

On October 8 Ole Miss played Vanderbilt on the Commodores home field in Nashville. The Rebels had been embarrassed at Memphis, and they were probably insulted to be playing the Dores in their homecoming game. In a game completely dominated by the visitors, 23,000 fans saw George Blair score on a 1-yard run, Hoss Anderson score on runs of 1 and 6 yards, and Art Doty score on a 16-yard run. Ole Miss regained their defensive dominance and their number-one rank by whipping Vanderbilt 26-0.

All the scoring came in the first half as the miscues of the prior Saturday were put in the rearview mirror. Ole Miss moved the ball well in the second half but failed to score. Backups played most of the way and the Rebs hurt themselves with several penalties. Art Doty fumbled going into the end zone, and Vandy intercepted a Glynn Griffing pass at their 10-yard line. The Rebels dominated game statistics, leading in first downs 17-10 and in yards gained 402-119. The Commodores gained a total of 11 yards rushing. Again, the Rebels were not up to par on their extra-point attempts; they missed three out of four, one on a kick and two on 2-point attempts, a failed pass and a run. After the last touchdown the Rebels finally converted as Doug Elmore threw to Billy Ray Adams for a 2-pointer.

On October 15 Ole Miss visited New Orleans to take on an improving Green Wave team in Tulane Stadium before 73,000 fans. Jake Gibbs put on an All-American-type performance, throwing three touchdown passes to Johnny Brewer and running 6 yards for another score. Often called the Rifleman, Mr. Gibbs had pretty much mastered the art of playing quarterback. In five games he had passed for eight touchdowns and run for six. The Rebels again struggled with extra points making two of four with Allen Green and George Blair both making one. The only first-quarter touchdown came when Gibbs hit Brewer from 42 yards out. George Blair kicked the extra point. The Rebels scored again early in the second quarter on a 37-yard seven-play drive after Ralph Smith recovered a Tulane fumble. Gibbs toted the ball over the goal line on a 6-yard run. Blair's extra-point attempt was blocked. Ole Miss led at the half 13-0. Late in the third quarter Rush McKay recovered a Tulane fumble on the Greenies' 14-yard line, and Gibbs promptly hit Brewer for another touchdown. It was 20-0 Rebs at the end of the third quarter. Gibbs connected with Brewer for another touchdown in the fourth quarter, this time a 24-yarder. All of Tulane's scoring came in the fourth quarter. The Green Wave scored an 11-yard pass from Phil Nugent to Tom Mason and on a 2-yard run by fullback Bill Ary. The Greenies made one of two extra-point attempts. The Rebels dominated the statistics, first downs 18-14, yards rushing 238-110, yards passing 256-145. It was back to number two in the polls, probably because Tulane scored 13 points.

In the fall of 1960, for the first time I got to see the Rebels play several games in person. Even though I didn't attend the game, I remember vividly the October 22 contest against the Arkansas Razorbacks. The game was played in War Memorial Stadium in Little Rock before 40,000 fans. I listened to Bill Goodrich's description of this thriller on the radio in Jackson with my dad. The fourteenth-ranked Hogs came into the game 4-1 having lost to fellow Southwest Conference member Baylor 28-14 and having beaten eleventh-ranked Texas the week before, 24-23.

With 11:30 left in the second quarter Arkansas scored first in this titanic defensive struggle on a 2-yard jump-pass from quarterback George McKinney to end James Gaston. Mickey Cissell added the extra point. The Rebels drew even in the third quarter thanks to an interception by Doug Elmore and a gutsy 80-yard drive. Gibbs sparkled in that drive, gaining 2 yards on a fourth and one at the Ole Miss 29-yard line and running twice to the 43. After Bobby Crespino was stopped for no gain, Gibbs uncorked a pass to Ralph "Catfish" Smith, who dashed down the sideline for a 57-yard touchdown. Allen Green kicked the extra point. In the fourth quarter, thanks to the running of Lance Alworth, Darrell Williams, and Curtis Cox, the Razorbacks moved the ball from their own 38-yard line to gain a first down at the Rebels' 18. On fourth and 9 from the 17 Cissell attempted a field goal, which fell short and to the left. Ole Miss took over at the 20. Runs by Doty, Anderson, and Gibbs moved the ball to the 50 where Gibbs fumbled it away to Arkansas's Dean Garrett. Arkansas soon punted, and the Rebels were in business again at their own 25. Gibbs quickly engineered an eight-play drive that put the ball to the Hogs' 18-yard line with 25 seconds left in the game. Gibbs was then sacked for a 2-yard loss. The *Clarion-Ledger*'s Wayne Thompson explained what happened next:

> Confusion joined bedlam as a reigning force in the final moments of play as Ole Miss after driving from its own 25-yard line to the Porkers' 18, went into field goal formation with 16 seconds left on the clock. Green's initial effort was good but a horn went off in the stands and the referee called time with 3 seconds still left on the clock. Ole Miss had

> another chance and Green got that referee and a horn blower off the hook by putting his second try straight and true and good for the victory. It went into the books as a 39-yard kick as Gibbs held from the 29.

The validity of that Rebels' 10-7 victory is still contested by Arkansas fans. While there was no dispute that Green's first kick was good, it seems that all Arkansas fans questioned the second kick. The second attempt hooked left but the officials ruled it crossed the goal post between the uprights. To make things worse, the kicker, Allen Green, hailed from Hanceville, Arkansas. Arkansas coach Frank Broyles said, "Everybody in the park knew it wasn't good." Even with their slim victory margin, the Rebels maintained their number-two national ranking.

The week after the Arkansas game, the Rebels played LSU in Oxford on October 29. For some reason I can't remember I was home in Jackson that weekend and watched the game on TV with my dad. This was one of the few LSU games that teams coached by Johnny Vaught played the Tigers in Hemingway Stadium on Mississippi soil. It was homecoming day when the Rebels faced their bitter rivals, and the Tigers were a 15-point underdog. Fans should have learned to expect the unexpected when these teams played. The game turned out to be a defensive struggle in which the two offenses combined produced only one touchdown and two field goals.

In the first quarter LSU drove to the Ole Miss 6-yard line where the Rebels held and the Tigers missed a field-goal attempt. The same thing happened to the Rebels in the second quarter as they drove to LSU's 6-yard line only to have Allen Green miss a field-goal attempt. At halftime neither team had scored a point. On the first play of the third quarter LSU's Jerry Stovall fumbled and Treva Bolin recovered at the Tigers' 24-yard line. When three plays gained only 1 yard, Allen Green kicked a 30-yard field goal. Late in the third quarter LSU drove 52 yards for a touchdown on a 1-yard run by Ray Wilkins. Wendell Harris's extra-point attempt failed, 6-3 LSU. In the last quarter an injured Jake Gibbs returned a punt from the Rebels' 11 to their 21 and then started a drive with 1:26 left in the game. Gibbs promptly drove the Rebels down field and with six seconds on the clock Allen Green kicked a 41-yard field goal to tie the game and preserve Ole Miss's undefeated season for the second straight week. Statistics accurately reflected the tightness of the game: first downs Ole Miss 14, LSU 9, total yards Ole Miss 208, LSU 221. LSU gained only 5 yards rushing.

LSU battered Jake Gibbs all day; he wound up with minus 13 yards rushing and only 89 yards passing. If I remember correctly Jake was actually limping (he had just run a punt back, and he was sacked for a 9-yard loss during the drive) when he led the final drive to set up Green's field goal. After the game, Coach Vaught said, "I was glad to get out of it with a tie—a Mexican standoff. With our team crippled so badly, I thought our boys played real well, everything considered." Coach Paul Dietzel said of his Tigers, "Our kids deserved to win that one. It's been like that all year. We've got a bunch of great [players] and I'm proud to coach them." The Tigers would go on to finish the season with a very unlikely LSU record 5-4-1.

After the tie with LSU, Ole Miss dropped to sixth place nationally in the polls. Chattanooga was up next, and the Rebels easily dispatched the lightly regarded Moccasins 45-0. But it was enough for the pollsters to move the Rebels to fourth place.

Tennessee was next in line, and the Mississippians' 24-3 victory over the Volunteers pushed the Rebels back up to third in the national rankings. The November 12, 1960, victory over Tennessee was especially sweet and memorable because it was the Rebels' first win ever at Shields-Watkins Stadium in Knoxville.

Taking the opening kickoff, the impolite visitors strutted down field 76 yards in nine plays capped off by Hoss Anderson's 2-yard burst for a touchdown. Allen Green kicked the extra point. The Vols got their first and only score when Doug Elmore fumbled and Larry Richards recovered at the Rebs' 23. The Vols were stopped by a great defense at the 11, but Cotton Letner was successful on a 28-yard field-goal attempt. The Rebels' next score came on a 32-yard Allen Green field goal. At the half, the score was Ole Miss 10, Tennessee 3. Neither team scored in the third quarter, but the Rebels put up 14 points against the outmanned Vols in the fourth. Hoss Anderson scored on a 43-yard run, and Bobby Crespino on a 5-yard pass from Gibbs. Allen Green, who had almost conquered his early kicking woes, kicked both extra points. Again, the stats reflect the Rebels' dominance—first downs 18-4, total yards 269-24. (That's right, the Vols gained a total of 24 yards!) Losing three fumbles and suffering 89 yards in penalties kept the Rebels from running up the score.

Both head coaches were magnanimous after the game. Coach Vaught called it "one of the finest victories of all time for us" and said it "was a fine a game as we have played in a long long time." Then the delighted head coach added, "Tennessee made us earn everything we got and they never quit." Coach Bowden Wyatt, who had dropped a game 37-7 to the Rebels in Memphis the year before, was complimentary and sanguine. Wyatt said the Vols had been beaten by "a real fine football team" and "we did as well as could be expected."

Ole Miss closed out its regular season November 26 with a 35-9 victory over in-state rival Mississippi State in Oxford. State took the kickoff and moved down field until they stalled at the Rebels' 35-yard line. Sammy Dantone then missed a 42-yard field-goal attempt. After a short Rebel drive Allen Green missed on a 52-yard field-goal attempt; he was human, after all. Neither team scored in the first quarter, but the home team found its mojo in the second quarter and posted 14 points. Early in the quarter Jake Gibbs bobbled a snap at State's 1-yard line and State's Lee Welsh recovered. State couldn't take advantage of the fumble recovery, and the Rebels regained possession on a punt at the Maroons' 38. Gibbs then negotiated a drive that ended with Johnny Brewer catching an 11-yard pass for a touchdown. Allen Green quickly got back on track as he kicked the first of what would become five consecutive extra points. State couldn't move the ball, and after a punt Doug Elmore came in and drove the Rebels to State's 16-yard line where Gibbs took over and fired a pass to Bobby Crespino for a touchdown. Ole Miss led 14 to nothing at halftime.

State went into a spread offense and scored first in the third quarter to draw within 7 points of its rival. Billy "Tootie" Hill directed a spectacular 78-yard drive that ended with a 3-yard touchdown pass to David Kelly. Dantone added the extra point. The unfazed Rebels responded by mounting a 94-yard touchdown march of their own. Gibbs ran the ball into the end zone from the 8. Ole Miss went on to put up a total of 21 points in the quarter. Wes Sullivan intercepted a Billy Hill pass and returned it for a touchdown, and Billy Ray Adams's 1-yard run ended the Rebels' scoring for the day. After Ole Miss stopped a State drive at the 1-yard line, 2 points were added to the Maroons' total when Doug Elmore rolled out to throw a pass but tripped in the end zone. Suffice it to say that by gaining over 400 yards and making 25 first downs Ole Miss dominated the game statistics. As unbelievable as it seems State's 9 points were the most they had scored against Ole Miss since they lost to the Rebels 20-14 in 1952.

MSU's head coach Wade Walker had nothing but praises for the Rebels after the game. In the postgame press conference, he said, "Ole Miss has a great football team and Jake Gibbs is the greatest quarterback in the United States, bar none." The Maroons were behind 14 points at the half, and Walker explained what happened. "We had to gamble to catch up and they got two quick touchdowns and we were out of the game. However, I don't want to take anything away from my kids, they were ready and did a good job but just couldn't stop Gibbs. We tried to do it by rushing and he ruined us with those short passes. Especially in the flat." Coach Vaught was asked about Gibbs after the game and he responded, "Without a doubt Jake is the best college back in America today. If there ever was such a thing as an All-American, he is it. I rate him the absolute tops."

At the end of the regular season and before the bowl games Ole Miss was ranked second in the final AP and third in the final UPI coaches poll. With an 8-1 record Minnesota finished first in both polls. Former Mississippi State head coach Murray Warmath's Golden Gophers' only loss was to Purdue by a score of 23-14. Iowa finished second in the UPI poll with an 8-1 record; the Hawkeyes' loss was to Minnesota 27-10. The only bowl game that Big 10 teams played in before 1975 was the Rose Bowl. Minnesota represented the Big Ten

Conference in the 1961 Rose Bowl where they lost to sixth-ranked Washington 17-7. The Huskies came into the game with a 9-1 record. It was a travesty that the AP and UPI did not rank the University of Mississippi number one in the nation.

Ole Miss (9-0-1) was matched against the Rice Owls (7-3) in the 1961 Sugar Bowl. In the 14-6 Ole Miss victory, the Rebels intercepted four passes, which killed Rice's hopes. Jake Gibbs, who was named most valuable player, led the Rebels to first- and fourth-quarter touchdowns. After the Sugar Bowl victory, the Football Writers Association of America named the Ole Miss Rebels national champions symbolized by the Grantland Rice Trophy. The writers got it right. Other ratings organizations who ranked the Rebels number one in 1960 included Billingsley, DeVold, Dunkel, Football Research, National Championship Foundation, and Williamson.

How could the 1960 edition of Rebel football not prosper? They were led by All-American quarterback Jack Gibbs and featured six other players who were drafted by NFL teams—Bobby Crespino, Jerry Daniels, Allen Green, Bob Benton, Doug Elmore, and Charlie (Chico) Taylor. The great Richard Price, an undersized guard and linebacker, was not drafted. According to a Rick Cleveland article in the July 26, 2019, edition of *Mississippi Today*, Johnny Vaught once said Price was not only the best linebacker he ever coached, he was the best he ever saw.

One memory of Bobby Crespino is still seared in my mind. While walking up the steps to the old campus post office I was struck by the sight of a guy coming down the steps. He was a large impressive figure and I gave him a wide path. When I got back to the dorm, I told my roommates that I had just encountered the biggest and meanest-looking guy I had ever seen. I also said that he was probably a football player and that if he wasn't first-team I wanted to see who was ahead of him. The big guy was Bobby Crespino, who starred in football, baseball, basketball, and track at Greenville High School and excelled as a Rebel running back and receiver. He was a member of the 1959 Ole Miss team that had been named the team of the decade in the SEC. After his great senior year, he was named the MVP of the Senior Bowl in which he set a Senior Bowl record with nine catches for 214 yards. Crespino played in the 1961 College All Star Game in which graduating seniors played the NFL champs. Drafted in the first round by the Cleveland Browns, this fabulous athlete went on to play three seasons with the Browns and five seasons with the New York Giants.

The year 1960 was a very good time for a sports fan to be a freshman at Ole Miss!

How Did the Other Teams Fare?

1960 Mississippi State Basketball

After winning the university's first SEC basketball championship in 1959 it seemed that the Maroons might be headed for hard times again. The great Bailey Howell had graduated and was beginning his hall-of-fame NBA career. Although standouts Jerry Graves and Jack Berkshire were still around, their presence was not enough to offset the loss of Howell. The 1959–60 Mississippi State basketball team finished 12-13 overall and 5-9 in the SEC. Not to worry, plenty of help was on the way. Coach Babe McCarthy was just reloading. The 1959–60 MSU freshman team included Leland Mitchell, W. D. "Red" Stroud, Joe Dan Gold, Bobby Shows, and Mack Whyte. During their upcoming varsity seasons this quintet would lead MSU to heights hardly imaginable by State fans.

1960 Ole Miss Basketball

Ole Miss basketball had finished in last place in the SEC in the 1958–59 season, but things were changing for the better. The 1959–60 basketball season was the best Ole Miss had experienced in 22 years. The Rebels finished 15-9 overall and 8-6 in the SEC. Junior forward Jack

Donnie Kessinger

Baseball: 1962, 1963, 1964 (All-American 1964)
Basketball: 1962, 1963, 1964 (All-American 1964). Ole Miss Athletics Photo.

Waters averaged 20 points per game and 7 rebounds. Senior center Ivan Richmann averaged 15 points and 10 rebounds while sophomore center Sterling Ainsworth averaged 13 points and 7 rebounds. Future basketball and baseball star Donnie Kessinger was a freshman in the fall. Because of Kessinger the old gym would fill up for freshman games and the Forrest City, Arkansas, product didn't disappoint. He regularly put on a show that kept the fans coming back. It seemed like things were looking up for Rebel basketball.

1960 Mississippi State Baseball

At the beginning of the 1960 baseball season, Mississippi State was set to rebound from Head Coach Paul Gregory's first losing season. His teams had posted overall and SEC winning records in both 1957 (13-5, 10-5) and 1958 (14-10, 8-6). But in 1959 the Maroons had slipped to 12-13 overall and 5-10 in the conference. The 1960 season would see Gregory's team bounce back to post a 16-11 overall record that included an 8-8 SEC mark. Left-handed pitcher Guy Parker led the SEC with a 2.84 earned run average. Gregory was in the process of building an SEC powerhouse that over the next 14 years (1961–1974) would play in five SEC championship series and win four of them. The only other SEC school that came close to Gregory's State teams' performance was Ole Miss, which won three championships during that period.

1960 Mississippi State Football

There were few positives associated with Mississippi State football in the fall of 1960 as the Maroons went 2-6-1 overall. For the second consecutive year the Maroons won only two games, and those victories were again against Arkansas State (29-9) and Memphis State (21-0). Arkansas State still did not play big-time college football, but Memphis State had moved into the major college ranks. State lost five and tied one (0-0 against Tennessee) in SEC competition. That SEC mark landed MSU dead last in the conference. This was Wade Walker's fourth losing season in his five years as head coach. Walker would start 1961 on the "hot seat."

1961

Another Championship, Basketball Rising

1961 SEC Basketball Champion—Mississippi State
1961 SEC Baseball Champion—LSU
1961 SEC Football Champion—Alabama/LSU (tie)
Final score: Mississippi schools 1 SEC championship, all other SEC schools 2

The Champion

1961 Mississippi State Basketball

As a sophomore Jerry Graves averaged 10 points and 8 rebounds per game for the Mississippi State basketball team that won the 1959 SEC championship with a 24-1 record. That season Graves played in the shadow of the great senior Bailey Howell. Like Howell, Graves was from Tennessee, hailing from Lexington, which is close to Middleton, Howell's hometown. During his junior year (1959–1960) Graves improved to 19 points and 10 rebounds per game and was named All-SEC. Sophomore point guard Jack Berkshire had averaged 7 points for the 1959–60 Maroons. Unfortunately, Graves's and Berkshire's performances could not keep MSU from slipping to a 12-13 overall record for the 1959–60 season. But these two stars got big-time help when the 1959 recruits, probably the best recruiting class in school history, joined the varsity in the fall of 1960. The 1959 recruiting class included Leland Mitchell, W. D. "Red" Stroud, Joe Dan Gold, Bobby Shows, and Mack Whyte. Those sophomores would go on to play huge parts in the greatest three-year period in Mississippi State basketball history.

Jerry Graves and Jack Berkshire co-captained 1960–61 Maroons. Graves, a superb leader, averaged 21 points and 10 rebounds. Point guard Berkshire, a superb game manager, again averaged 7 points a game. On a team that averaged 77 points per game the great sophomore class combined to average 43 points and 22 rebounds. Three of the sophomores averaged scoring in double figures, Mitchell 13, Stroud 12, and Gold 10. In contrast to the 1959 champions who played a fairly conventional style, Coach Babe McCarthy's 1961 team liked to play fast most of the time but ran the stall to perfection when the occasion called for it.

The Maroons went 7-3 against non-SEC foes in their first 10 games. The super sophomores were just getting their bearings and developing confidence. The three losses were to Louisiana Tech 61-60, to Loyola of New Orleans 83-60, and to Texas 93-82.

Opening SEC play January 7, 1961, State upset defending SEC champion Auburn 56-48 while snapping the Plainsmen's 15-game winning streak and their 36-game home winning streak. Twenty-five hundred fans packed Auburn's gym to witness the contest, which was broadcast on television statewide in Alabama. State began playing its stall offense midway through the first half, sometimes going five minutes without taking a shot. Auburn had to foul, and they sent State to the free-throw line 25 times, where the Maroons canned 24 points. Auburn took 21 free throws and made 16. Free throws won the game. Jerry Graves scored 24 points, making 6 field goals and

12 of 12 from the charity stripe. He was named SEC co-player of the week along with Georgia Tech's Roger Kaiser. Auburn was ranked tenth in the Associated Press poll before the game. After the defeat, the Plainsmen dropped out of the poll and didn't return for the rest of the season.

Posting their second road victory in four nights, MSU spanked Alabama 80-63 on January 10. There was no slowdown this time as the Maroons ran the fast break almost to perfection. Graves, who scored 20 points, rested on the bench 10 minutes, and Berkshire chipped in with 14. Two of Coach McCarthy's super sophomores scored in double figures: Red Stroud 16 and the steadily improving Joe Dan Gold 17. Brookhaven native Henry Hoskins led Alabama in scoring with 27 points. Larry Pennington from Jackson also scored 7 points for the Tide even though he was hampered by foul trouble. After the game the Maroons stood atop the SEC standings with a 2-0 mark.

Vanderbilt came into the Maroons' gym January 14 riding a 13-game win streak with SEC wins over Kentucky and Tennessee, both by 2 points. State snapped another opponent's win streak, prevailing 74-65. Coach McCarthy called for the stall offense with less than five minutes to play when Vandy closed to within one point, 59-58. Frustration set in for the visitors while State sacked 14 free throws and only one field goal in those last five minutes. The Maroons attempted 43 free throws and made 32. Graves made 21 of 27 from the line to break Bailey Howell's record of 19 successes against Florida in 1959. Graves ended the game with 29 points, and Jack Berkshire scored 12. The sophomores did their part; Stroud hit for 13 points while Mitchell and Gold added 9 points each. The battle on the boards was fairly even with State grabbing 50 rebounds and Vanderbilt 47. State stayed atop the SEC standings at 3-0.

Georgia Tech took MSU to overtime January 16 in Starkville. The score was tied 56-56 at the end of regulation. Jerry Graves put on a show as the overtime period drew to a close. The *Clarion-Ledger*'s Robert (Steamboat) Fulton wrote:

> He [Graves] scored two free throws, hit an important jump shot with 1:31 left, stole the ball from a driving tech guard and his grittiness was called on once again with State clinging to a 60-59 lead with 13 seconds left and he, with a two-point foul. Under tremendous pressure the six-six senior from Lexington, Tenn., calmly sank both shots, pulling the game out of Tech's frantic reach despite an unguarded Jacket layup and a desperation timeout with three seconds left. "There isn't a player in basketball with more guts than Graves," said a jubilant Babe McCarthy after the game, "especially when he walked to that free throw line under pressure."

Tech's Roger Kaiser, the SEC's leading scorer, put up 31 points against the Maroons while breaking Tech's all-time scoring record of 1,363 points. But MSU's Jerry Graves pretty much canceled out Kaiser's performance by scoring 28 points including 12 of 13 free throws. Graves also grabbed 10 rebounds while Joe Dan Gold contributed 11 rebounds and 16 points. After the victory the Maroons stood alone at the top of the SEC with a 4-0 conference record.

When State played Ole Miss in Starkville January 21, the Maroons had just played two home games and had five more to go. The Rebels were 2-2 in the SEC and 7-6 overall. The game featured the SEC's second and third leading scorers, MSU's Jerry Graves (22) and Ole Miss's Jack Waters (21). State led 31-25 at the half, but the Rebs closed to within one point 35-34 in the first seven minutes of the second half. Then W. D. Stroud made a layup to push the lead to 3 points and State went into its stall game. MSU took only one shot over the next seven minutes. Then the Maroons switched to a fast-breaking scheme and put the visitors away before 5,000 screaming fans. MSU won 63-40 to maintain its lead in the SEC. Ole Miss scored only three points during the last 14 minutes of the game.

The anticipated matchup between Graves and Waters never materialized. The Rebels' sophomore twins, guards Mel and El Edmonds, double-teamed Graves and held him to 10 points. Waters went down in the first half with a sprained ankle. The Rebels' star snatched 3 rebounds, but he attempted only three shots and converted none. Two of Mississippi State's sophomores shined. Red Stroud hit 10 of 14 field-goal attempts and scored 23 points and Leland Mitchell chipped in with 18 points while making 8 of his 14 field-goal attempts. Both teams had 38 rebounds, with Graves snatching 16 for the Maroons and Sterling Ainsworth 15 for the Rebs.

The LSU Tigers came to Starkville February 4 and were promptly drubbed by the home team 77-61. The victory was a typical team effort with all five Maroon starters scoring in double figures. W. D. Stroud led the way with 21 points while Leland Mitchell and Jerry Graves each contributed 15 points. Jack Berkshire scored 13 points and Joe Dan Gold 11. State simply dominated the second half as LSU failed to score a field goal during the first 10 minutes. The Maroons' dominance is reflected in field-goal percentages and the number of free throws converted—field goals, State 48 percent, LSU 37 percent; free-throw conversions, State 23 of 30, LSU 11 of 16. Before the game the Maroons were tied with Florida atop the conference but when the day ended, State sat alone at the top; Kentucky had knocked off Florida.

State chalked up its seventh straight conference win February 6 when it became Tulane's time to visit the Maroons' gym. Before 4,500 State fans the Green Wave fell 73-59. It was Coach McCarthy's 100th victory at State, a feat achieved in fewer than six seasons. With the Maroons leading 14-12 midway through the first half, MSU put its foot down on the pedal and over the next two and a half minutes upped their lead to 27-14. It was all over. With Berkshire scoring 10 points while triggering the offense, Graves scored 28, Mitchell 15, and Gold 11. Graves, Mitchell, and Gold dominated the boards grabbing a total of 31 rebounds. State was still in first place in the conference, but Tennessee and Kentucky would soon show up in Starkville.

The Tennessee Volunteers proved to be a rugged challenge when they arrived. Before a full gym the Maroons won by only 5 points, 72-67. But the game was not that close, leading by 15 toward the end of the game Coach McCarthy put in four subs. The Maroons had masterfully employed their speed-up, slow-down tactics. Tennessee, a very physical team, sent State to the free-throw line 39 times where the nonplussed Maroons calmly sank 28 points. Again, four MSU players finished in double figures. Three sophomores—Mitchell, Gold, and Stroud—each scored 17 points, and their reliable senior leader Graves chipped in with 16. Despite the Vols physical style, State prevailed in the battle for rebounds 38-35. MSU was still perfect in the conference and atop the standings by two games.

Then the Kentucky Wildcats showed up in Starkville. State's SEC winning streak had to stop sometime, and Kentucky put an end to the eight-game run on February 13. Before an overflow crowd of about 6,000 fans, the Wildcats defeated the home team 68-62. At the half, Kentucky led 33-32 when the Cat's Larry Pursiful hit two free throws after the buzzer. State went cold early in the second half, allowing the Cats to build up a lead that couldn't be overcome. Jerry Graves led the Maroons with 27 points and 12 rebounds. For a change, only two other MSU players cracked double digits in scoring, Joe Dan Gold scored 12 points and Red Stroud 11. Kentucky's Roger Newman scored 24 points and grabbed 10 rebounds, and he was supported by three other Wildcats in double figures. After the game Babe McCarthy explained, "We hit a cold streak about five minutes deep in second half and that was the turning point." McCarthy also said, "Newman killed us. He was the difference."

During the game, a State student put a dead skunk in a bag under Kentucky coach Adolph Rupp's chair. In somewhat of a mystery, a black wreath appeared on State's dressing room door. Was that wreath ordered by Coach Rupp? Babe McCarthy ordered that the wreath be saved; he had plans for its future use.

Despite the loss, Coach McCarthy had encouraging words for his team after the game, saying, "This doesn't mean a thing." He could afford to make such a statement because the Maroons still held a two-game lead in the conference. Second-place Vanderbilt lost to LSU 65-61 that same night. The lead meant the Maroons were still in good shape with four league games to play. After the game, both State and Kentucky received votes in the AP's poll, but neither was in the top 10.

After seven consecutive home games the Maroons ventured to Gainesville February 18 to play Florida. The Gators had an 11-9 record but had not lost a home game all season. The results were a second straight SEC loss as the Gators edged the Maroons 59-57. State led 40-39 at halftime, but in the second half the Gators went to a zone defense and the Maroons went into their stall offense. State maintained the lead until there were 2 minutes and 13 seconds left when Florida's George Jung hit two free throws to tie the game. With four seconds left in the game Florida's center Cliff Luyk hit a 15-foot jump shot to seal the Gators' victory. Luyk's shot came after the Gators' Bobby Shiver stole the ball from Jack Berkshire, who was dribbling as he attempted to set up a shot that would win the game for the Maroons or send it into overtime. Graves led State's scoring with 15 points followed by Mitchell's 14 and Stroud's 12. State's two-game SEC lead had melted to one game over the Gators and Vanderbilt.

Next came the Georgia Bulldogs on the road and a much-needed victory. The Maroons' running game simply overwhelmed the home team 99-77. It was not much of a contest. Georgia had already lost nine SEC games and would end the season 8-18 overall and 4-10 in the conference. Jerry Graves scored 34 points and secured 10 rebounds. Three of the sophomores scored in double figures: Stroud 17, Mitchell 14, and Gold 11. Mitchell also grabbed 14 rebounds. Standing 9-2, the Maroons still led the conference with three games to play.

A February 25 game against LSU in Baton Rouge provided an opportunity for Mississippi State to win on a last-second shot. Super sophomore Leland Mitchell did not disappoint as he drained a 15-foot jump shot to give the Maroons 56-54 win in a hotly contested game. State did not score during the first four minutes of the game and trailed by as much as 13 points in the first half. Red Stroud countered the initial four-minute drought by scoring 10 points during the following four minutes. The game took place before 5,000 fans, LSU's largest crowd of the season. The score was tied 50 apiece with 10:32 left when LSU went into a freeze. State soon matched the Tigers with its own stall game. The two teams scored a combined total of only

10 points the rest of the contest. In the end, Mitchell's last-second shot secured MSU at least a tie for the SEC championship with two games remaining on its schedule.

On the last day of February 1961, a *Clarion-Ledger* sports section headline proclaimed, "State Defeats Tulane 62-57 to Clinch SEC Cage Crown." Babe McCarthy's Maroons had secured their second Southeastern Conference title in three years the night before in New Orleans when they defeated the Green Wave. In the process, Babe's Boys had to overcome a 12-point second-half deficit to put away the home team. State also had to overcome the loss of Leland Mitchell, who fouled out early in the second half. Plus, the Green Wave was terrific from the foul line, hitting 21 of 24 shots. Both teams played the slow-down game, especially in the second half. But Joe Dan Gold scored 13 points and Jerry Graves 9 in that half. State was perfect from the charity stripe when the game was on the line. Red Stroud, Jack Berkshire, and Jerry Graves each hit a pair of free throws with less than three minutes left in the game. Again, Graves led State's scoring with 16 points while Gold chipped in 15 and Stroud 14.

State's final game of the season was played on March 4 against Ole Miss in Oxford. While it was a rivalry game, it was nevertheless somewhat anticlimactic for the Maroons. They had already defeated the Rebels by 23 points in Starkville and had secured the conference championship four days earlier. The Maroons also knew they were not advancing to the NCAA tournament because of Mississippi's racial segregation policy. Ole Miss came to the contest with a 9-14 overall record and a 4-9 conference mark. The Maroons dug themselves a deep hole in the first half; they trailed the Rebels 37-22 at halftime. State made a valiant effort to recover, but in what Ole Miss coach Bonnie Graham called an outstanding team effort the Rebels prevailed 74-70. A team effort it was as four of the Rebel starters scored in double figures.

I saw this game up close and personal. Like about 3,000 other folks I watched it unfold in the Rebels' tiny gym. That game is still one of my best basketball memories more than 50 years later. I really wanted to see the Rebels' great senior Jack Waters excel against MSU. He did not disappoint.

Unlike the earlier game in Starkville when Waters had gone down with a sprained ankle in the first half, the anticipated scoring dual between the Rebels' Waters and State's Jerry Graves materialized. They shared scoring honors as both pitched in 22 points. Waters hit 12 of 12 free throws. In the confines of their own cozy gym the Rebels simply out-shot the Maroons. Ole Miss shot 48 percent from the field while State shot only 34 percent. Sterling Ainsworth scored 20 points while making 10 of 11 field-goal attempts. The Maroons' 52-44 rebounding advantage could not counter the Rebels' shooting. Two of State's sophomores scored in double figures: Joe Dan Gold made 17 points and Leland Mitchell 15. For some reason the author was unable to discover, sophomore Red Stroud did not play at all.

Coach Babe McCarthy's 1960–61 Maroons finished 19-6 overall and won Mississippi State's second SEC basketball championship with an 11-3 conference record. But the Maroons never appeared in the AP College Basketball Poll. Preseason media prognosticators had predicted that State would finish in the second division of the SEC. The pundits knew about Jerry Graves and Jack Berkshire, but they had no idea how well the super sophomores would play.

Jerry Graves and Leland Mitchell were named first-team All-SEC by the Associated Press. Coach McCarthy won his second SEC Coach of the Year Award. The three conference losses were by a total of 12 points. The other three losses were to Loyola of New Orleans 83-60, Texas 93-82, and to Louisiana Tech 61-60. The loss to Loyola in an early season game on the road was the only bad loss of the year. The loss to Ole Miss was the most disappointing.

Jerry Graves averaged 21 points and finished second in the SEC scoring race behind Georgia Tech's Roger Keiser's 23-point average. The senior also grabbed 12 rebounds per game, fifth best in the conference. Graves was a good teammate and student, and he was popular on campus. In fact, Jerry Graves was elected Mr. Mississippi State his senior year.

Graves should have gone from MSU to a promising career in the National Basketball Association. It didn't happen. Unfortunately, Graves was caught up in a gambling scandal uncovered by the FBI that rocked college basketball in 1961. In his book *Wizard of Odds* published in 2001 Charley Rosen fingered Graves as one of the players who gave information to gamblers and/or shaved points to benefit gamblers during the 1960–61 season. Graves was said to be part of former college basketball player Jack Molinas's national network that cooperated with gamblers. Graves was never prosecuted, and he has consistently denied that he ever shaved points, but he has admitted that he took small amounts of money to provide information. Rosen wrote that the gamblers considered Graves a coup because he was a bonified All-American. Graves was drafted in the NBA's second round by Chicago, but he was banned by the league based on what the FBI had found. There is little or no evidence that Graves ever shaved points. Opposing teams sagged on Graves all year or double-teamed him. He consistently scored in double figures and made many shots from the floor and free throws in key situations.

W. D. Stroud described Graves as "a great player and a really good guy." Stroud also said, "I remember we found out about the whole thing after the season. We found out the FBI had been watching him and had been at our games. I don't know if he did what they said he did, but I do know he couldn't have done it much because he helped us win a lot of games."

Graves has spent his adult life as an educator, and in the early 2000s he was teaching in his hometown of Lexington, Tennessee. The *Clarion-Ledger* concluded a June 22, 2003, article about Graves and the scandal as follows:

> Jerry Graves was a splendid player, an outstanding and popular student, a nice person. Indeed, he was co-captain both his junior and senior seasons and "Mr. Mississippi State" his senior year. He has lived a productive life. Whatever mistakes he made, he more than paid for them when he wasn't allowed to pursue an NBA career.

So true! It must be added that one of MSU's greatest athletes, Jerry Graves, has never been inducted into the MSU Sports Hall of Fame or the Mississippi Sports Hall of Fame. What a shame.

How Did the Other Teams Fare?

1961 Mississippi State Baseball

Mississippi State's 1961 baseball team finished the season 12-7 overall record and 7-6 in the SEC, which ranked third in the Western Division and seventh overall. In his only season at MSU, future major leaguer Sammy Ellis set an SEC strikeout record by whiffing 19 Tulane hitters. Ellis was inducted into the MSU M Club Sports Hall of Fame in 2012. Under Coach Paul Gregory, State's baseball program was steadily improving. Since becoming head baseball coach in 1957 Gregory's teams had gone 38-35 in league play and had posted only one losing season. As we will see, the future was bright for MSU baseball.

1961 Mississippi State Football

The Mississippi State football team posted an overall 5-5 record for the 1961 season, but the SEC mark was one win against five losses. The one SEC win was an 11-10 affair against Auburn in Birmingham. State won all of its nonconference games but was competitive in only three of its six SEC contests. The season ending 37-7 loss to Ole Miss was the last game for MSU's head coach and athletic director Wade Walker, who had been under pressure from alumni. Walker, whose six-year record at MSU was 22-32-2, gave up his coaching duties but remained athletic director. In 1966 Walker would resign as athletic director and return to his home state of Oklahoma. Walker was named athletic director at his alma mater, the University of Oklahoma, in 1971, and he would remain in that position for 15 years. Walker experienced great success as an athletic director as Oklahoma won three national football championships in the years 1974, 1975, and 1985.

1961 Ole Miss Basketball

Coached by Bonnie "Country" Graham, an Ole Miss legend, the Rebels compiled a less than stellar 10-14 record while going 5-9 in the SEC, which placed the Rebels last in the conference. The finish was disappointing especially given the optimism at the start of the season. Ole Miss had the great senior guard Jack Waters, the SEC's second leading scorer during the 1959–60 season. Waters was surrounded by another senior guard, playmaker Larry Wagster, talented juniors center Sterling Ainsworth and forward Bill White, and the exciting sophomore twins El and Mel Edmonds, who could play forward and guard. The season produced few high points, but the Rebels did manage to squeak out four 2-point victories over SEC teams—69-67 over Georgia Tech, 74-72 over Vanderbilt, 57-55 over Tennessee in Oxford, and 48-46 over LSU in Baton Rouge. The Rebels other SEC win was a 74-70 victory over SEC champion Mississippi State in Oxford. Four of the SEC wins came in Oxford and the Rebs outscored their foes by a total of 10 points in those games. The Rebels worst SEC loss was by 26 points to Alabama 80-54 in Tuscaloosa. Not being a fair-weather fan, I went to most of the home games that were played in the old gym. You can tell by the scores that the Rebel games were exciting.

In his senior year All-SEC and All-American Jack Waters played great, averaging 20 points a game while displaying a classic jump shot that I will never forget. Originally from Gilbertown, Alabama, Jack grew up mostly playing football. But as a high school freshman he played basketball in Cedartown, Alabama. When the family moved to Madison, Indiana, before his sophomore year, he found himself in a school that did not field a football team. Indiana was basketball country, and Waters turned to basketball, which became his passion. After an outstanding high school career, Waters compiled three All-SEC seasons at Ole Miss. At 6'5" he was the original big guard in the

SEC. He would take smaller defenders inside and take advantage of his height and he would take taller defenders outside where they didn't match up well with his guard skills. During the 1959–60 season he led the nation in free-throw percentage (87%). Over his entire career he scored 1,384 points and averaged 20 points per game. Waters went on to play briefly in the NBA and the ABL with a stint in the military sandwiched in between. After his playing days were over, Waters went on to a successful coaching career that included stops in high schools and colleges. He was an assistant coach at Georgia Tech, and he served as head coach at Delta State and twice at Georgia State. In 2008 Jack Waters was named to the Ole Miss All-Century Basketball Team. Jack Waters should be but isn't in the Mississippi Sports Hall of Fame. In 2014 Waters was inducted into the Indiana Basketball Hall of Fame, high cotton!

Freshmen couldn't play varsity sports in 1960–61. That rule consigned Don (Donnie) Kessinger, one of the best to ever play basketball for Ole Miss, to the freshman team. But the word was out that he was a phenom and I, like many others, gravitated to the old gym when the freshman team played. I don't know the attendance figures, but it appeared to me that the freshmen out drew the varsity that season. In any event it was a pleasure to watch the freshmen play and especially to be introduced to the athleticism of Don Kessinger.

I play with the Ole Miss Seniors Golf Group on Tuesdays when I am teaching at Ole Miss. We play a 4-ball scramble, and sometimes I play in a group that includes Larry Wagster. He played varsity basketball and golf for Ole Miss during the period 1958–1961. In September 2019 Larry and I rode in the same cart, and I interviewed him for 18 holes. We talked about what it was like to be a varsity athlete at Ole Miss during those long-ago days and to play for Coach Bonnie Graham and with his great friend Jack Waters.

I asked Wagster if Ole Miss's basketball facilities were the worst in the SEC when he played for the Rebels. He shocked me by immediately replying that they were not, Georgia's were. Then he told me this story. Ole Miss played Georgia in Woodruff Hall in Athens on

February 18, 1961. The Bulldogs won the game under conditions that would not be allowed today. It had been raining for a while and the roof leaked. When the teams came out from the dressing room for the second half, towels covered a large part of the right side of the Rebels' end of the court where they would be attempting to put the ball in the basket. The results were that the part of the floor that was playable was crowded with 10 players and the Rebels had little room to maneuver to get off good shots. After a few trips up and down the court, Jack Waters told Larry that he had figured out what to do. Larry was a guard who generally handled the ball, and one of his duties was to get it to All-SEC Waters so he could score. Jack had spied a fairly small bare spot not covered by towels on the right side of the court about where the 3-point line is today. Waters told Wagster that he was going to get to that spot and Larry should get the ball to him. It worked like a charm the first time down the court as Waters swished one of his beautiful jump shots. The same thing happened the second time down the court. Then the Bulldogs caught on and a defensive man raced to beat Waters to the bare spot the next time the Rebels had the ball. Not to worry, the Rebels were then five on four on the left side of the floor that had no towels and scoring was much easier for the disadvantaged visitors. In fact, the Rebels almost pulled a rare road win losing by 4 points, 73-69.

Wagster, who is from Missouri, told me how he got to Ole Miss. As a high school junior, he played on a team that lost in the state playoffs to the eventual state champions. That team was led by super senior Gene Jordan, who signed with Ole Miss. Cobb Jarvis, an Ole Miss graduate assistant at the time, came to Missouri to recruit Jordan and saw Wagster play. Long story short, Wagster was also a golfer and Ole Miss wanted to start a golf team. Coach Bonnie Graham offered Wagster a partial scholarship, which would waive out-of-state tuition and allow him to eat at the training table during basketball season, possibly earn a full scholarship depending on his play as a freshman, and allow him to play golf. After the basketball season, Wagster kept eating at the training table. Coach Graham challenged him about it, reminding him that eating at the training table after the basketball season was not in the agreement. Wagster admitted it wasn't and soon Graham gave him a full basketball scholarship. Wagster went on to play in 66 games for the Rebels over his three-year varsity career. As noted above Wagster was also a Rebel golfer. Many years after his varsity golfing days were over, he won the 1989 Mississippi Senior State Amateur Championship.

Coach Graham didn't appreciate players laughing after a loss, according to Wagster. Against Kentucky one season, the Rebels were being blown out of the gym. With 47 seconds left in the game, guard Bill "Wicky" White, who had played the whole game, fouled out. Graham inserted Wagster. With just a few seconds left in the game, Kentucky scored again and Wagster was about to throw the ball inbounds to a Rebel streaking across midcourt. Tom "Goose" Farley shouted from the bench, "Hit the SOB [the Kentucky player who scored] in the head." Wagster attempted to throw the ball to the Rebel player running for the basket. The ball barely missed the Kentucky player's head and Wagster began laughing. Coach Graham saw him laughing and after the game read the riot act to the whole team about laughing after a loss. Graham told Wagster if he ever did it again, he would soon be on a train on his way back to Missouri. Very soon after that, something else funny happened and Wagster laughed again. Graham said that was it and he was sending the youngster back to Missouri. Wagster thought that was it for him as an Ole Miss basketball player. The next morning at breakfast Graham sent Bill White over to talk to Larry. White asked Wagster if he were ready to go and Wagster thought for sure he was headed home. White then said you better be because you are starting Monday instead of me! Wagster started the next Monday against Tennessee.

In his junior year, Wagster was treasurer of the M Club, an activity club for varsity athletes. Robert Khayat was president and Wobble Davidson, a famous disciplinarian, was the sponsoring coach. Davidson told Wagster to let him know every time he was about to write a check on club funds for anything so he could approve it, and he was to bring Davidson the actual check to approve before it was mailed.

At the end of the year Rebel lettermen wanted to give Davidson a gift to show their appreciation for what he had done. Davidson was extremely demanding but the players loved him. Robert Khayat told Wagster to write an M Club check for the gift, but Wagster explained Davidson's requirements for checks. Khayat said write the check and he would handle Davidson. Reluctantly Wagster agreed to do so. When Davidson received the gift, he graciously thanked the club, but he soon made a beeline to Wagster and asked how the gift was financed. Wagster explained and suffered Davidson's wrath; Khayat apparently never said anything about it to Davidson. Wagster said that to this day he regretted going against Davidson's instructions.

1961 Ole Miss Baseball

In the spring of 1961, Ole Miss was the defending SEC baseball champion, having won titles in 1959 and 1960. The baseball team was populated by several Rebel football players—Jake Gibbs, Frank Halbert, Chuck Morris, Whaley Hall, Doug Elmore, and Billy Ray Jones. Gibbs was the team leader, having been named All-SEC in 1959 and 1960 and All-American in 1960. He would repeat as All-SEC and All-American in 1961. Gibbs drove in 31 runs to repeat as the SEC RBI champion. Don Porter led the SEC with 5 home runs. The Rebels finished the 1961 season 15-8 with a 10-5 SEC record, which was good for second place in the Western Division and in the Southeastern Conference. Gibbs played third base and finished with a career batting average of .384. Being a big Rebel fan and loving baseball, I went to just about all of the home games. What impressed me most about Gibbs was his great throwing arm. The Yankees later made him a catcher, possibly because of that arm.

1961 Ole Miss Football

Ole Miss did not win the SEC football championship in 1961, but Johnny Vaught again fielded a dominant team. Outscoring their opponents 326-40, the gridiron Rebels finished the season 9-1 overall and 5-1 in the SEC. The Rebels defeated Arkansas, Kentucky, Florida State, Houston, Tulane, Vanderbilt, Chattanooga, Tennessee, and Mississippi State. The only loss was to the hated LSU Tigers in Baton Rouge (10-7). Having been ranked as high as number one nationally by the AP after the October 14 victory over Houston, at the season's end Ole Miss was ranked number five by both the AP and the UPI coaches poll. Two games stand out in my memory.

One was the Arkansas game September 28 at the new Mississippi Memorial Stadium in Jackson. The rivalry between the universities had recently become more heated because of the Rebels' controversial 1960 victory and the fact that Lance Alworth, a Mississippi product out of Brookhaven, played for Arkansas. Alworth was a running back/receiver/punter. He was simply a great athlete and would go on to become "Bambi" as a receiver for the San Diego Chargers and Dallas Cowboys. Alworth was instrumental in the Cowboys winning the 1971 Super Bowl, catching a key third-down pass and a touchdown pass both thrown by Roger Staubach. Alworth's football skills eventually landed him in the College Football Hall of Fame and the Professional Football Hall of Fame. He should have played for Ole Miss.

Lance Alworth grew up wanting to play for the Rebels, and he signed with Ole Miss after high school. Alworth married Betty Jean Allen in 1958 before he was supposed to report for football practice in Oxford. It is reported that Johnny Vaught told him that he was welcome to come to Ole Miss but not as a guest of the athletic department. Vaught had a rule against married guys playing football for the Rebels, and he would not break it even for a great athlete such as Lance Alworth, who soon took his skills to Arkansas. Ole Miss fans take some consolation from the fact that the Rebels defeated Arkansas all three seasons Alworth played varsity football for the Razorbacks.

The 1961 Ole Miss vs. Arkansas game turned out to be the only time I ever saw Lance Alworth play in person. What I remember most about that game, which the Rebels won 16-0, was Alworth's punting skills. I first noticed in warm-ups that he boomed punts long and extremely high. That carried over into the game, and his punting contributed to the Rebels being held to what proved to be their second-lowest scoring total of the season.

Vaught would soon change his rule about married players. It is futile but fun to speculate about the difference Alworth could have made in Rebel football fortunes had he played for Ole Miss during the 1959–1961 seasons. The Rebels lost a total of three games and tied one during those seasons. One loss was to Texas in the 1962 Cotton Bowl (12-7), and two losses and the tie were to LSU: 1959 (7-3), 1960 (6-6), 1961 (10-7). The Rebels lost those three games by a total of 12 points. There is a high probability that had the great Lance Alworth been playing for Ole Miss during that stretch they would have been undefeated.

The loss to LSU in 1961 was nearly as bitter as the 1959 loss because it kept Ole Miss from winning the SEC championship. The Rebels finished the regular season 5-1 in the SEC while LSU finished 6-0 in the conference. LSU started the season by losing to Rice 16-3 but beat Colorado in the 1962 Orange Bowl 25-7 to finish the season 10-1. The Rebels lost to Texas in the January 1, 1962, Cotton Bowl 12-7 and finished the season at 9-2. Including the Cotton Bowl, the scoring differential between the Rebels and their opponents for the season was 333-52, which was a good indication of the Rebels' dominance. The two losses would prove to be the most losses the Rebels would suffer in any one season during my four years as an undergraduate.

There is a familiar saying that a picture is worth a thousand words. A picture on page 13 of the 1962 Ole Miss yearbook dramatically tells the story of the 1961 LSU game. It shows the great Rebel quarterback Doug Elmore walking off the field in tears with his girlfriend after the loss. You can find that picture on the internet by going to theolemis-syearbook. It's enough to break your heart if you are a Rebel.

Johnny Vaught became the Rebels' coach in 1946, and by the end of the 1961 season his teams had played LSU 15 times in the regular season and once in the Sugar Bowl. After the 1961 loss Vaught's record against the Tigers was 8-6-2. That record is much more impressive considering where those games were played. Thirteen of the 16 games were played in Baton Rouge, 2 in Oxford, and 1 in New Orleans. That is, in 14 of the 16 games Vaught's teams had faced LSU teams that had the home field advantage. Ticket sales figured in because the Rebels had a small stadium in Oxford and the Tigers had a large stadium in Baton Rouge.

There were a number of outstanding players on the 1961 Ole Miss team, including four first-team selections on various All-American teams: fullback Billy Ray Adams, tackle Jim Dunaway, guard Treva Bolin, and quarterback Doug Elmore. I will focus on only one here, Doug Elmore.

When the great All-American Jake Gibbs used up his eligibility at Ole Miss and signed with the New York Yankees baseball team, Fred Russell of the *Nashville Banner* wrote this ditty:

Alas!
When Gibbs joined the Yanks
The Conference thanks
Rose up to the height of the sun.
But we are getting no break
For right behind Jake,
Stand Elmore, Griffing and Dunn.

In the fall of 1961, it was Elmore's time to be the Rebels' field general. In those days Coach Vaught always played at least three quarterbacks, and Elmore had played significant snaps during his sophomore and junior seasons behind Bobby Franklin and Jake Gibbs.

Not often remembered is Elmore's first play as a sophomore member of the varsity. On that play he ran a quarterback sneak against Kentucky for a 51-yard touchdown. Elmore made a name for himself in the 1959 nightmare of a game in Baton Rouge remembered for Billy Cannon's 89-yard return of a Jake Gibbs punt. After that punt the sophomore Elmore drove the Rebels to the Tigers' one-yard line where he was stopped on fourth down.

During his senior year Elmore started ahead of Glynn Griffing and Perry Lee Dunn, who would both play significant snaps that fall. Vaught really liked seniors, and as usual he had a senior leader in quarterback Doug Elmore. With All-American fullback Billy Ray Adams leading the way, Ole Miss was mostly a running team. Elmore made contributions in several aspects of the game. He completed 50 of 84 passes for 741 yards and a 60 percent completion rate. He rushed for 345 yards on 77 carries averaging 5 yards per carry. He also played defensive back and had two interceptions, punted 24 times for a 32-yard average, returned one kickoff for 18 yards, and returned four punts for 26 yards. After the season Elmore was named by various media outlets All-American, Academic All-American, Academic All-SEC, and All-SEC (second team). He played in the 1962 Coaches Association All-American Bowl. Elmore went on to punt for the NFL's Washington Redskins in 1962 and the CFL's Calgary Stampeders in 1963. He was inducted into the Mississippi Sports Hall of Fame in 1993.

The passing and rushing statistics show that Elmore, Griffing, and Dunn truly shared the quarterback duties. Griffing actually threw more passes (91) than Elmore (84) and completed only 4 fewer passes (46-50). Griffing's passing yardage exceeded Elmore's (785-741), and Griffing rushed 24 times for 135 yards. Dunn threw 27 passes, completing 13 for 301 yards and he rushed 39 times for 175 yards. It's fun to play the what-if game. Had Elmore taken every snap and compiled the other two quarterbacks' statistics, he would have thrown 202 passes and completed 123 passes (60 percent) for 1,827 yards. He would also have rushed 655 yards on 140 carries. That is, he would have accounted for 2,482 total yards and 24 touchdowns. Mr. Elmore was an outstanding player and an outstanding person.

1962

Maybe the Best Year in Mississippi Sports History

1962 SEC Basketball Champion—Mississippi State University*

1962 SEC Baseball Champions—Florida

1962 SEC Football Champions—Ole Miss

Final score: Mississippi universities 2 championships, all other SEC schools 1

*Tied with Kentucky; MSU wins the tie breaker because they beat Kentucky.

The Champions

1962 Mississippi State Basketball

By 1962 the Mississippi State Maroons had become the Mississippi State Bulldogs.

A university website explains:

> Mississippi State University athletic teams are called Bulldogs, a name earned and maintained over the decades by the tough, tenacious play of student-athletes wearing the Maroon and White. The official school

1962-63 S. E. C. CHAMPS
Members of Mississippi State's 1962-63 Southeastern Conference Championship basketball team: Front Row, left to right - Coach Babe McCarthy, Doug Hutton, Stan Brinker, Captain Joe Dan Gold, Bob Shows, Leland Mitchell, W. D. (Red) Stroud, Assistant Coach Jerry Simmons. Second Row - Manager Jimmy Wise, Don Posey, Larry Lee, Jackie Wofford, Howard Hemphill, Bi Anderton, Aubrey Nichols, Freshman Coach J. D. Gammel. Missing from picture Richie William

The 1962–63 Mississippi State University SEC Champion Basketball Team

During their three varsity years, seniors Joe Dan Gold, Bobby Shows, Leland Mitchell, and W. D. (Red) Stroud won the SEC championship each year. Those years produced an overall record of 65 wins and 13 losses (83%) and an SEC record of 36 wins and 6 losses (86%). There has never been an MSU basketball class like them before or since. Photo courtesy of Mississippi State Athletics.

mascot is an American Kennel Club registered English Bulldog, given the inherited title of "Bully."

As with most universities, State teams answered to different nicknames through the years. The first squads representing Mississippi A&M College were proud to be called Aggies, and when the school officially became Mississippi State College in 1932 the nickname Maroons, for State's uniform color, gained prominence. Bulldogs became the official title for State teams in 1961, not long after State College was granted university status [1958]. Yet references to school teams and athletes as Bulldogs actually go back to early in the century, and this nickname was used almost interchangeably with both Aggies and Maroons, since at least 1905.

Coach Babe McCarthy and Mississippi State basketball lost the great Jerry Graves to graduation in the spring of 1961. But in 1962 the reliable Jack Berkshire was a senior and the super sophomores of 1960–61 would soon prove to be super juniors. The loss of Graves proved to be manageable largely because another outstanding player, Doug Hutton, joined the varsity and several other players stepped up in key situations.

The newly minted Bulldogs started the 1961–62 season by ripping off nine straight nonconference wins against Southeast Louisiana, Southwest Louisiana, Louisiana Tech, Delta State, Louisiana College, Murray State, Memphis State, Maryland, and LSU. The Maryland and LSU games were played in the Sugar Bowl Tournament and the LSU game did not count as a conference game. Then the fun began as MSU embarked on a rugged 14-game SEC schedule. When the conference schedule began, the Associated Press ranked MSU ninth in the country.

Auburn came to Starkville on January 6 and the Tigers gave the Bulldogs all they could handle. State trailed by 13 points early in the first half but led at halftime 31-30. Doug Hutton, who scored only 4 points, combined with W. D. Stroud to put the Tigers away very late in the game. The score had been tied at 48 all for three minutes and 32 seconds when Hutton banked in a layup with eight seconds left in the game to put State up by 2 points. After a timeout Stroud intercepted the in-bounds pass, was fouled, hit the front end of a one-and-one free-throw opportunity, and sealed the 51-48 victory. Six Bulldogs scored in the closely contested slow-paced game. Stroud played the role of bell cow scoring 20 points while making 7 of 14 shots from the floor and 6 of 9 free throws. Leland Mitchell scored 11 points and grabbed 13 rebounds. Auburn was led by Layton Johns with 14 points and 10 rebounds. The Dogs moved up to seventh in the AP poll.

Next the undefeated and seventh-ranked Bulldogs went on the road to play Vanderbilt in Nashville. Vanderbilt came into the game 6-6 overall and 0-2 in the conference. State left the January 13 contest humbled by the Commodores, who ended the Bulldogs' 10-game win streak with a 100-86 victory. State had lost four straight games on Vandy's home court, and things didn't go well for the visitors from the beginning of what would prove to be the fifth. The Bulldogs didn't score a field goal in the first six minutes of the game and ended the game shooting only 34 percent from the floor. By contrast the Commodores shot 45 percent from the floor. Vandy had a slight edge in rebounds 58-57. Coach McCarthy said he had never seen his team so flat and cited "tightness" and a lack of "get-up-and-go on defense" as the apparent causes. The comment about defense was telling. Led by John Russell's 23 points and Jerry Hall's 21, five Commodores racked up double figures. Four Bulldogs had double-figure games with Stroud leading the way with 27 points. The game resembled a street brawl, six players fouled out. The teams combined to commit 57 fouls, which resulted in 89 free-throw attempts and 66 points being scored from the foul line.

The Associated Press dropped State to tenth place in the national rankings before Georgia Tech took State to the wire on January 15 in Atlanta. The *Clarion-Ledger*'s Robert Fulton captured the hero and the drama, writing:

> W. D. Stroud, Mississippi State's nonchalant red-head from Forrest, who is becoming accustomed to carrying the Maroons to cliffhanger victories, was obligingly carried off the floor by his teammates in a triumphant march here last night. Stroud's clutch layup a scant second before the buzzer gave Babe McCarthy's Bulldogs a come-from-behind 57-56 victory over hell-bent Ga. Tech before 4,892 unbelieving partisans.

State started cold again going five minutes and 52 seconds before scoring from the floor. Stroud soon led a comeback that quickly erased a 10-point lead. It was nip and tuck the rest of the game. The last minute and 15 seconds of the game were simply bizarre. Tech's Frank Landry missed the front end of 2 one-and-one opportunities. An all-alone Landry then missed a layup with six seconds left. Joe

Dan Gold grabbed but dropped the rebound, and Leland Mitchell recovered the ball. Mitchell slung the ball up-court to Doug Hutton, who went two-on-one with Stroud toward State's basket. The redhead scored the last-second bucket with an assist from Hutton.

Going into MSU's January 17 game against Alabama in Starkville the Bulldogs' chances of defending their SEC championship were not promising. State had played three conference games and had won two by a total of 5 points and had dropped the other one by 14 points. The Alabama game could prove to be just the tonic the Bulldogs needed to jumpstart a drive to defend their championship. Bama played the part as scripted, falling to State 67-40.

Alabama tried different approaches. In the first half the Tide tried to freeze the ball, and in the second half they attempted to outshoot the Bulldogs; neither tactic worked. State led 21-5 at halftime and outscored Alabama 46-35 in the second half. With 13:30 left in the game and State leading by 25 points, Coach McCarthy called off the big dogs and sent in the subs. Nine of the 12 Bulldogs who saw action scored. Three scored in double figures with Leland Mitchell leading the way with 20 points. Gary Blagburn was the only visitor to score more than 10 points. He hit 7 of 20 from the floor and made two free throws.

Next up for the Bulldogs were the Ole Miss Rebels in Oxford, January 20. The defending SEC champion Bulldogs had lost to the Rebels in Oxford the year before, 74-70. The game would be played before a packed Ole Miss gym. The *Clarion-Ledger*'s Carl Walters, who had predicted a close game and a possible upset, described the environment the Bulldogs could expect in Oxford. "Regardless of the outcome, the antiquated, outmoded, inadequate and wholly unsatisfactory Ole Miss gym, which seats approximately 3,000, will be jammed to the gunwales or rafters."

This time the Maroons escaped the hostile Ole Miss environment with a 4-point victory 61-57. Red Stroud was again State's leading scorer with 18 points while Leland Mitchell chipped in 14 and Doug Hutton 11. Sophomore sensation Don Kessinger led the Rebels with

21 points, and Bill White contributed 15. The Rebels kept the game close by winning the rebound battle 36-28. Ole Miss had been handicapped by the loss of its second-leading scorer and leading rebounder, center Sterling Ainsworth, whose mother died in Meridian the day of the contest.

Carl Walters's prediction about the closeness of the game and his comments about the environment in which it would be played had been insightful. The antiquated gym was full and I was among the crowd. The atmosphere was electric. After the game the Rebels were 1-4 in the SEC. About the only consolation for Rebel fans was that they had two more years to watch Don Kessinger play basketball. On the other hand, with the Bulldogs standing 4-1 in the conference, State fans now had a better chance of celebrating a second-straight SEC championship. State could also look forward to another year of basketball from the class that included Red Stroud, Leland Mitchell, and Joe Dan Gold.

The AP poll kept MSU at tenth. State next took a needed two-week break from the rigors of conference play. In the Maroons' last two nonconference games of the season, they registered easy victories over Northeast Louisiana and Delta State. It was back to the SEC grind as State played LSU in Baton Rouge February 3.

Both MSU and LSU came into the contest with SEC title hopes alive. Those flickering hopes could be all but extinguished by a loss as Kentucky had yet to be defeated. The Bulldogs took care of business, outclassing the Tigers 87-66 in LSU's Agricultural Center. State's extremely quick guards Red Stroud and Doug Hutton sparked a fast-breaking attack by scoring 22 and 20 points, respectively. Before the 10-minute mark of the first half, the fast-break tactic put Babe's Boys up by 19 points. That tactic would also spotlight the value of sophomore Doug Hutton, who would soon prove himself to be one of MSU's greatest athletes ever by excelling in basketball, baseball, and track. Leland Mitchell sacked 17 points and grabbed 11 rebounds while Joe Dan Gold scored 15 points and corralled 14 rebounds. With a 19-point lead, State slowed down to stall mode, and LSU switched to a full-court press, which reduced the Bulldogs' lead to 7 points with less than five minutes left in the half. Leland Mitchell stopped the bleeding by stealing the ball and making a layup. He was fouled intentionally on the play and politely converted two free throws, putting the Dogs back up by 11. By halftime State had a 15-point lead. It was fast-break time again in the last half and State got up as much as 24 points. MSU won the battle of the boards 54-44 while holding the nation's fifteenth leading rebounder, Maury Drummond, to 8 rebounds. State was now 5-1 in the SEC and undefeated in nonconference games.

The Bulldogs traveled down the road from Baton Rouge to New Orleans to play Tulane February 5. State won 70-59 and in the process handed Tulane its first SEC loss while inching to within half a game of league-leading Kentucky. A full house of 5,600 hostile Tulane fans watched as their Greenies proved no match for the Bulldogs. The fans got out of hand in the second half and interrupted the game by throwing paper on the floor. This game was Leland Mitchell's time to play the starring role for an almost unbelievable talented and balanced Bulldog team. Mitchell contributed 29 points by making 13 of 25 shots from the field and hitting three of five free throws. He also grabbed 10 rebounds. The ultrareliable Red Stroud was State's second-leading scorer with 19 points, and Joe Dan Gold scored 9 points and collected 5 rebounds before fouling out early. Another of the prior year's super sophs, center Bobby Shows, was emerging as a rebounder; he grabbed 9 as State again won the battle of the boards 44-38. Tulane's outstanding Jim Kerwin, who was averaging 24 points per game and had tossed in 41 against Ole Miss two days earlier, was held to 12 points by the Bulldogs. Leaving Louisiana, MSU was 17-1 overall and 6-1 in the conference. AP ranked the Maroons ninth in the country.

State next played its third consecutive road game against the University of Tennessee February 10 in Knoxville. Even on their home floor the Volunteers were no match for the Bulldogs; State won 91-67. Always a very physical team, the Vols committed 27 fouls that turned into 40 free throws and 33 points for the visitors. The Bulldogs committed 20 fouls, which turned into only 13 points for the home team. Tennessee placed three players in double figures with their high scorer Orb Bowling, a 6'10" giant who grabbed 9 rebounds, contributing 18 points. Four State players scored in double figures: Mitchell 23, Gold 21, Hutton 18, and Stroud 16. Doug Hutton, who came off the bench to spell captain Jack Berkshire, had a special game, hitting 6 of 6 field-goal attempts and sacking 6 of 7 free throws. State left Tennessee having won 18 of 19 games and 7 of 8 in the conference. They were headed to Kentucky for their fourth-straight road game and a chance to take down the conference leading and number 2-ranked Wildcats.

Babe McCarthy's remarkable team was ranked ninth by the Associated Press by the time they got to Lexington for their showdown with Kentucky. The Bulldogs forced Adolph Rupp's Wildcats to play Babe's game and left town with a hard-earned 49-44 victory that shocked the sports world. By all accounts Kentucky fans thought their team was invincible when playing big games on their home floor. The loss to MSU was only the thirteenth on their home court since 1943! The 13,500 who had expected a victory over the upstart Bulldogs left Memorial Coliseum in shock. Babe's game was flexible and, in this encounter, the slow-down version worked to perfection, producing the Maroons' first-ever victory over the Cats in Kentucky. The Maroons gained an early 3-2 lead and didn't trail for the rest of the game. When State got the lead, McCarthy replaced 6'7" center Bobby Shows with 5'10" Doug Hutton, and the Dogs ran a three-guard offense the rest of the game. It should be noted that although Hutton was only 5'10" he was super athletic and could "jump out of the gym."

Robert Fulton wrote: "Because of this [the slow-down] the invincible Wildcats never got started. They had to play State's game which featured meticulous, precise ball-handling and a very effective zone defense." State took only good shots and hit an amazing 69 percent of their 26 shots from the floor. Three Maroons scored in double figures: Stroud 17, Mitchell 13, and Hutton 10. Kentucky took 45 shots from the floor (19 more than State) but hit only 15 (one fewer than State) for 33 percent. Kentucky's sensational sophomore Cotton Nash led the Cats in scoring with 23 (9 for 15 from the floor) points, but the rest of the team made only six field goals and mustered only 21 points. Jack Berkshire held Kentucky's leading scorer Larry Pursiful to 5 points. State lost the battle of the boards 26-18, but the team's ultrasharp shooting more than compensated. The Dogs moved up a notch to eighth in the AP poll.

Babe and his team had to feel comfortable as they left the Blue Grass State headed home to Mississippi. They now held a 19-1 overall record and a 7-1 conference mark that tied them with Kentucky for first place in the SEC. The Dogs' next five games were scheduled for McCarthy Gymnasium on the MSU campus. At this point in the season State did not lead the SEC in any team statistical category except wins. The Maroons averaged scoring 79 points per game and giving up 62. They were second in field-goal percentage (44) and free-throw percentage (75). While Leland Mitchell averaged 18 points per game (sixth in the SEC) and W. D. Stroud averaged 17 and two other Dogs, Doug Hutton and Joe Dan Gold, averaged in double figures, not a single State player was among the conference's top-five scorers. This was a team in the best sense of the word.

Visiting Florida did not prove much of a challenge on February 17 as MSU downed the Gators in routine fashion 67-45. The Bulldogs played slow-down in the first half and fast-break in the second to demoralize the outmanned Gators. State led 24-14 at the half but quickly pulled away to a 23-point lead with 12 minutes left in the game. In a packed McCarthy Gymnasium, State placed three players in double figures led by Leland Mitchell's 17 points. Carlos Morrison led Florida with 15 points. State played stifling defense all game and dominated the boards, grabbing 41 rebounds to Florida's 31.

Two days later, February 19, the Georgia Bulldogs rolled in to Starkville and, despite the fact that Georgia was last in the league, the game proved to be a fairly stiff test of the home variety Bulldogs. State won this conference battle 83-74. A packed gym watched a 19-point first-half State lead diminish to 9 by the end of the contest. The Babe wasn't very happy. "We got off to a good start and had a good lead, but everybody started horsing around. We didn't have a good team effort." Evidently the "horsing around" occurred while the Maroons were playing defense. But not on the boards, as State outrebounded Georgia 45-32. There seemed to be little or no "horsing around" on offense. Six of Babe's Boys scored in double figures: Mitchell 17, Gold 14, Hutton 13, Stroud 11, Shows 10, and Gene Chatham 10. A team effort indeed. Postgame State stood at 21-1 overall and 9-1 in the conference, and the next day they were ranked fifth in the country by the AP.

LSU's Fighting Tigers came to Starkville on February 24 and fight the Tigers did. The *Clarion-Ledger*'s Robert Fulton captured what transpired, writing, "If ever there was a game that was closer than the score would indicate, it was played here last night as LSU pushed Mississippi State to the wire before the Maroons pulled a hard-earned 58-48 victory out of the fire in the final hectic minutes."

State had already beaten LSU by 22 points in the Sugar Bowl Tournament and by 21 in Baton Rouge in SEC play, but this was a different contest. It looked like State would chalk up another routine win against the Tigers when they went up 23-11 near the midway point of the first half. But the suddenly cold-shooting Bulldogs did not score another field goal in the last 11 minutes of the half. By halftime the lead had shrunk to 30-27. State's 29 percent shooting night against the Tigers' fierce zone press defense proved to be their worst effort of the season. LSU shot 38 percent from the floor. Joe Dan Gold's 22-point, 13-rebound performance proved to be the key to the Bulldogs' victory. MSU led 50-48 with 2:15 left in the game and then added six straight free throws and a last second field goal by Leland Mitchell to escape with the win. State as usual won the battle of the boards 50-39. LSU's Maury Drummond and Ellis Settler scored 14 points each. With two games to play, the AP ranked the Bulldogs, who stood 11-1 in the conference and 22-1 overall, fifth in the nation.

Tulane visited the friendly confines of McCarthy Gymnasium on February 26. The Maroons were back on their game as they put away the Greenies 83-62. An overflow crowd watched as State systematically overpowered the visitors. Tulane managed to lead the game only once and that by a score of 1-0 in the first minute of the game. W. D. Stroud led State's scoring with 21 points, and he had a lot of help as three other Dogs notched double figures: Joe Dan Gold 12, Bobby Shows 14, and Dave Glasgow 10. Tulane was led by Jack Ardon's 26 points, but the SEC's leading scorer, Jim Kerwin, was held to a season low of 9 points. The Bulldogs connected on 41 percent of their field-goal attempts, Tulane 29 percent. The boards were again swept clean by the Bulldogs as they outrebounded the Greenies 60-42. With a 23-1 overall record and a 12-1 SEC mark, only Ole Miss stood between fifth-ranked State and a second consecutive SEC championship.

One thing was certain after this game, MSU had conquered Louisiana. The Bulldogs were 9-0 against teams from the Bayou Country. In addition to defeating Tulane twice and LSU three times, State had beaten Louisiana Tech, Northeastern Louisiana, Southeastern Louisiana, and Southwestern Louisiana.

Ole Miss showed up in Starkville March 3 with a 12-12 overall record, including a 5-8 conference mark. The visitors were coming off SEC wins against LSU and Tulane. The five starters had played every minute of those two games. The Rebels' outstanding guards, Don Kessinger and Mel Edmonds, had scored a combined 112 points in those two games. McCarthy Gymnasium filled up again with State fans hoping to see their team that was ranked fifth nationally secure its second-straight SEC championship and its third in four years. Although the visiting Rebels put up a valiant fight, the home team and its fans went home happy, State 63, Ole Miss 58.

It didn't come easy. The Rebels led at halftime 37-28 and for all but 11 minutes of the game, but the Dogs rallied to outscore the visitors by 14 points in the second half. Joe Dan Gold tossed in 16, Bobby Shows 14, and Red Stroud 13 for State, while Mel Edmonds scored 20, Don Kessinger 15, and Sterling Ainsworth 14 for Ole Miss. With Bobby Shows, who had come on strong for the Dogs in the latter part of the season grabbing 10 rebounds, the Dogs won the battle of the boards 41-33. The March 6 AP poll ranked State fifth in the country immediately after the victory.

Mississippi State University ended its basketball season with a 24-1 overall record and a 13-1 SEC mark. The 24-1 record tied the great 1959 team for the best record in MSU's basketball history. State had now won three of the last four SEC basketball championships. Kentucky and Mississippi State ended the season tied with 13-1 conference records. But MSU had handed the Wildcats their only conference loss. State held the tie breaker, which would award the Bulldogs the SEC's automatic invitation to the NCAA Basketball Tournament along with an opportunity to win the national championship. Alas, again Mississippi's egregious policy that barred state-supported schools from competing in integrated athletic events prevented the great 1962 MSU basketball team from playing in the NCAA tournament. Once again Kentucky with a 23-2 overall record would represent the SEC in the NCAA tournament when Mississippi State should have been the conference's representative. Mississippi sure knew how to cut off its nose to spite its face.

In the NCAA tournament Kentucky beat Butler 81-60 but lost to a great Ohio State team led by Jerry Lucas and John Havlicek 74-64. Ohio State, which was ranked number one all season by the AP, lost the championship game to the University of Cincinnati 71-59. The final AP poll looked like this: number one Ohio State 26-2, number two Cincinnati 29-2, number three Kentucky 23-3, number four Mississippi State 24-1. Had the Mississippi State Bulldogs played in the NCAA tournament, the results of both the NCAA tournament and the final AP poll might have been quite different.

After the season W. D. Stroud was named the SEC's Most Valuable Player and Best Playmaker. Jack Berkshire was named the conference's Best Defensive Player.

1962 Ole Miss Football

As has been noted, Fred Russell of the *Nashville Banner* predicted after the 1960 football season the great Jake Gibbs would be followed by three other outstanding Ole Miss quarterbacks who were just waiting their turns—Doug Elmore, Glynn Griffing, and Perry

Lee Dunn. Elmore had excelled during the 1961 season. Now it was Griffing's turn and he did not disappoint.

The 1962 Ole Miss football Rebels went 10-0 to post their only undefeated, untied record in school history. Along the way they defeated Memphis State, Kentucky, Houston, Tulane, Vanderbilt, LSU, Chattanooga, Tennessee, Mississippi State, and Arkansas. The Rebels scored 247 points to their opponents 53, won the SEC championship, and Johnny Vaught was named SEC Coach of the Year. The Ole Miss roster was loaded with outstanding players including future NFL players Allen Brown, Glynn Griffing, Perry Lee Dunn, Jimmy Heidel, and Jim Dunaway. Ole Miss finished third nationally in both the AP and the UPI coaches polls. The Rebels were actually named national champions by Billingsley, Litkenhous, and Sagarin.

The first game of the season was played against Memphis State on September 22 on the Tigers' home field. The Rebels dispatched the Tigers in routine fashion 21-7. Memphis State's only touchdown came on an 88-yard punt return in the fourth quarter. The Rebels dominated the statistics in first downs 18-10, rushing yards 161-45, and passing yards 101-32. Coach Vaught was breaking in a new offensive unit and didn't show much for future opponents to dissect.

Forty-two thousand fans, many of them waving Confederate flags, crowded into Jackson's Memorial Stadium September 29 to see the Kentucky game. The contest featured two of the SEC's best passing quarterbacks. The Wildcats' Jerry Woolum had finished second in the conference in 1961 and Glynn Griffing had finished third. As has been noted, Griffing played behind Doug Elmore in 1961 but finished one place ahead of him in passing. Kentucky also brought to town the SEC's leading receiver from 1961, Tom Hutchinson, who had 32 catches for 543 yards and four touchdowns.

In a hotly contested game that the Rebels won 14-0 the Wildcats were held to a net 4 yards rushing and 123 yards passing. Ole Miss rolled up a total of 329 yards in the contest. The Rebels scored on a 4-yard run by Griffing, a 6-yard run by A. J. Holloway, and two extra points kicked by Wes Sullivan.

Carl Walters of the *Clarion-Ledger* captured the game well in a single paragraph: "The Rebels were much the best and showed it in just about every way except in piling up a big score. Fumbles, pass interceptions and penalties—plus a determined defense by the invading Cats—stymied all touchdown threats but two." Billy Ray Lea and I went to Jackson for the Kentucky football game. We cheered the Rebels on to victory and witnessed Governor Ross Barnett's infamous halftime speech encouraging defiance of a federal court order to admit James Meredith as Ole Miss's first black student. When we returned to Oxford late on September 30, we found the University Avenue entrance to the front of the campus blocked by law enforcement officers. The Riot at Ole Miss was underway. We didn't realize that we were about to witness a pivotal part of Mississippi history and an important event in the civil rights movement in our country.

Our dormitory, Baxter Hall, was located on the west side of the campus so we decided to drive around there to see if we could get to our room. It worked but when we got to Baxter it was surrounded by federal marshals who allowed us to pass through to our room. We soon learned that we had an unexpected resident in our dorm. Across the hall from our room was an apartment where dorm parents had once lived. The federal government had moved James Meredith into that apartment.

Being curious about what was happening in the front part of the campus we made our way through loud noises and tear gas to the circle in front of the Lyceum building. Since we were not belligerent, we did not actually participate in the rioting, but we did watch the tragedy as it took place. We would stay as long as we could stand the tear gas, retreat to our room, massage our eyes with wet towels, and then return to watch the action. This routine was repeated several times. It soon became obvious that we should not stay in our room that night. We drove to my cousin Virginia Crockett Hall's home in Oxford where we watched what was unfolding on television for most of the rest of the night.

Two people (neither one of whom were students or employees of Ole Miss) died and about 300 were injured in what has been called the Riot at Ole Miss, the Battle of Oxford, and the Last Battle of the Civil War. The riot and its tragic consequences have been documented in hundreds of newspaper and journal articles and several books. Suffice it to say here that it took Ole Miss at least 25 years to fully recover from the riot and to some extent it still suffers from the stigma associated with the night of September 30, 1962.

George "Buck" Randall was a star fullback and linebacker for Coach Vaught's 1962 team. The Greenwood native had a well-earned reputation for being an extremely tough guy. Buck stood especially tall the night of the riot. A 2013 Associated Press story reporting Randall's death included the following:

> A U.S. marshal told Randall to go outside near the university's main administrative building, the Lyceum, to try to talk to the mob and to urge people to leave, The *Sun Herald* reported. "It was a war, really," Randall said in a 2008 interview with the newspaper. "I didn't want anybody to get killed. It was a bad situation back then."
>
> In 2008, the U.S. Interior Department designated the Lyceum and the surrounding area, known as The Circle, as a National Historic Landmark. In the 2007 nominating form for the landmark status, an architectural historian described how Randall implored rioters to stop attacking the marshals.
>
> "Randall, unarmed, forced his way through the combatants to the flagpole in the center of The Circle," the nomination says. "He shimmied up the flagpole, which sported a Confederate flag, and yelled at the agitators to go home. After bullets hit the pole, he slid down, resuming his mission at the Confederate Monument and other strategic places in The Circle. A few demonstrators obeyed the Rebel football player."

The 1962 homecoming game was set for October 6 in Oxford against the University of Houston. It didn't work out that way. Because of the prior week's riot there was fear of further violence if the game were played on campus. After approval by the US Army and the Justice Department the game was switched to Mississippi Memorial Stadium in Jackson. Dianne Klyce would be the first and hopefully the last Ole Miss homecoming queen crowned in Jackson. The Rebels blew out Houston 40-7. There were no incidents and some maintain that the game actually saved Ole Miss from being closed down. In his book *Rebel Coach*, Johnny Vaught wrote: "Boys became men that day, and I think then and there they sensed that no one would be able to stop them, and a university rode on their shoulder pads."

In the second quarter Glynn Griffing threw three touchdown passes to Louis Guy to put the game out of the Cougars' reach. In the fourth quarter Griffing capped a spectacular day by throwing another touchdown pass to Reed Davis. Sophomore quarterback Jim Weatherly (who would later make quite a name for himself in the music industry) threw a fourth-quarter touchdown pass to fellow sophomore Allen Brown (who would make a name for himself in pro football). Three statistics reflect how one-sided the game was: first downs 23-5, rushing yardage 187-72, and passing yardage 264-36, all in favor of the Rebs.

After a much-needed open week, the Rebels took on Tulane in a rainy Mississippi Memorial Stadium in Jackson October 20. It was the Rebels' third straight game in the capital city. Playing in far from ideal conditions and against a scrappy Green Wave team, the Rebels kept their record clean, if not their uniforms, posting a 21-0 victory. Despite constant rain, the Rebels threw 20 passes and completed 8 for only 84 yards. Three of the 8 completions went for touchdowns. Glynn Griffing threw 2 to Woody Dabbs, and Jim Weatherly threw one to fellow sophomore Billy Carl Irvin. Moving the ball on a sloppy field was not easy for either team, but the Rebels won the total yardage battle 270-154.

The undefeated Rebels had been favored to win by 34 points against a team that came into the game with an 0-4 record. After the game Coach Johnny Vaught had this to say:

> Man. I'm glad this one is over. I couldn't help but think back to 1956 when Tulane beat us 10-3 on the same field in another rainy-night game. We started awful slow and Tulane was playing some good football too. They made it rough and a couple of fine quick kicks set us back on our heels and it looked for a while that we were not going to get started. But you have to give the boys credit. They got organized and played good football for the last part of the second quarter and for the rest of the game.

An estimated crowd of 23,000 showed up for the game. Rain started falling before the kickoff and lasted the whole game. By the game's end few fans were left. I sat through the whole rainy ordeal and the next day I had a bad cold. I vowed never to do that again even to see the Rebs play.

Next the Rebels played Vanderbilt in Crump Stadium on October 27. Ole Miss coasted to a 35-0 win in a Vanderbilt home game that had been moved from Nashville to Memphis. A week earlier Vanderbilt's head coach Art Guepe had tendered his resignation effective at the end of the season. The Commodores had not won a game all season, and only 16,262 fans showed up to see Ole Miss beat Vanderbilt for the ninth straight time. Relying on their run game the Rebels accumulated 313 of their 390 total yards on the ground. Vanderbilt's total offense amounted to only 164 yards. Perry Lee Dunn scored two touchdowns, and Buck Randall, Woody Dabbs, and Fred Roberts scored one each. One of Dunn's touchdowns was scored on a recovered blocked punt in the end zone. Dabbs's score came on a pass from Jim Weatherly. It was really no contest and the Rebels stood 5-0 after the game.

The game against fourth-ranked LSU played in Tiger Stadium in Baton Rouge on November 3, 1962, is one of my best memories. It was the first game I ever attended in Baton Rouge. Ole Miss had not won in the Tigers' den since 1956. LSU had spoiled perfect seasons for the Rebels in 1959 (loss) and 1960 (tie) and LSU was the only team they lost to in the 1961 regular season. The Rebel seniors had won only one game against the Tigers and that was the 1960 Sugar Bowl rematch after the Halloween nightmare of 1959. It was pay-back time.

Billy Ray Lea and I made our way to Tiger Stadium in his reliable '54 Chevy. I have attended hundreds of Ole Miss athletic events and this one was the most satisfying of all. Ole Miss won 15-7, but the score does not reflect the Rebels' total domination of the game, total yards—Ole Miss 393, LSU 107. The 1963 Ole Miss yearbook captured the night very well.

> A. J. Holloway, Louis Guy, and Wes Sullivan demoralized the Tigers with two touchdowns and a field goal. The impact of these scores will long be remembered by every fan and most assuredly by those who call the Rebels "Tiger Bait." A deciding factor was Glynn Griffing's running and passing. The accurate ball-handler had been held back all season to make sure he sustained no damaging injuries. It was not the same at LSU. Griffing, playing probably one of the best games of his collegiate career, ran and passed Ole Miss up and down the field with the fury of an un-leashed tornado. Praise could not be too high for any Ole Miss participant. Every player took his task and performed to his utmost abilities. In a game which was dedicated to "Doc" Knight, the Ole Miss trainer, a better outcome could not have been asked for by him or Coach Vaught and his staff.

Throughout the game, the almost total silence of the LSU fans was golden. The sound of silence never sounded so good to these Rebel ears. The sound of Rebel fans cheering at the top of their voices at game's end and the looks on the faces of Tiger fans as they trudged silently out of the stadium were priceless. They are still seared in my memory.

In a game that was played at Hemingway Stadium on November 10, the University of Chattanooga proved to be the Rebels' next victim, 52-7. *Sports Illustrated* had recently labeled the contest a "cupcake" game for Ole Miss and indeed it was. The Rebels were a major college team and the Moccasins were small college. Statistics from this game are almost meaningless. Nevertheless, here are a few that are interesting: Ole Miss rushed for 454, Chattanooga 21, the Rebels had 31 first downs (a school record), the Mocs 6, Ole Miss punted only once, Chattanooga punted eight times. Most Rebel fans were not interested in the game as only 9,200 showed up. I was one of the 9,200. With two regular-season games left, the Rebels stood 7-0.

Ole Miss had already dispatched two Tennessee schools, Memphis State and Chattanooga, when the Rebels visited the state's flagship, the University of Tennessee, in Knoxville November 17. Coach Bowden Wyatt's Volunteers had begun their season with four straight losses, but two of those losses were by one point. When the Ole Miss team showed up at Neyland Stadium the Vols were riding a three-game win streak. Tennessee certainly wasn't a cupcake. In another rain-soaked game the Rebels prevailed 19-6. The closeness of the game is better reflected in total yards than in the final score. Ole Miss outgained the Vols by only 60 yards 280-220. The rain had a lot to do with those low numbers as the wet field negated much of both teams' speed.

Coaches sometimes say that two or three plays often determine a game. This game provided a perfect example of that adage. On the first play from scrimmage Chuck Morris sprinted 52 yards to the Vols' 28-yard line to set up a touchdown. In the third quarter Louis Guy intercepted a pass at the goal line and returned it for a 100-yard touchdown. Before the interception Ole Miss led 7-0 and Tennessee had driven to the Rebels' 4-yard line. *Clarion-Ledger* sportswriter Wayne Thompson called Guy's play "perhaps the biggest play for the Rebels since Paige Cothren's conversion in the 1956 Cotton Bowl which beat TCU 14-13."

Postgame the two coaches commented about the contest that was played before 37,000 fans in the rain and featured a brawl after the Volunteers scored their only touchdown. Wyatt said, "There's no doubt this was as good a game we could put together. Louis Guy's interception was the turning point." Vaught agreed saying, "We beat a fine team. I have seen every Tennessee game film and I feel this was their best game of the season."

Ole Miss squared off against rival Mississippi State December 1 in Oxford. The Bulldogs had a chance to prevent the Rebels from posting their first regular-season perfect record. It was not to be.

Ole Miss prevailed in a great defensive struggle 13-6. For a change the Rebels played in good weather backed by a home crowd that numbered 30,000.

Capping an 81-yard drive, State's outstanding running back Ode Burrell put the Bulldogs ahead 6-0 four minutes into the game with a 2-yard run. Fred Roberts blocked Sammy Dantone's extra-point attempt. Ole Miss's first score came in the second quarter after a beautiful 15-play, 82-yard drive capped by Louis Guy's 1-yard run. Billy Carl Irvin kicked the extra point and the home team led 7-6. The Rebels' final score came in bizarre fashion late in the fourth quarter. Jim Weatherly, after executing a great fake to tailback Dave Jennings, ran untouched 43 yards down the sideline for a touchdown. Weatherly's fake fooled just about everyone in the stadium, and some State players said they thought a referee had blown a whistle. Irvin's extra-point attempt failed.

The game produced some statistics that would be shocking in college football today. Ten (10!) Rebels had at least one carry and the contingent rushed for a net of 212 yards on 48 attempts. Eight MSU players had at least one carry, but they gained a net of only 47 yards on 31 attempts. The defensive line-play actually dominated the game. There were several tackles behind the line of scrimmage. Ole Miss lost 31 yards rushing and State 30. Perry Lee Dunn led the rebels in rushing with six carries for 51 yards. Mackie Weaver led State in rushing with six carries for 22 yards. Playing from behind most of the game State had the passing honors; quarterbacks Charlie Furlow and Sonny Fisher completed 14 of 25 passes for 179 yards. Ode Burrell led Bulldog receivers with six catches for 65 yards. Ole Miss threw only 16 passes for 101 yards. Glynn Griffing threw 12 and completed 5 for 58 yards. Jim Weatherly threw one pass that was complete for 12 yards. Halfback Chuck Morris threw three passes and completed them all for 36 yards. Louis Guy led the Rebel receivers with six catches for 69 yards.

State, a 25-point underdog, came into the game with a 3-5 overall record and a 2-5 SEC mark. The Bulldogs' stout defense made the spread look ridiculous. After the game MSU's first-year head coach Paul Davis (who played his college football at Ole Miss) said, "No question about it, this was our best effort of the year." Rebel head coach Johnny Vaught noted that State had given his team as tough a struggle as they encountered along their way to a perfect season and an SEC championship.

Immediately after the game the 9-0 Rebels accepted a bid to play the Arkansas Razorbacks, runner-up in the Southwest Conference, in the 1963 Sugar Bowl. Arkansas had a 9-1 record, the loss coming at the hands of SWC champion Texas by a score of 7-3. As has been noted, Arkansas dropped Ole Miss from their regular-season schedule after the 1960 season.

The Rebels put a red-and-blue bow on their perfect season in New Orleans January 1, 1963. Final score Ole Miss 17, Arkansas 13. The score better reflects the grittiness of the Razorbacks than the actual dominance of the Rebels on the field. Ole Miss won the statistical battle by a much larger margin: first downs 22-7, rushing yardage 160-47, passing yardage 269-123, and total yards 429-170. The Rebels' touchdowns came on a 33-yard pass from Griffing to Guy and a 1-yard run by Griffing. Irwin kicked both extra points and a field goal. Arkansas's scores came on a pass from Billy Moore to Jesse Branche and Tom McKneley's extra point and two field goals.

While the Hogs' defense was extremely tough in the clutch, the Rebel defense, which had been the nation's best statistically, simply dominated. The Hogs had led the SWC in offense but were stifled by the Rebels. Arkansas's first field goal came from 27 yards. How did the Hogs get the ball at the Rebs' 27-yard line? Frank Lambert's punt from the 5 had sailed out of bounds at the 27. Three plays later the ball was still on the 27, hence the field goal. Arkansas scored its only touchdown after recovering a Buck Randall fumble on the Rebel 13-yard line. Arkansas's quarterback Billy Moore had been the total offense leader in the SWC. Carl Walters of the *Clarion-Ledger* wrote that the Rebels stopped Moore "stone cold dead." Moore finished with 53 yards total offense. The Rebels had several defensive heroes, including linemen Don Dickson, Tommy Lucas, Jim Dunaway, and Whaley Hall and linebackers Buck Randall and Perry Lee Dunn.

Following in the footsteps of former Ole Miss quarterbacks Ray Brown, Bobby Franklin, and Jake Gibbs, Glynn Griffing set a Sugar Bowl passing record and was named Most Valuable Player. Frank Broyles noted that Griffing's passing especially on big third-down plays when he would elude Hog rushers and complete the pass was the difference in the game. The Arkansas coach went on to say, "He's the greatest quarterback in America. In fact, he is the best college passer I have ever seen." Much later in his book *Rebel Coach*, Johnny Vaught said that Griffing was the best third-down quarterback he had ever coached.

Johnny Vaught's teams consistently beat Frank Broyles's teams. The Rebels beat the Hogs in the regular season in 1958, 1959, 1960, and 1961. Then Arkansas canceled the series based on Broyles's wishes. In the October 2, 1961, edition of *Sports Illustrated*, Coach Broyles explained why the series was canceled, saying, "I don't like to say this but the field goal last year [1960] had very little to do with our discontinuing the series after this year. Mississippi is just too big, too deep and too rough. They wear you out and leave you in bad shape for your conference games." Despite the regular-season games being canceled, teams coached by Johnny Vaught and Frank Broyles would meet in the 1963 and 1970 Sugar Bowls. Johnny's Rebs triumphed on both occasions. Final score card, Vaught 6, Broyles 0. It has been reported that Frank Broyles always avoided being in the same room with Johnny Vaught at coaches' meetings. Is there any wonder why?

With the Sugar Bowl victory, Ole Miss finished their first undefeated and untied season 10-0 and ranked number three in the country by both the Associated Press and the United Press International. Postseason honors were heaped on Rebel footballers. Several organizations awarded first-team All-American and All-SEC honors to Jim Dunaway. Don Dickerson was named Honorable Mention All-American and first-team All SEC. Woody Dabbs and Chuck Morris were named Honorable Mention All-American, and Morris was named third-team All-SEC. Louis Guy and Allen Brown garnered All-SEC status.

Glynn Griffing was named first-team All-American by the Football Writers of America—*Look* magazine, second-team All-American by NEA Services and the Associated Press, and third team by the Sporting News. He was also accorded first-team All-SEC by the Associated Press and United Press International. He played in the 1963 College All-Star Football Classic—the last time the "College Joes" beat the pros. Started in 1934 as the Chicago Charities College All-Star Game as an exhibition between the NFL champions and selected college all-stars, the game was played until 1976. Of the 42 games played in the series, the Pros won 31, the All-Stars won 9, and there were 2 ties. The 1963 college kids upset the mighty Green Bay Packers 20-17.

Griffing was drafted in the fourth round of the 1962 NFL draft by the New York Giants and in the fourteenth round of the AFL draft by the Houston Oilers. He signed with New York right after the Rebels' Sugar Bowl victory and played the 1963 season with the Giants. During his only season of pro ball, he played in 13 games and completed 16 of 40 passes and three touchdowns while suffering four interceptions. The Giants lost 14-10 to the Chicago Bears in the 1963 NFL championship game. After leaving football, Griffing entered the business world where he has flourished. He now heads Glynn Griffing and Associates. Located in Jackson, the company administers employee benefits programs for clients nationwide.

As an aside, another college football team from the state of Mississippi deserves recognition although it did not play in the SEC. Mississippi Southern College became the University of Southern Mississippi early in 1962. Southern Miss coached by the legendary Thad "Pie" Vann posted a 9-1 record, and UPI named the Southerners the 1962 college division national champions. As a small college team, USM was not invited to play in a bowl, but this was the second national football championship for the Southerners. During the 1958 season Vann's Mississippi Southern College Southerners posted a 9-0 record and copped its first UPI national college division crown. That was the year LSU won the major college championship and many MSC fans lobbied for a matchup with LSU in the 1969 Sugar Bowl, but no bowl extended the Southerners an offer. Pie Vann, who played tackle for Ole Miss from 1926 to 1929, coached MSC/USM from 1949 through 1968 and recorded a 139-59-2 (.700) record. Along the way Vann's teams played in two Sun Bowls and two Tangerine Bowls. Vann's teams regularly played such opponents as Alabama, Auburn, Georgia, Mississippi State, Ole Miss, Louisville, Florida State, North Carolina State, and other schools which were or became major college powers. Under Vann the Southerners beat Alabama twice and tied the Tide once. They also beat Georgia the only time they played the Bulldogs, and they beat Mississippi State two out of five. Vann's teams played Ole Miss twice and lost both games. In the writer's opinion, Johnny Vaught and Thad Vann are the two best college football coaches that ever walked the sidelines for Mississippi universities.

How Did the Other Teams Fare?

1962 Mississippi State Baseball

Mississippi State took the last two games of the regular season from Ole Miss in Oxford May 5 and 6 to finish 14-1-1 in the SEC and claim the Western Division SEC baseball championship. The tie was a 2-2 affair with Tulane in New Orleans. State's lefties junior Frank Montgomery and senior Guy Parker, both Jackson Murrah products, outdueled the Rebels' Larry Higginbotham and Robert Siedell 4-1 and 5-0. Montgomery also collected two hits and drove in two runs while holding the Rebels to 1 run. Parker pitched a gem of a 1-hit shutout as Don Kessinger produced the only Rebel hit. Having beaten Ole Miss twice earlier in Starkville, the Bulldogs registered their first sweep of their rivals in 14 years. State lost to Eastern Division champion Florida two games to one in the SEC playoff. Playing at home, Florida won the first game 8-3. State bounced back in Starkville on the strength of Montgomery's six-hitter to take the second game 3-1. The Gators won the deciding game on State's home field in an 8-7 slugfest. Paul Gregory's team finished the season with a 21-5-1 record. The .700 winning percentage is one of the best in school history. Things were really looking up for Mississippi State baseball.

Frank Montgomery was simply phenomenal in 1962. He had a 0.81 earned run average, struck out 102 batters, and posted a 9-0 record (10-0 counting his playoff win). All of those numbers were tops in the SEC. After going 4-0 in freshman ball and 3-0 and 10-0 in his two varsity seasons, Montgomery had yet to lose a game at MSU. He was named to the NCAA All-District III team, and garnered All-SEC, and All-American honors. Third-baseman Hal Green, first-baseman Bill Etheridge, and catcher Art Nester were also named All-SEC. Bill Etheridge drove in 22 runs and finished with the league's third-best batting average, .412. H. K. Etheridge was the SEC's home run king with 6 dingers.

1962 Mississippi State Football

Paul Davis, who had been an assistant coach on Wade Walker's 1961 squad, was named head coach of the Maroons when Walker resigned after the 1961 season. In his first year Davis's Maroons went 2-5 in the conference and 3-6 overall. After starting the season by losing to Florida 19-9 in Jackson, the two SEC wins came back to back in early October. MSU got by Tennessee 7-6 in Memphis and Tulane 35-6 in Starkville. Playing at home the next week the Maroons posted their third win, 9-3 over Houston. Four games into the season things were going well for Coach Davis and his Maroons. MSU stood 3-1 overall and 2-1 in the conference. But things quickly soured as MSU would not win another game. They would score only 16 points and give up 88 over the last five games of the wicked season. The Maroons scored only 76 points in all nine games and 35 of those came in the Tulane game. In their other eight games MSU averaged scoring only 5.13 points.

The offense averaged rushing for 87 yards a game and passing for 104. Future Houston Oiler Ode Burrell was by far the Maroons' biggest offensive weapon. Burrell rushed 71 times for 310 yards and caught 24 passes for 204 yards. Excellent defense, which would prove to be a mark of Paul Davis's teams, was the team's strong point. They gave up only 232 yards per game.

1962 Ole Miss Basketball

Despite the loss of All-SEC Jack Waters, excitement surrounded the Rebel basketball team as it entered the 1961–62 season. Don Kessinger had moved up to the varsity, and he soon ushered in what might be called the Kessinger era of Ole Miss basketball. Donnie thrilled the fans that crowded into the old gym by averaging 24 points per game during his first varsity season. In a late-season game played in Knoxville, Kessinger scored 48 points, a record for the most points scored against the Tennessee Vols on their home floor. In the very next game, he scored 33 against Georgia on their home court. After the season Kessinger was named All-SEC, an honor he would also receive for his junior and senior seasons. My roommate, Billy Ray Lea, and I attended nearly all of the home games that season. Under Coach Bonnie Graham the Rebels finished 11-12 overall and 5-9 in the SEC. We enjoyed Kessinger's playing tremendously but bemoaned the team's overall performance.

Billy Ray and I were especially drawn to basketball because of Kessinger and the Edmonds twins, Mel and El. An early season injury to El Edmonds, who started at forward, dealt the Rebels a devastating blow. The Edmonds had played for Brookhaven High School during the 1958–59 season. Brookhaven won the South Big 8 championship that season and went on to defeat North Big 8 champions Jackson Central for the overall Big 8 title. Billy Ray played on the Jackson Central team that lost to Brookhaven and that loss was seared into our minds. The Edmonds, who were about 6 feet tall, played one season for Brookhaven as did center Bobby

Shows, who stood about 6'7" and went on to have an outstanding career at Mississippi State.

Controversy surrounded Brookhaven's basketball team that season as it was rumored that local citizens had "bought" the Edmonds twins and Shows for their senior years and in essence bought the Big 8 championship. That controversy led to the death of one of the Jackson Central players. Kellon Sullivan was a senior at Jackson Central during the 1959–60 school year. He was a starting halfback for the football team and a starting guard for the basketball team that lost the Big 8 championship game to Brookhaven. Kellon also ran track and was voted most athletic in his senior year. He was shot and killed on graduation night, June 4, 1959. Sullivan was not at the graduation exercise that night because he lacked one credit and could not graduate with his class.

Sullivan had gotten into an argument with 31-year-old Robert T. Foster at a local restaurant, and a fight later ensued on a Jackson street. Foster was a former resident of Brookhaven and the argument that led to the fight was over whether Brookhaven had bought the Edmonds twins and Bobby Shows and thus the Big 8 championship. Foster said that some of Sullivan's friends were involved in the fight and that he thought they were about to beat him to death. Foster said he went to his vehicle, got a gun, and fired to frighten them. Sullivan was hit with two bullets and died at the Baptist Hospital after undergoing surgery. Foster was charged with manslaughter. Kellon had been a lieutenant in Central's JROTC program. Billy Ray and I went to Wright and Ferguson Funeral Home to Kellon's viewing. I will never forget seeing his body in a casket in his ROTC uniform. That was one of the saddest experiences of my youth.

My roommate Billy Ray Lea was an athlete. At Jackson Central he had been a two-year starter in baseball, and he started at point guard on its 1960 Big 8 champion basketball team. He was also a two-year starter on American Legion baseball teams that won state championships. Before changing majors and transferring to Ole Miss he excelled on MSU's 1961 freshman baseball team. After coming to

Ole Miss he briefly worked out with the basketball team as a walk-on. Realizing that he was not going to displace Mel Edmonds or Don Kessinger that adventure soon ended. While working out with the basketball team he and 6'4" sophomore forward Harry Johnston became friends.

Harry Johnston had starred in both basketball and baseball at Gulf Port High School. He was tall, handsome, and smart, and girls loved him. He was also full of himself. After averaging 8 points per game during the 1962 season Harry decided to transfer basically because the offense was not designed to get him very many shots. He moved out of the athletic dorm and into an apartment downtown, but he mostly lived with Billy Ray and me. Harry was a charismatic guy and we did a lot of things together. Harry didn't like what he called snooty social-climbing girls. One night when we were doing the twist on the dance floor at a frat party, both of us turned around from facing our girl partners and faced each other. Harry said to me, "I am tired of this social climber" and politely walked off the floor without her. I felt sorry for the poor girl when she turned around and could not find him.

Harry had been a pitcher in high school, and before the end of the semester he convinced Billy Ray to be his catcher as he ventured to West Point to try out for the West Point Packers semipro team. They went to the tryout and the Packers offered Billy Ray a place on the team, but not Harry—a big jolt to his ego. Billy Ray caught for the Packers that summer. One of his teammates was Claude Reeder, a pitcher for MSU whom he had played with at Central and in American Legion ball. Harry Johnston transferred to Memphis State and was never heard from again.

1962 Ole Miss Baseball

The 1962 baseball team finished with 15 wins and 10 losses, but 9 of those losses were to SEC opponents (4 to Mississippi State), dropping the Rebels to 6-9 in the SEC. This less-than-stellar record landed the

Rebels in second place in the SEC Western Division and fourth overall in the SEC. Nevertheless, sophomore super athlete Don Kessinger excelled. Kessinger led the team by hitting for a .402 average, stealing 9 bases, and driving in 15 runs. Kessinger's 41 hits led the SEC. Finishing with a .306 average Billy Lamb was the only other Rebel who batted above .300. Doug Elmore finished third with a .292 batting average. Fred Roberts, who also played fullback for the Rebel football team, was my ping-pong playing pal and fellow accounting major. In 1961 Roberts was the baseball team's most productive long-ball hitter collecting nine extra base hits, 3 home runs, 3 triples, and 3 doubles. Three Rebel pitchers finished with ERAs of less than 3.00, Robert Siedell 2.02, Larry Higginbotham 2.52, and Jan Adelman 2.79. Siedell also threw a no-hitter against Alabama.

With most of the team's young talent coming back, the Rebel fans could see better days ahead under their great baseball coach Tom Swayze.

How Good Were Mississippi Collegiate Athletic Teams in 1962?

In the writer's opinion, 1962 was the best year ever for Mississippi collegiate sports. Mississippi State won the SEC basketball championship and the SEC Western Division baseball championship. Ole Miss won the SEC football championship by compiling its only perfect season. Although the Rebels finished third in the AP and UPI national ranking, they were named the best team in the nation by three rating services, Billingsley, Litkenhous, and Sagarin. Southern Mississippi won the college division national football championship with a 9-1 record. There has never been another year like it, but 1959 came close. In 1959 MSU won the SEC in basketball and Ole Miss won the SEC in baseball. In addition, the 1959 Ole Miss football team was named the team of the decade in the SEC and won the Grantland Rice Award as the national champions. The writer's generation was young during those salad days.

1963

Two out of Three Again and History Made in the NCAA Basketball Tournament

---

1963 SEC Basketball Champions—Mississippi State University

1963 SEC Football Champions—Ole Miss

1963 SEC Baseball Champions—Auburn

(Ole Miss won the Western Division title)

1963 Final score: Mississippi universities 2 SEC championships, all other members of the SEC 1

The Champions

Mississippi State University—1963 SEC Basketball Champion

Mississippi State basketball was ranked sixth in the country by the AP's 1962–63 preseason poll. The Bulldogs defeated Arkansas A&M, Louisiana Tech, Northeast Louisiana, Louisiana College, Christian Brothers College, Memphis State, Xavier, and Delta State but lost to Virginia Tech and Houston to start the season. Having lost 2 of 10 nonconference games the Bulldogs fell out of the AP top 10 before their first SEC game against Auburn January 5, 1963.

The defending SEC champions picked it up a notch on the road by besting the previously undefeated and tenth-ranked Tigers 62-53. The super sophomores of 1961 were now seniors and three of them, Leland Mitchell, W. D. Stroud, and Joe Dan Gold, played like they expected to top off their brilliant careers with another SEC championship. State's scoring was paced by Mitchell with 15 points, Stroud pitched in 19 while juniors Doug Hutton and Stan Brinker scored 11 and 7 points, respectively. The Tigers were coming off a Sugar Bowl Tournament championship and were shooting 52 percent from the floor. Against the Bulldogs' defense Auburn would shoot only 35 percent while State's hot shooters made 58 percent from the floor. The Bulldogs won the battle of the boards 36-33 and made 24 points from the free-throw line compared to Auburn's 19. Coach McCarthy said after the game that he thought Leland Mitchell, who snatched 13 rebounds, had played his best game ever. Layton Johns starred for Auburn grabbing 17 rebounds and scoring 17 points. The victory in their first conference game and an overall 9-2 record were not enough to lift Bulldogs back into the AP top 10.

Two days after dispatching Auburn, the Bulldogs returned to Alabama and took on the Crimson Tide in Foster Auditorium. The game went to overtime before 3,500 Tide partisans who cheered their team on as they upset the favored Dogs 77-72. Bama basically led all the way, and it took a Doug Hutton jump shot with a minute to go in regulation and a Joe Dan Gold steal with 17 seconds left to send the game into overtime. Hutton gave State its only lead with another jumper early in the overtime period. But the Crimson Tide scored 9 points in overtime while State managed only 4. This time the Bulldogs lost the battle of the boards 45-41. Four Bulldogs scored in double figures, Mitchell 17, Stroud 16, Hutton 10, and Brinker 13. Gold led both teams in rebounding with 13 boards. An unhappy Babe McCarthy said, "No it wasn't the bad start that beat us. It was our free-throw shooting [20 of 33] and missing all those layups. Those are the kind of shots that will win for you and when you miss them you are in trouble." State shot 44 percent from the floor while Bama shot 45 percent. State hit 60 percent of their free throws while Bama hit 77 percent. Now 9-3 overall and 1-1 in the SEC, Mississippi State would remain absent from the AP top 10.

Back home in Starkville, MSU welcomed the Vanderbilt Commodores on January 12. The Bulldogs regained their winning ways with a 58-55 victory that was not very impressive. It took reliable Leland Mitchell's heroics in the last seconds for State to avenge the only blemish on the previous year's stellar record. Mitchell, who played with 4 fouls most of the second half, scored 8 of State's final 12 points including two free throws with 8 seconds left to clinch the victory. The Commodores led 55-53 with 31 seconds left. Eleven seconds later previously cold-shooting Red Stroud hit a jump shot to tie the score. Mitchell then secured a rebound after a shot by Vandy's John Russell and was immediately fouled with 8 seconds left on the clock. Mitchell promptly sacked both ends of a one-and-one opportunity to put State up by 2. Joe Dan Gold was fouled when he rebounded Vanderbilt's final shot and he sank a free throw with one second left that provided the final 3-point margin.

This was a most unusual game for two of State's stars, W. D. Stroud and Leland Mitchell. Although he hit a crucial shot late in the game Stroud scored only 5 points. Mitchell led both teams in scoring with 22 points, but he collected only 3 rebounds, early foul trouble probably contributed to that season low. One of the reasons for State's continuing success was that when the regulars were not up to par their teammates generally stepped up. Despite Mitchell's lack of rebounds the Bulldogs still won the battle of the boards 47-33 with Joe Dan Gold, grabbing 10 and Stan Brinker 8. Vanderbilt shot 40 percent from the floor and the Bulldogs 35 percent. State hit 69 percent from the line with Mitchell making 8 of 10 while Vandy hit 75 percent from the line. The Bulldogs gritted and hustled their way to this, their tenth victory.

On January 14 undefeated and seventh-ranked Georgia Tech faced the Bulldogs and 5,100 fans in McCarthy Gymnasium. In sharp contrast to the Vanderbilt game Red Stroud and Leland Mitchell were about as hot as the fire that severely damaged the campus cafeteria that very afternoon. Stroud scored 30 points while Mitchell scored 25 and pulled down 12 rebounds as the Bulldogs defeated the Yellowjackets 81-69. Stroud made 11 of 19 shots from the floor and 8 of 8 from the free-throw line. Mitchell's rebounds triggered State's fast-break offense to perfection. Coach McCarthy captured the essence of the game, saying, "The difference in the game was our ability to get the ball off the boards and get it to the other end so quick. This made their press ineffective." State shot 48 percent from the floor and 68 percent from the foul line. The Jackets shot 36 percent from the floor and 71 percent from the line.

Rebounding was indeed the key to the Bulldogs' victory. State had 65 rebounds to Tech's 47. Coach McCarthy praised the team's rebounding and praised Stan Brinker and Bobby Shows for their rugged work under the boards. Again the game exemplified how the Bulldogs picked each other up. Joe Dan Gold, one of the team's most consistent rebounders and scorers, grabbed only 6 rebounds and scored only 6 points. Gold got in early foul trouble and didn't play much in the second half before finally fouling out. Up stepped Brinker with 8 points and 7 rebounds and Shows with 6 points and 5 rebounds. Red Stroud also grabbed 5 rebounds. Tech's coach Whack Hyder praised State's fine ball-handling and its student body for their tremendous support.

State jumped back into the AP's top 10 at number 9 before taking on Ole Miss in Starkville January 19. The home fans showed up again to crowd McCarthy Gymnasium and root their team on to a 78-64 victory over the Rebels. Leland Mitchell, Red Stroud, and Joe Dan Gold showed out again with Mitchell scoring 16 points and grabbing 12 rebounds, Stroud pouring in 26 points, and Gold scoring 12 points and securing 12 rebounds. The victory along with Kentucky's loss to Tennessee and Alabama's loss to Auburn put the Bulldogs in first place in the SEC with a 4-1 conference mark. Defensively, State's guards, Stroud and Hutton, countered the Rebels' two most prolific scorers, guards Mel Edmonds and Don Kessinger, by holding them to a total of 28 points. But again, it was State's ability to sweep the boards that was the major factor; State won the rebounding battle 58-40. The victory over Ole Miss did not move the needle in the AP poll as State maintained its number-nine ranking.

The Bulldogs went to the Bluff City to take on the 12-4 Memphis State Tigers on January 26. A month earlier Mississippi State had administered one of the Tigers' defeats in a 77-66 game played in Jackson. This time things didn't go as well. Before 4,951 approving fans in Ellis Auditorium the home standing Tigers defeated the Bulldogs 71-65. State's cold shooting and the Tigers' strong rebounding gave the home team an 18-point lead, 36-18, with 4:20 left in the first half. State closed the gap to 37-28 at halftime and actually went ahead 52-49 midway through the second half. That lead didn't last long as the Tigers were back on top by 5 points with 6:50 to go. The Tigers played tenacious defense and outrebounded the Bulldogs by 12 (a very unusual occurrence). Memphis State also converted 61 percent of their field attempts to State's 38 percent. Led by Leland Mitchell, who fouled out with 6:26 left in the game, and Doug Hutton, both of whom scored 15 points, five Bulldogs scored in double figures. The Tigers also had five players who posted double-digits scoring nights. State was led in rebounding by Joe Dan Gold and Stan Brinker, who each grabbed seven.

Coach McCarthy assessed the defeat, saying, "It was our bad start that beat us. We got behind and that put the pressure on us. We weren't able to get them out of their zone defense as long as we were behind so we had to play their game."

Mississippi State played its second game of the season in the new Mississippi Coliseum in Jackson on January 28. The historic contest matched State against the University of Southern Mississippi (USM) Southerners. Mississippi Southern College (MSC) had become a university the year before, and this was the first time the schools' basketball teams had ever played each other. Although USM came into the contest with a 5-10 record, the Southerners had experienced great success in basketball over the past few seasons under head coach Fred Lewis. During the 1959–60 and the 1960–61 seasons the Southerners, often referred to as the Golden Giants, won a total of 45 games and lost only 5. Along the way they produced a 26-game win streak. The 1959–60 squad posted a 23-2 record and ranked fourth in the United Press International College Division final poll. The 1960–61 team finished 23-3 and finished second in the UPI poll. USM finished the 1961–62 season, Coach Lewis's last, 13-13. After the season Lewis took his overall 89-38 record and decamped for Syracuse University, a major college power. Lee Floyd, who would soon build quite a name for himself, took over as USM's head coach at the beginning of the 1962–63 season.

Going into the game, MSU was heavily favored over USM. Although the Bulldogs won 62-52, things didn't go exactly as scripted. The *Clarion-Ledger*'s Robert Fulton put it this way, "Lee Floyd's ambitious Southerners employing an effective 2-3 zone defense and a deliberate drive-for-the-bucket offense, gave the Bulldogs all they could handle for two-thirds of the game." USM led by 3 points at the half, and State did not go ahead for good until 14:20 was left in the second half. Once ahead, the Bulldog defense shut out the Southerners for 6 minutes 20 seconds and iced the game. Stan Brinker and Leland Mitchell poured in 12 points during USM's long drought. Double-digit scorers for the Bulldogs were Stan Brinker 21, Leland Mitchell 18, and W. D. Stroud 13. State won the battle of the boards 44-38 as Mitchell pulled down 14 rebounds and Brinker grabbed 11. Jack Laird with 14 points and Jim Walker with 12 led USM in scoring. Walker also grabbed 11 rebounds.

One of the 4,951 fans in attendance marred the historic contest by throwing a chair on the court that almost hit Leland Mitchell. The chair hit the court with seven seconds left in the game, and it took five minutes to clear the floor and escort the offender out of the coliseum before the game could be resumed. Coach Floyd said, "That was real terrible about the chair-throwing incident. That was a Hattiesburg business man who threw it but it sure made Southern look bad."

It was back to the SEC grind as ninth-ranked State played host to LSU on February second and posted a hard-earned 73-66 win. While both teams made 23 field goals, State won the battle of the boards 44-39. In a contest that included 42 personal fouls it is no wonder that the game was won at the free-throw line. LSU made 20 free throws and the Bulldogs 27. Reliable Red Stroud made all 14 of his free throws. Three tigers scored in double figures: Ellis Cooper 19, Dick Malie 14, and Maury Drummond 11. Four Bulldogs scored in double figures: Mitchell 18, Stroud 18, Hutton 11, and newcomer Richie Williams 18. Joe Dan Gold led the Bulldogs with 9 rebounds and Dick Maile led the Tigers with 9. The game was a bad-news-good-news situation for State. Richie Williams was a transfer from Southern Illinois who had just become eligible at the beginning of the second semester. He contributed 18 points, making 8 of 10 field-goal attempts and 2 of 2 free throws, and he pulled down 5 rebounds. Williams also fouled out with five and a half minutes left in the game. The bad news was that Williams was needed badly because starter Stan Brinker was in the infirmary with a 103-degree fever.

February 4 saw Tulane visit McCarthy Gymnasium and leave on the short end of a 91-73 score. Twelve Bulldogs played in the lopsided contest as the home team completely outclassed the Greenies in the second half. Leland Mitchell sacked 29 points and Red Stroud added 20. With 10 boards Joe Dan Gold led State rebounding. In a real team effort, a total of 10 Maroons snagged an amazing 68 rebounds. Mitchell hit 12 of 18 field-goal attempts and was 5 for 5 from the charity stripe. The score was actually tied at the half 37-37, but with its fast-break clicking State outscored Tulane 54-36 in the second half. Five thousand fans witnessed the win that made State 16-5 overall and 6-1 in the SEC. The Maroons were now tied with Georgia Tech in the SEC, and they were ranked eighth nationally by the AP.

Tennessee came to Starkville February 9 and became State's seventh SEC victim 63-59. This one didn't come easy as the Vols shot the lights out, hitting 61 percent of their 33 field-goal attempts and 83 percent of their 23 free-throw attempts. On the other hand, State had a cold shooting night making only 36 percent of their 69 shots from the floor and 62 percent of their 21 free throws. The normally reliable Leland Mitchell was stone cold as he made only 2 of 17 field-goal attempts and fouled out with about six minutes left in the game. State won the battle of the boards 39-30 and took 36 more shots from the floor than Tennessee; volume shooting helped. The score was tied 28-28 at the half, and the Maroons never had a secure lead until Doug Hutton netted two free throws with seven seconds left in the game to give State its 4-point margin. Joe Dan Gold scored 15 points, Stan Brinkman 14, and W. D. Stroud 13 to lead State's attack. Gold grabbed 10 rebounds to lead both teams' board play. With Georgia Tech's loss to Tulane, the victory moved State to first place in the SEC with a 7-1 conference record.

Adolph Rupp brought his Kentucky Wildcats with a record of 14-6 to Starkville February 12 to face the league-leading Maroons plus an overflow crowd of 5,500 highly partisan fans in McCarthy Gymnasium. The Baron of the Bluegrass and his Cats had not forgotten that MSU had taken them down in their home gym the year before, 49-44. Babe's Boys would make sure Kentucky would not taste sweet revenge on MSU's home court. State won by a final score of 56-52. Brilliant coaching, a tenacious defense, a stall offense, and balanced scoring produced the victory. Led by Doug Hutton's 17 points three other Maroons scored in double figures, Stroud 12, Mitchell 10, and Gold 10. Kentucky's Ted Deeken, filling in for the ailing Don Rolfs, led Kentucky's scoring with 25 points. Apparently, Coach McCarthy decided to let Deeken shoot; he made 9 of 24 shots from the floor, and shut down everybody else. Joe Dan Gold held All-American Cotton Nash to 10 points. With Gold grabbing a rebound and slinging in a last-second 15-foot hook shot, State led at the half 38-32. The Cats outscored the Maroons 20 to 18 in the second half. Kentucky and MSU mistakes kept the Maroons scoreless for the first seven and a half minutes of the second half. When State finally started scoring again, McCarthy abandoned the stall tactic and switched to a shuffle that worked almost to protection. State won despite being outrebounded by Kentucky 41-31, a tribute to the Maroons' tenacious defense.

The victory kept State, now ranked sixth nationally by the AP, in first place in the SEC with an 8-1 conference mark. It was also a milestone in Babe McCarthy's career. The Babe had this to say: "I said before the game that if I could win this one, I'd be even with Adolph for the first time in my life [4-4] and now I am."

Although they were elated by the win over Kentucky and in first place in the conference, the Maroons had a real challenge ahead—five straight SEC road games to end the season. The first obstacle was Florida at Gainesville February 16 and the Gators let some air out of State's sails by defeating the Maroons in convincing fashion 73-52. Florida came into the game 5-5 in the conference and 11-10 overall. Shooting percentages in the first and second halves capture the game. In the first half the three seniors who had carried the Maroons to new heights for three years, Mitchell, Stroud, and Gold, could not find the bucket. The threesome combined sank only 3 of 22 shots from the floor, 14 percent. The Maroons' great radio voice Jack Cristil probably said, "They can't throw it in the ocean." Even with that shaky performance Florida led by only 4 points at the half, 24-20. In the second half it was Florida's free-throw shooting that killed MSU's chances. The Maroons' poor shooting in the second half put them further behind, and they had to foul to get the ball back. The Gators simply went to the foul line and connected on 29 of 32 or 91 percent of their free throws. After getting hot late in the game Red Stroud led State's scoring with 22 points; no other Maroon scored in double figures. Four Gators scored in double figures: Tom Baxley 23, Bud Bales 15, Tom Barbee 15, and Taylor Stokes 11. Florida won the battle of the boards 37-33. The performance had to have humbled an outstanding MSU basketball team. They were now 8-2 in the SEC and still in first place, but they had four more SEC road games to play.

The trip up the road to Georgia must have rejuvenated the Maroons. On February 18 they handled the Georgia Bulldogs 86-75. This time State got off to a good start scoring 8 points in the first 2 minutes and

32 seconds of the game. Although Georgia closed to within one point twice the Maroons led all the way. In contrast with what happened in the Florida game, State's big three seniors were simply outstanding. Joe Dan Gold scored 20 points and pulled down 10 rebounds; Leland Mitchell scored 17 points and grabbed 12 rebounds; and Red Stroud pitched in with 16 points and 5 rebounds. Junior Doug Hutton joined the scoring parade with 18 points. Led by Mitchell's 12 rebounds MSU won the battle of the boards 43-33. After the game Coach McCarthy hailed his players performance, saying, "This was a game we needed. After that bad night in Florida I was beginning to wonder if we could recover."

The Maroons were 9-2 in the conference and ranked eighth in the country by AP when they ventured to Louisiana February 23 to take on the LSU Tigers. Playing like they were still upset about the Florida loss, the Maroons punished the Tigers 99-64. As the score indicates, State truly dominated the game in which 11 Maroons saw action. The big three seniors showed out again, combining for 53 points and 25 rebounds. Another member of the great 1959 recruiting class, Bobby Shows, also contributed significantly, snagging 14 rebounds and scoring 9 points. Super reliable Doug Hutton did his part by pitching in 14 points. State outrebounded the homestanding Tigers 65-42. Maury Drummond scored 18 points and Dick Maile 13 to lead LSU's scoring.

Going into the LSU game MSU had been tied with Auburn for first place in the SEC with both sporting 9-2 conference records. With State's victory over LSU and Auburn's loss to Kentucky, MSU stood alone atop the conference with two games to play. With an eye toward the SEC championship and a bid to the NCAA tournament, Babe McCarthy said, "[This was] one of our greatest performances against an SEC opponent on the road." Then the great coach added, "It would be a shame for a team capable of playing as well as our boys did away from home tonight, not to get a chance to play in the NCAA."

Leaving Baton Rouge with a 10-2 conference mark State went south to play Tulane in New Orleans on February 25. The Maroons continued their remarkable run of road victories by dispatching the Green Wave 78-67. The Greenies never really had a chance because State's big three seniors came to play. Mitchell, Gold, and Stroud combined for 66 points and 23 rebounds. The Maroons shot 57 percent from the floor in the first half and held a 13-point lead at halftime. The *Clarion-Ledger*'s Robert Fulton explained how that lead was built midway through the first half: "The Bulldogs then began to pull away as they took command of the game by blending their shuffle offense with a deadly fast break. At one stretch the Bulldogs scored four consecutive effortless layups off the shuffle." State led by as much as 17 points early in the second half, but the Greenies were determined not to be blown out of their own gym and gradually cut into the lead. But the outcome was never in doubt. The Maroons finished the game having shot 50 percent from the floor and having converted 62 percent of their 16 free shots. Tulane shot 37 percent from the floor but cashed in 80 percent of their 26 free-throw attempts. Tulane actually won the battle of the boards 43-40. Tulane's star Jim Kerwin led all scorers with 34 points. State's top scorers were Stroud with 28 points and Gold, who contributed 26.

When they departed Louisiana the next day, Babe's Boys stood 11-2 in the conference and had clinched at least a tie for the SEC championship for the fourth time in five years. Tennessee's 55-47 win over Auburn had left the Tigers with a 9-4 SEC record and destroyed their hopes for an SEC title. But Georgia Tech's 89-69 win over Florida gave the Yellowjackets a 10-3 conference mark and a chance to tie State for the championship. If State were to lose their final game to Ole Miss and Georgia Tech would win their last game over Vanderbilt, both teams would finish with 10-3 conference marks. But State had defeated Georgia Tech earlier in the season and held the tie breaker. Thus, Mississippi State for the third consecutive year had earned an invitation to the NCAA Basketball Tournament. Whether Mississippi officials would allow this team to participate in the racially integrated NCAA Tournament remained to be determined. The February 26 AP poll listed Mississippi State as the seventh-best team in the country.

MSU's final regular-season game and its fifth consecutive road game was played March 2 at Ole Miss. Two years earlier under similar circumstances (State had already clinched the SEC championship) the Maroons went to Oxford and lost to the Rebels 70-74. Surely, Babe McCarthy reminded his players of that downer. This time the Maroons won a squeaker 75-72. State's big three seniors were still at the top of their game, and they combined to score 56 points and grab 28 rebounds. With 24 points and 11 boards Joe Dan Gold led the game in both scoring and rebounding. The Rebels, who were playing for new head coach Eddie Crawford, had struggled badly early in the season but had recently gained their footing by winning 5 of their last 8 games. Doing their best to match State's big three, the Rebels' outstanding guards, All-SEC Don Kessinger and Mel Edmonds, each scored 23 points and they kept Ole Miss in the game all the way. State won the rebounding battle 44-38, but the Maroons shot 38 percent from the floor and 72 percent from the line. The Rebels shot 49 percent from the floor and 82 percent from the foul line. My roommate Billy Ray Lea and I were at the game. I can attest to the fact that this was one of the most exciting and draining games that both of us ever witnessed.

The Maroons' win allowed Babe McCarthy's team to leave Oxford with a 12-2 SEC record and an undisputed SEC championship. Georgia Tech had lost to Vanderbilt on the Commodores home floor 75-74 to finish the SEC season tied with Auburn 9-4. But that didn't matter; even if the Jackets had won, State would have been the undisputed champions. Would the undisputed champs actually get to play in the NCAA tournament? The subterfuge that MSU officials had to execute to make it possible for State to play in the 1963 NCAA Basketball Tournament is described in detail in chapter 1. Suffice it to say here that the Maroons played in the tournament and in the process destroyed the prohibition against state-supported schools playing in integrated athletic events.

Surrounded by much controversy, seventh-ranked Mississippi State met third-ranked Loyola-Chicago in the semifinals of the NCAA

Mid-East Regional Tournament March 15, 1963, in East Lansing, Michigan. Loyola had already defeated Tennessee Tech in the first round while State had drawn a bye. It was MSU's first-ever appearance in the NCAA tournament. MSU started five whites and Loyola started four African Americans and one white. Led by All-American Jerry Harkness, the Loyola Ramblers had outscored their opponents by an average of 24 points per game during the season. Harkness averaged 21 points and 7 rebounds. Five Loyola players averaged scoring in double figures, and the Ramblers were the highest scoring team in the nation. Playing before 12,143 appreciative fans, the Bulldogs and Ramblers gave the spectators their money's worth. Doug Hutton told the writer that the fans were super. They appeared to have become MSU fans, probably because of what the team had done to get to the tournament. State's stall offense and tight defense held Loyola to its lowest scoring total of the season, but State was still unable to match the Ramblers' fire power. Loyola-Chicago won 61-51. Rebounds and free throws carried the Ramblers to the win. Loyola made 13 of 16 from the foul line and pulled down 48 rebounds. State converted only 11 of 20 free-throw attempts and grabbed only 35 rebounds. Harkness, who pulled down 9 rebounds, made 7 of his 11 shots from the floor and 6 of his 9 free-throw attempts to lead all scorers with 20 points. The Ramblers' Vic Rouse and Les Hunter registered double-digit games in both points and rebounds. Rouse scored 16 points and dominated the boards for the Ramblers by grabbing 19 rebounds while Hunter grabbed 10 rebounds and scored 12 points. State was led by Leland Mitchell, who scored 14 points and pulled down 11 rebounds. State stayed close to the Ramblers most of the game and trailed by only 3 points with 10:55 left. But Mitchell fouled out with six minutes and 47 seconds left and that pretty well ended the Maroon's chances.

Both coaches praised the other team after the game. Babe McCarthy said: "I still think Loyola is the fastest big team I have ever seen. We played as well as we were capable. We needed a perfect game to win and we didn't get it." McCarthy went on to say, "Let's talk about the way they played basketball not their color." Loyola coach George

Ireland said, "One of the things that came out of this game was the fact that you didn't see any pushing, shoving or needling among the players. That shows that Mississippi State has a good bunch of kids, just like we have." Captain Joe Dan Gold spoke for the Maroons, saying, "They were perfect gentlemen—just like any other team."

State's season wasn't quite complete. The Maroons played Mid-America Conference champions Bowling Green State of Ohio for third place in the NCAA Mid-East Regional. The 19-7 Falcons, led by the great 6'11" All-American center Nate Thurmond, started three African American players and were favored to win. The Maroons had already proved they could go toe to toe with the best in the land defeated the Falcons 65-60. Suffering with a broken hand, Joe Dan Gold had to set this one out so only two of the big three seniors, Leland Mitchell and Red Stroud, saw action in the season's final game. Mitchell scored 23 points and grabbed 8 rebounds and Stroud pitched in 13 points. Juniors Doug Hutton and Stan Brinker picked up the slack; Hutton scored 14 points and secured 3 rebounds while Brinker pulled down 10 rebounds and scored 7 points. State won the contest in highly unconventional fashion. The Maroons did not score a field goal in the last 12 minutes and 20 seconds of the game. Employing its shuffle/fast-break offense, State jumped out to a 12-point lead at the half, 34-26. When Mitchell, Brinker, and Richie Williams got in foul trouble, Coach McCarthy switched to the stall offense. The Maroons did not make a field goal the rest of the game. But the stall forced the Falcons to foul to get the ball and the Maroons scored their last 17 points from the charity stripe. Bowling Green had trailed the whole game, but with 1:29 left the Falcons closed to within one point of State, 59-58. In the last two minutes Leland Mitchell hit 6 free throws to preserve the victory. Mitchell led all scores with 23 points and he pulled down 8 rebounds. Mr. Thurman made his presence known by grabbing a school record 31 rebounds and scoring 19 points. Neither team shot well. State shot 36 percent from the floor and the Falcons shot 26 percent. Poor shooting resulted in a total of 111 rebounds of which State grabbed 51 and Bowling Green 60.

Loyola-Chicago went on to finish the season 29-2 and to win the NCAA tournament by defeating number-one ranked Cincinnati 60-50 in overtime. Loyola finished third nationally, behind Cincinnati and Duke in the AP poll. Mississippi State finished the season with a 22-6 record and the Maroons ranked sixth in the final AP poll. Why Loyola-Chicago did not finish number one in the AP poll, which was apparently conducted after the NCAA tournament, is a mystery. Perhaps, those who voted concluded that Cincinnati and Duke had played more demanding schedules.

The Mississippi State seniors closed out their brilliant three-year run in which they won 70 games and lost only 13 (84 percent) with three SEC championships. MSU has never had another class as successful as the one led by Leland Mitchell, W. D. (Red) Stroud, and Joe Dan Gold. No Mississippi State basketball coach other than the great Babe McCarthy has ever won 3 straight and 4 out of 5 SEC basketball championships.

Ole Miss Football—1963 SEC Champions

Fred Russell's premonitions about Elmore and Griffing following Gibbs published in the *Nashville Banner* had proved to be spot on. Would Perry Lee Dunn continue the string for Johnny Vaught's 1963 Rebels?

In 1959 Natchez High School's Perry Lee Dunn was one of the most highly recruited quarterbacks in the country. He had lettered in basketball, baseball, football, and track and had even been featured in a *Time* magazine article his senior year. Natchez, Mississippi, is a lot closer to Baton Rouge, Louisiana, than it is to Oxford and LSU's coach Paul Dietzel coveted Dunn. Johnny Vaught tells an interesting story of how he signed Perry Lee. In his book *Rebel Coach*, Vaught wrote: " . . . a couple of days before signing day in December, I invited Perry Lee and his father to the campus. Then we went on a hunting trip and we kept moving. On the day before you could sign in the SEC we decided to drive to Jackson and spend the night at a hotel there. I signed Perry Lee one minute after midnight. At that hour Paul sat at the Dunn home in Natchez."

Like Perry Lee, I was a freshman in the fall of 1960. Being a freshman Perry Lee could not play on the varsity that year, but he soon became an established presence on campus. Even the veteran football players seemed to be in awe of him. I remember coming out of the student union building one day and hearing a bunch of burly guys singing a little ditty that went like this:

One, two, three,
Look at Perry Lee,
Three, four, five,
He's the best alive.

Jake Gibbs, Doug Elmore, and Glynn Griffing were on campus at the time!

Although he took some snaps at quarterback in his sophomore and junior years, Perry Lee did not (and was not expected to) dislodge Doug Elmore and Glynn Griffing as starters in their senior campaigns. However, Dunn was such an outstanding athlete that he found his way onto the field playing both fullback and defensive back and some linebacker while he waited his turn to start at quarterback. It is interesting that Perry Lee played some at the fullback position. There were two other really good players from the 1960 class that lined up at fullback for the Rebels during Dunn's three varsity seasons: Buck Randall and Freddie Roberts. Both of those guys were more than capable of playing the position fulltime, a real testimony to the depth of the Rebels at the time.

As anticipated Perry Lee was the Rebels' starting quarterback for the 1963 season. He led the Rebels to a 7-0-2 regular-season record and the SEC championship. The two ties came against Memphis State in the first game of the season (0-0) and Mississippi State in the last game of the regular season (10-10). The website Saturday Down South says that Ole Miss won the Mississippi State game played November

30 at Davis Wade Stadium in Starkville by a score of 10 to 10. In a way that is true since a tie was as good as a victory in the race for the SEC championship. I remember Coach Vaught being criticized for settling for a tying field goal rather than going for a touchdown and a win when the Rebels had a scoring opportunity late in the game. Vaught had a simple explanation—going for a TD was riskier than going for 3 points and a tie, which would make his team champions of the SEC.

In their first game on September 21 the defending SEC champion Ole Miss Rebels played home-standing Memphis State in Crump Stadium. It was not an auspicious beginning for a team with great potential despite the fact that it had lost 9 of its first 15 players to graduation. The AP preseason poll ranked the Rebels second in the country. Ole Miss was favored by 14 points and was riding a 17-game winning streak against the Tigers. The game turned into a ferocious defensive battle that ended in a 0-0 tie. Ole Miss had not been shut out since LSU turned the trick 14-0 in 1958. The *Clarion-Ledger*'s Wayne Thompson captured the game in a single paragraph: "The Memphis State Tigers knocked on the door of heaven here Saturday night while the Ole Miss Rebels were ringing the door bell of Purgatory. One might say, after a scoreless tie, that the Tigers came closest [to] getting an answer." The Rebels did not move into Tiger territory or register a first down during the first quarter, and they turned the ball over on downs on their only serious scoring threat. That opportunity came in the second quarter, but Buck Randall was stopped inches from the goal on a carry from inside the Tigers' 3-yard line. Memphis State's biggest scoring threat also came in the second quarter when, after a short Rebel punt, the Tigers moved to Ole Miss's 23-yard line before turning the ball over on downs. The statistics reflect the defensive nature of the game. Ole Miss gained only 57 yards rushing while the Tigers garnered 87. The Rebels passed for 139 yards with Perry Lee Dunn and Jim Weatherly hitting on 11 of 26 throws. Memphis State quarterbacks connected on four of eight attempts for 41 yards, but they ended the game with a 13-5 advantage in first downs. The Rebels suffered from three pass interceptions, the Tigers from one.

Drive-stopping penalties hurt both teams. The Rebels accumulated 55 yards in penalties, the Tigers 83.

Coach Vaught's teams always seemed to bounce back from a subpar performance. The Rebels started living up to their potential the next week against Kentucky. The September 28 game was played on the Wildcats' home field in Lexington. For the eleventh time in 13 years the Rebs beat the Cats, this time 31-7. Perry Lee Dunn threw touchdown passes of 12 and 21 yards to end Allen Brown and one to Larry Smith for 70 yards. Jim Weatherly threw a 28-yard touchdown pass to Billy Sumrall, and Billy Carl Erwin kicked four extra points and a field goal. In pilling up 223 yards through the air, Dunn and Weatherly enjoyed superb protection from rotating linemen Stan Hindman, Rodney Mattina, Whaley Hall, Bob Robertson, Kenny Dill, and Cecil Ford. The line also led the way as Freddie Roberts, Mike Dennis, and Weatherly combined for 165 yards rushing. The Rebels' 388 yards of total offense produced 16 first downs.

The Ole Miss defense dominated as usual, giving up just 28 yards on the ground and 107 through the air. The Rebels also picked off 5 of the Cats' 21 passes. Kentucky managed only nine first downs. The Wildcats had fewer penalty yards than Ole Miss, 49-78, and they lost no fumbles while recovering two Rebel miscues. After two games the Rebels had dropped from preseason number two to tenth in the AP poll.

On October 5 the Rebels were on the road again, this time in pursuit of their eleventh consecutive victory over the University of Houston Cougars. Quarterback Jim Weatherly, who led the Rebs in rushing with 80 yards on 11 totes, scored on a quarterback sneak in the first quarter, and Billy Carl Irwin kicked the extra point to put Ole Miss up 7-0. Midway through the second quarter the Cougars recovered Larry Smith's fumble on the Ole Miss 19-yard line. It took eight plays, but with the help of a pass interference penalty, which gave them a first down at the 14, the Cougars earned a touchdown on a 2-yard pass from Jack Skog to Clem Beard. After a successful extra-point kick was nullified by a penalty, the Cougars' Bill McMillian missed the second attempt and the Rebels led 7-6. Trailing by only 1 point at halftime to a 21-point favorite, the Cougar homecoming crowd had to be feeling good. But the Rebels controlled the second half. In the third quarter Perry Lee Dunn threw a 23-yard touchdown pass to Mike Dennis, but Billy Carl Irwin missed his first extra-point attempt of the year. As the third quarter ended, Jimmy Heidel intercepted a Skog pass at Houston's 28-yard line. The ensuing Rebel drive stalled at the 14, and Irwin missed a field-goal attempt. The Cougars soon punted, and Ole Miss started a drive on its own 47-yard line. Three plays later the Rebels cracked the end zone on a 30-yard pass from Dunn to Dennis. Irwin's kick was true this time. That ended the game's scoring and Ole Miss won 20 to 6.

The Rebels' defense was once again magnificent. The Cougars gained 159 total yards and managed 12 first downs. Fifty penalty yards against the Rebs extended several drives. When Houston got close to the Rebel goal line, Ole Miss's defense invariably stiffened. The Rebels punted only twice and mustered 372 yards of total offense and 18 first downs. The Cougars intercepted one pass and recovered two Rebel fumbles, which limited the Rebel scoring. Ole Miss didn't beat the point spread and remained ranked tenth by the AP.

After three games Ole Miss had not played in Mississippi and the fourth game would be played on October 19 against Tulane in New Orleans. The Green Wave had already lost four games and only 17,000 fans populated the 83,000-seat Tulane Stadium.

In the second SEC game of the season the Ole Miss defense pitched another shutout and the Rebels won 21-0. The offense scored on its second possession, marching 59 yards in six plays that included a 19-yard pass from Perry Lee Dunn to Billy Clay. Dunn capped off the drive with a 3-yard scamper around right end. It looked like the beginning of a big scoring day but that was not to be. A stubborn Green Wave defense, two pass interceptions, and penalties slowed the Rebel offensive machine. After a frustrating first half that featured a 15-yard penalty that halted a drive, a key Tulane interception, and a goal-line stand by the Greenies, the Rebels led 7-0. Like the first half, the second half started well for the Rebels, who received the kickoff and in eight plays marched down field for a touchdown. Dunn again did the honors with a quarterback sneak from the one. An unusual series of events occurred when Tulane secured possession of the ensuing kickoff. Mike Dennis recovered Dave East's fumble at the Tulane 22. Bill Goss intercepted a Jim Weatherly pass at the 5 and returned it to the 14. Three plays later Bo Aldridge recovered Al Burguieres' fumble at the 21. Weatherly promptly threw a touchdown pass to Dennis. Irwin's third successful extra-point kick ended the scoring for the day. Tulane's good defensive play was in sharp contrast to its offense. While the Rebels gained a total of 355 yards, the Green Wave defense was tough in key situations. Tulane's offense simply never got going. It generated only 4 first downs, 69 yards rushing, and 5 yards passing!

Earlier in the season Tulane had lost to number-one-ranked Texas by 21 points. After succumbing to the Rebels by 21 points, Tulane coach Tommy O'Boyle said the passing of Dunn and Weatherly put Ole Miss on par with Texas. The pollsters were impressed too; the road-weary but undefeated Rebels jumped from tenth to fifth in the AP poll. It could be because the Rebel defense had given up only 13 points in four games.

The 1963 Ole Miss-LSU game was almost as memorable to me as the 1962 encounter. I don't remember where I was at the time, but I watched the game on TV. During my freshman year I had suffered through a heartbreaking 6-6 tie with the Tigers and in my sophomore year a humiliating 10-7 defeat at their evil hands. The spell was broken during my junior year with the Rebels' 15-7 victory in Baton Rouge. The 1963 game would simply be icing on the cake for me as the Rebels destroyed LSU 37-3 in Baton Rouge. The margin of victory was the largest by Ole Miss over LSU since 1917.

Rebel fullback Freddie Roberts scored three touchdowns in that game. Freddie and I met between our junior and senior years of high school at Boys State where we started playing ping-pong. We played off and on while at Ole Miss. Freddie was also a fellow accounting major as was my friend Richard Calvasina. Richard told me this story about Freddie's three touchdowns in the LSU game. He and Freddie were taking an accounting course under Professor Joe Cerny at the time. Before the LSU game Mr. Cerny told Freddie that if he scored two touchdowns against LSU, he would earn some extra credit points. After Freddie scored three touchdowns, Mr. Cerny reneged, saying, "I said two." Many will remember Mr. Cerny! Richard Calvasina and his two brothers all earned baccalaureate, masters, and PhD degrees from Ole Miss. In the 1980s Richard and I were faculty colleagues at the University of West Florida.

One of the most celebrated series of plays in my generation's great memories of Rebel football took place that night. Here is how Buddy DiLiberto of the *Times-Picayune* described it:

> Mississippi led 23-3 when Joe Labruzzo gathered in a punt at his own 18, waited for a block, and set sail up the sidelines right in front of the LSU bench.
>
> Stan Hindman, Ole Miss' 230-pound sophomore guard, did the impossible, catching Labruzzo from behind and knocking him out of bounds at the Rebel one. How fast that makes Hindman is anybody's guess but until Saturday Labruzzo was considered the fastest thing this side of Cape Canaveral.

But that's not the end of the story. Starting from Ole Miss' one-yard line, the Tigers ran four plays against the Rebels' defense which was rated number one in the nation. That series ended when the Rebels took over on downs at the Ole Miss five-yard line.

This game marked the eighteenth time that Johnny Vaught's Ole Miss teams had played LSU. After the 1963 victory Vaught's overall record against the Tigers stood at 11 wins, 5 losses, and 2 ties. In the 16 games that did not result in a tie, Vaught won 69 percent of the time. That record is simply amazing considering the fact that all but two of the games were played in Louisiana. One of the two games played in Mississippi ended in a tie and the other one in an Ole Miss win.

That is, 10 of Vaught's 11 victories had been achieved before hostile fans on Louisiana soil. Nothing illustrates the greatness of Coach Johnny Vaught more than his record against LSU.

It has always been pleasant for me to remember the Rebels' overall performance against the Tigers during my undergraduate years. The final slate—Rebels 2, Tigers 1, and one tie. The tie was the only game played in Mississippi; all three of the other games were played in Tiger Stadium in Baton Rouge.

On November 9, Ole Miss played the University of Tampa in Oxford. Tampa did not play major college football at the time, and the game wasn't much of a contest. The Rebels won 41-0 with the younger members of the team leading the way. Ole Miss used 43 players, gained 399 total yards to Tampa's 81, and led in first downs 21-4. Although the Rebels didn't score until the second quarter, they posted seven touchdowns including four in the fourth quarter. The nation's best defense was never seriously challenged by the visitors from the Sunshine State. From a physical perspective, the win was costly as starting guard Bobby Robinson went down with an injury that kept him out of the season's last two games and starting quarterback Perry Lee Dunn got his left hand hurt, which prevented him from playing offense the next week against Tennessee. But Ole Miss benefited that day from Mississippi State's victory over Auburn. The Bulldogs 13-10 win over the Tigers gave the Rebels undisputed possession of first place in the SEC.

Third-ranked Ole Miss played Tennessee in Memphis November 16 and the defense though severely challenged pitched another shutout allowing the Rebels to prevail 20-0. Because of Perry Lee Dunn's injured left hand, Jim Weatherly was the main trigger man for the Rebels. Before a Crump Stadium crowd of 27,022, Weatherly threw a first-quarter 33-yard touchdown pass to Larry Smith. Early in the second quarter Weatherly drove the Rebels 78 yards to the Vols' 2-yard line where Freddie Roberts bulled into the end zone. Ole Miss gained possession for the first time in the third quarter when Jimmy Heidel returned a punt 24 yards to the Vols 22. The Rebels moved by land to the 2-yard line where Frank Kinard (Bruiser's son) flew over the left side of the line for a touchdown. Billy Carl Irwin made two of three extra-point attempts. The Rebels managed 274 yards of total offense, 160 passing and 114 rushing. Tennessee actually generated 168 yards rushing and 92 yards passing for a total of 260 yards.

Although the Volunteers gained a lot of yards, they were unable to score on Ole Miss's magnificent defense. *Jackson Daily News* sportswriter Lee Baker paid tribute to the Rebels' number-one defense, writing:

> The defense of guards Stan Hindman and Rodney Mattina, tackles [Whaley] Hall, [Cecil] Ford, Bo Aldridge, and James Harvey, ends [Allen] Brown and [Reed] Davis and linebackers [Kenny] Dill, [Robert] Upchurch, [Freddie] Roberts and [Frank] Kinard made the forward wall tough to penetrate when the goal was threatened. In the defensive backfield [Jimmy] Heidel was a shining light in breaking up the Vol passing, but he had his share of help with a large contribution coming from [Perry Lee] Dunn who made his appearances on defense count quite as much as though he was running the Rebel scoring machine.

The Mississippi State game was played November 30 in windy Starkville. Ole Miss took the lead in the first quarter when Jim Weatherly hit fullback Mike Dennis with a 30-yard touchdown pass completing an 80-yard drive. After Billy Carl Erwin kicked the extra point, the Rebs led 7-0. State didn't register a first down in the first quarter but began the second quarter by moving to the Rebels' 31-yard line where they faced a fourth-and-four situation. Justin Canale, who had missed a 21-yard attempt earlier after the Bulldogs intercepted a Dunn pass, promptly kicked a 49-yard field goal to make the score to 7-3 in favor of the visitors. In the third quarter Frankie Lambert punted from the Rebels' 14-yard line into a strong north wind. The ball traveled only 18 yards and State was in business at the 32. At that point MSU coach Paul Davis pulled a rabbit out of a hat and called on his outstanding halfback Ode Burrell to throw his first pass of the season. Taking a pitch out from the quarterback and making the play look like a sweep, Burrell threw to end Tommy Inman, who caught the ball at the 15 and took it in for a touchdown. State led 10-7 until the scoreboard showed that there were only 3 minutes 10 seconds left in the game. Ole Miss had just driven 73 yards and had a fourth and goal at State's 3-yard line.

With time running out, Coach Vaught faced what could have been a difficult decision but it wasn't for him. Would he attempt to score a game-winning touchdown or would he attempt a field goal to tie the game at 10? Vaught quickly opted for a field-goal attempt. Billy Carl Irwin's kick tied the score and the game ended in a 10-10 standoff. Some context is in order. Fullback Freddie Roberts had been stopped by a stubborn State defense for no gain on the last play before the field goal. Quarterback Perry Lee Dunn was limited offensively because of his hand injury. Billy Carl Irwin had been successful on only 2 of 5 field-goal attempts during the season. He had, however, converted 23 of 27 extra-point attempts. The ball would be snapped from the 3 and placed down at the 10. The kick would be just like an extra-point attempt. But the most important consideration was that a tie would make Ole Miss the SEC champion.

Had State won, the Maroons' record would have been 5-1-1 in the SEC and Ole Miss's record would have been 5-1. That scenario would have made Auburn with a 6-1 conference record SEC champs. The tie put the Rebels' final SEC mark 5-0-1 and made them SEC champs. The game statistics clearly show that this had been an epic defensive battle. The Rebels gained a total of 220 yards and made 14 first downs. Mississippi State gained only 102 yards and made only 4 first downs. But the Bulldogs intercepted 3 passes to stop Rebel drives while Ole Miss did not intercept a pass.

The field-goal decision was severely questioned and the Rebel head coach caught flack for settling for a field goal. But Coach Vaught explained his choice very succinctly after the game, saying, "Concerning that field goal, we're conference champions and undefeated." It was Vaught's sixth SEC championship and his third in the last four years.

In his 17 years as head coach of the Rebels, Vaught still had not lost to their in-state rivals Mississippi State. Vaught made no excuse for the tie but gave his perspective on the game: "I thought the strong wind was a definite factor in our game. State played a real fine defensive game. The wind bothered us both, though." He also mentioned that several players were injured and unable to play and that a couple of others saw limited playing time because of injuries.

Immediately after the game Ole Miss accepted an invitation to play Alabama in the 1964 Sugar Bowl. Marshall Davis, president of the Sugar Bowl, said this of Coach Vaught's decision to go for the tie: "Vaught did perfectly right. He was playing for the championship and he won it and we of the Sugar Bowl are happy he took the action he did. It gives us the SEC Champion in our bowl."

Ole Miss lost 12-7 to Alabama in the January 1, 1964, Sugar Bowl in snow-covered Tulane stadium. From the beginning there seemed to be a damper on the Sugar Bowl. Alabama's famed coach, Paul (Bear) Bryant, had suspended starting quarterback Joe Namath from the game (apparently for carousing). The weather had not cooperated. Snowbanks surrounded the field at the old Tulane Stadium and at game time the temperature was in the mid-40s and the ground and air were very moist.

I watched on TV in Jackson with my dad. It was memorable and excruciating for several reasons, starting with the snow in New Orleans that hampered both teams' offenses. There were a total of 17 fumbles in the game! Alabama fumbled 6 times and lost 3 while Ole Miss fumbled 11 times and lost 6. Ole Miss had 5 penalties for 45 yards and Alabama had 3 for 15 yards. When a team loses 6 fumbles and has three times more penalty yards than its opponent, it's almost impossible to win. All of Alabama's points came on field goals by Tim Davis (31, 46, 22, and 48 yards). Three of those field goals came after Ole Miss had fumbled the ball away. The last one, a 48 yarder, was the longest field goal ever kicked in any bowl game up to that day. I am of the opinion that if the two teams were still playing, Alabama would still have not scored a touchdown. Ole Miss's lone touchdown came on a five-yard pass from Perry Lee Dunn to Larry Smith, who graduated a year before me from Jackson Central. Going for the win late in the game, the Rebels lost a fumble at Alabama's 9-yard line. The teams' total yardage illustrates the closeness of the game—Alabama had 69 plays for 194 yards while the Rebels had only 48 plays for 248 yards. Perry Lee Dunn went 8 for 10 passing for 125 yards and a touchdown and he rushed 6 times for 24 yards.

When Coach Bryant suspended Joe Namath for the Sugar Bowl, the starting quarterback role for the Crimson Tide fell to 18-year-old Steve Sloan. The youngster didn't play well. He threw 11 passes, completed 3 for 29 yards, and had one intercepted. He also ran the ball 16 times for 51 yards. Steve Sloan would go on to become a star at Alabama and Ole Miss's head football coach for five very disappointing seasons.

The Rebels' backup quarterback for the 1963 team would become famous and highly successful in another calling. Jim Weatherly, who became the starting quarterback in 1964, made his mark in music. He became a singer-songwriter and Gladys Knight and the Pips made him rich and famous by recording his "Midnight Train to Georgia." The original title of the song, which was inspired by Weatherly's friend Farrah Fawcett, was "Midnight Plane to Houston." Weatherly recorded several singles and albums and wrote songs recorded by Ray Price, Lynn Anderson, Brenda Lee, and Bob Luman. Jim Weatherly was inducted into the World Songwriters Hall of Fame in 2014. I remember him playing for a street dance on the Ole Miss campus in the early sixties.

How Did the Other Teams Fare?

1963 Mississippi State Baseball

MSU opened the 1963 baseball season in the Loyola Coca-Cola Invitational in New Orleans March 14–16. State sandwiched losses to LSU

(2-1) and Loyola (5-4) around a 2-0 win against Illinois to finish in third place in the four-team tournament. Coach Paul Gregory had been slowly building a powerhouse, and the Dogs promptly went on an eight-game win streak beating Arkansas State twice, Alabama twice, Illinois Wesleyan twice, and Southern Mississippi twice. Then they dropped a two-game set to LSU to bring their overall record to 9-4 and their SEC mark to 2-2. The next two series were played against Alabama and Ole Miss. The Crimson Tide again fell twice to the Dogs, but Ole Miss beat MSU in both games. State got back to its winning ways in the SEC by defeating Tulane twice. At this point MSU stood 13-6 overall and 6-4 in the conference.

Before closing out the season against three SEC foes, the Dogs played three out-of-conference games in which they went 1-1 against Arkansas State and beat Southern Mississippi. Returning to conference play MSU played two-game sets against Tulane, LSU, and Ole Miss. State split the series with Tulane, were swept by LSU, and split with Ole Miss. The Bulldogs ended the season 17-11 overall and 9-7 in the SEC. The SEC record tied LSU for second place in the Western Division behind Ole Miss.

1963 Mississippi State Football

Nineteen sixty-three was a good year for Mississippi State football. Fielding one of its best teams ever under Coach Paul Davis, State would finish the season with a 7-2-2 record, including a 4-1-2 mark in the SEC. The Maroons had not won 7 or more games since they finished 7-3 in 1947, and they had not won more than 4 SEC games since they won 5 in 1942. State's 1963 team gave up only 94 points in 11 games. The Bulldogs shut out Howard, Tennessee, and Houston, and gave up 10 points or fewer to Florida, Tulane, Auburn, LSU, and Ole Miss. The most points State gave up was 20 in their 1-point loss to Alabama. MSU scored 175 points during the season and featured two outstanding running backs, Hoyle Granger and Ode Burrell, who would go on to fine professional careers.

Mississippi State was rewarded for its outstanding season with an invitation to play in the December 21, 1963, Liberty Bowl in Philadelphia, Pennsylvania. In State's first bowl game in 23 years, the Bulldogs defeated the North Carolina State Wolfpack 16-12 before 8,309 fans in Municipal Stadium where the temperature was 22 degrees and the wind was out of the north. Coached by Earle Edwards, the 8-2 Wolfpack came into the game as co-champions of the Atlantic Coast Conference.

MSU's Bill McGuire blocked a North Carolina State punt in the first quarter and Tommy Inman picked the ball up at the Wolfpacks' 11-yard line and took it to the endzone for a Bulldog touchdown. State's second score came after a 23-yard pass from Don Edwards to Dan Bland, an 11-yard tote by Burrell and a 3-yard sweep by Sonny Fisher around left end. After Justin Canale missed the extra-point attempt, the Dogs led 13-0. The next MSU drive started after they received a punt at midfield and ended on the first play of the second quarter when Canale kicked a 43-yard field goal. That put the Dogs up 16-0 and ended MSU's scoring for the day. NC State scored a touchdown in the second quarter but misfired on the 2-point conversion attempt. In the fourth quarter the Pack got into the end zone again on a 4-yard pass from Jim Rossi to Ray Barlow. The 2-point conversion attempt was unsuccessful. Final score Mississippi State 16, North Carolina State 12. Hoyle Granger rushed for 94 yards on 13 carries, quarterback Sonny Fisher carried 11 times for 81 yards, and MVP Ode Burrell 10 times for 69 yards.

Mississippi State has the distinction of winning the fifth annual Liberty Bowl, the last one played in cold-weather Philadelphia. The next year the game that had been labeled "The Deep Freeze Bowl" moved to an indoor facility in Atlantic City, New Jersey. In 1965 the Liberty Bowl found a permanent home in Memphis.

1963 Ole Miss Basketball

By the time 1962–63 basketball season started Ole Miss had a new head coach. Bonnie Graham had been replaced by Eddie Crawford, who had been an assistant football coach under Johnny Vaught in 1962. Crawford had been an amazing athlete at Ole Miss in the mid-1950s. He played halfback and defensive back for Vaught's 1954–56 football teams that won 26 games and two SEC championships, and he played in both the Cotton and Sugar Bowls. He was a center fielder in baseball and as a senior led the SEC in home runs and was named All-SEC. Crawford was also a standout in basketball and ran sprints for the track team. This great athlete was enshrined in the Mississippi Sports Hall of Fame in 2012.

During Eddie Crawford's first year as Ole Miss's basketball coach the Rebels won 5 of their last 9 games to finish 7-17 and 4-10 in the SEC. The four SEC wins came against Tulane, LSU, and Tennessee at home and Florida on the road. Of course, there were a few highlights. For the second time Don Kessinger was an All-SEC selection, averaging 22 points per game. Against Tulane, Kessinger made 22 of 28 shots from the floor and scored 49 total points to set new school records.

Billy Ray Lea and I went to the Kentucky game at the new Mississippi Coliseum in Jackson on February 9 anticipating a duel between Kessinger and the Wildcats' All-American Cotton Nash. Kentucky won the shootout 75-69, but the expected duel did not disappoint. Kessinger sacked 27 points and Nash pitched in 22. But Ole Miss point guard Mel Edmonds, who scored 30 points and dished out several assists, was the star of the game. The Rebels, who were not expected to give the mighty Cats much of a game, exceeded the Rebel fans' expectations that night. As they often say, "The game was closer than the score indicated."

1963 Ole Miss Baseball

Ole Miss had been a real power in SEC baseball for several years. The Rebels won the conference championship in 1959 and 1960, and in 1961 they finished with the second-best record in the conference. The 1963 season saw Ole Miss and Mississippi State go head to head for the Western Division title. The Rebels beat State 5-0 April 15 in

Oxford as Bill Keyes pitched a 5-hitter. State's starter Frank Montgomery departed in the fourth inning after having given up 5 hits and 5 runs and making a throwing error that allowed 2 runs to score. The next day the Rebels downed State 6-1 as Dennis Huffman hit 2 solo home runs for the Rebels and Tommy Keyes hit a 3-run homer. Larry Higginbotham was the winning pitcher as the Rebels picked up their tenth straight win. Ole Miss went to Starkville May 3 to face State in the final SEC series of regular season. The race between the intrastate rivals for the Western Division championship had ended the week before when Ole Miss beat Alabama 11-5 (the second game was rained out) and State lost two games to LSU, 8-4 and 7-3.

The Rebels had a 10-3 SEC mark compared to State's 8-6 record. Ole Miss had already clinched a berth in the SEC championship series against Eastern Division champs Auburn. But pride was on the line in this series. The Bulldogs had swept all four games against Ole Miss in 1962, and the Rebels wanted to return the favor. It didn't happen as the two rivals split the final series 1-1. State won the first game 5-3. State's H. K. (Butch) Ethridge hit a 3-run homer in the sixth inning and the Bulldogs added two more in the eighth. Doug Hutton gave up 3 runs over 9 innings while boosting his record to 5-0 for the season. Ole Miss bested State 5-4 in the final game when Dave Jennings, who played third base for the baseball team and tailback on the football team, hit a home run in the fifteenth inning.

The Rebels went 19 and 7 overall and won the 1963 Western Division championship, their fifth since 1954, with an 11-4 conference record. Along the way Coach Tom Swayze posted his 200th win as the Rebels' head coach when Ole Miss beat LSU 5-4 April 20. First-baseman-pitcher Tommy Keyes set a school record for triples with eight and posted a 3-0 record as a pitcher. All-SEC honors went to Keyes and Don Kessinger, who led the team by hitting .371 and stealing 15 bases.

Auburn defeated Ole Miss in the championship series two games to one. The Rebels won the first game 7-6, but Auburn took the last two 7-4 and 6-2. Ten of the Rebels' first 12 players were either sophomores or juniors; the future looked good for Ole Miss baseball.

CHAPTER 7

1964

A Baseball Championship and Freedom to Play in the College World Series

---

1964 SEC Baseball Champions—Ole Miss (The Rebels also won the NCAA District III championship and advanced to the College World Series.)
1964 SEC Basketball Champions—Kentucky
1964 SEC Football Champions—Alabama
Final score: Mississippi universities 1 championship, other SEC schools 2

The Champions

1964 Ole Miss Baseball

Coach Tom Swayze had his Ole Miss Rebels baseball team at the top of their game during the 1964 season. Swayze's Rebels finished the regular season with a 19-4 overall record and an 11-1 SEC slate, which gave them the SEC Western Division title. Ole Miss defeated Tulane four times, LSU twice, Alabama three times, and Mississippi State twice. The Rebels' only regular-season SEC loss was a 5-2 decision to Mississippi State. Four scheduled conference games were rained out, two against LSU and one each against Mississippi State and Alabama. The three non-SEC losses came against the University of Southern Mississippi, Southeastern Louisiana, and Nicholls State. Ole Miss split a two-game series with each of those schools. After losing the first game of the best two-of-three SEC playoff series 10-9 to Eastern Division champs Auburn, the Rebels defeated the Tigers 7-0, 5-0 to take the overall SEC championship.

Key players for the 1964 Rebels included catcher Chet Bergalowski, first baseman Tommy Keyes, second baseman Billy Sumrall, shortstop Don Kessinger, third baseman Richie Perkins, left fielder Freddie Roberts, center fielder Glenn Lusk, and right fielder Dennis Huffman. The pitching rotation stacked up as Richie Prine, Larry Higginbotham, Jimmy Jones, and Russell Johnson.

The Rebels were scheduled to play a regular-season ending two-game series with Mississippi State on Friday and Saturday, May 8 and 9. Sporting a 11-0 conference record and a 19-3 overall mark the Rebs would be playing in Oxford against a Bulldog team that they had defeated twice in Starkville. Going into the series Ole Miss was ranked number three in the nation by the Collegiate Baseball newspaper poll. On Friday the Bulldogs spoiled the Rebels' perfect SEC record by winning a 10-inning 5-2 game. It was an ugly game for the Rebels as they stranded 18 base runners. Rain washed out the game scheduled for May 9. The rainout was the sixth Ole Miss had encountered at home during the season. Rain had washed away two games with LSU, two games with Arkansas State, and single games against Alabama and Mississippi State.

Auburn won the SEC Eastern Division crown with a 12-5 conference mark, setting up a rematch of the 1963 SEC playoff in which the Plainsmen defeated the Rebels 2-1. It soon looked like sweet revenge was not to be had. Things didn't go well for the Rebels in the first game played May 13 at Auburn when the home team won 10-9 in a game decided in the ninth inning. Ole Miss started their number-one pitcher Richie Prine, who finished the regular season 6-0. Auburn saved their best pitcher, Jimmy Crysel, who had a 7-0 record for the second game. The Rebels fell behind 4-0 in the first inning and scrambled the rest of the game to close the gap. Auburn had 14 hits, including 5 doubles and a triple, while the Rebels managed 13 hits including 2 doubles a triple and a home run.

The Rebs were down but not out when they came back to Oxford to play the second game where they had to face Auburn's ace Jimmy Crysel in a contest that could clinch the SEC title for the visitors. The trip to Oxford didn't work out well for Auburn. While the hitters and fielders did their jobs, the Rebel pitchers took over, shutting out the Plainsmen 7-0 and 5-0. In the second game Larry Higginbotham didn't just close down Auburn's hitters over 9 innings, he hit a grand-slam home run to help his own cause. Russell Johnson and Richie Prine combined for the third game shutout. Prine had given up 4 runs in the first inning of the first game, but he blanked Auburn for 4 innings in this game. In the final two games Rebel pitchers gave up a total of 9 hits and no runs. Meanwhile, Rebel bats were hot. Over the entire series the Rebels hit .311 while Auburn hit .233. Kessinger hit .462, Lusk .417, and Bergalowski .300. With the playoff victories over Auburn, Coach Swayze and his Ole Miss Rebels had won their third SEC baseball championship in six years.

Unlike the 1959 and 1960 SEC champions, the 1964 Ole Miss baseball team was not forced to sit out the NCAA playoffs. Thanks to the courageous actions of Mississippi State's administration and its 1963 basketball team, Mississippi-supported schools were now allowed to play in integrated sports events.

The Rebels traveled to Gastonia, North Carolina, where they would join East Carolina, North Carolina, and West Virginia in the NCAA District III playoffs. North Carolina played East Carolina in the first round, and Ole Miss was matched against West Virginia in the double elimination tournament. North Carolina defeated East Carolina 8-0, and Ole Miss defeated West Virginia 11-0. In the Rebel victory Larry Higginbotham gave up 5 hits, struck out six, and ran his scoreless innings streak to 20. The Mountaineers came into the game with a 24-3 record. Ole Miss shelled West Virginia pitchers for 15 hits with Don Kessinger, Jimmy Keyes, and Fred Roberts each collecting 3. North Carolina and Ole Miss advanced to the winners' bracket. West Virginia and East Carolina played an elimination game in the losers' bracket and East Carolina eliminated the Mountaineers 6-5.

Richie Prine pitched a 7-hitter in the Rebels' 4-3 victory over North Carolina in their second game. The score was tied 1-1 in the top of the ninth inning, but the Rebels scored 3 runs in their half of the inning. Mr. Prine helped his own cause immensely by driving in 2 runs with a triple and scoring what would prove to be the winning run. The Rebels led 4-1 going into the bottom of the ninth. Two hits scored a run, making the score 4-2. Two more hits put runners on first and third with one out. Then a ground ball was hit to Tommy Keyes at first base. Keyes stepped on the bag to register the second out while holding the lead runner at third and allowing the runner on first to advance to second. Prine issued an intentional walk to load the bases and set up a force play at any base. The next batter hit a grounder to second base where Bill Sumrall fumbled the ball allowing the runner who had been on third to score. But the runner who had been on second attempted to dash home too. Big mistake, Sumrall threw to Bergalowski, who made an outstanding play to tag the runner out and preserve the 4-3 victory. Tar Heel fans thought the runner was safe at home, and after the game law officers had to usher some of them off the field. Sumrall led the Rebels' 8-hit attack with 3 singles. Ole Miss stranded 7 runners on the base paths while the Tar Heels got 7 hits and left 7 runners stranded.

At that point Ole Miss stood 2-0 in the tournament, and both East Carolina and North Carolina were 1-1. The Tar Heels won the elimination game and had an opportunity to win the tournament by defeating the Rebels in two straight games. On May 30 the Rebels quickly brought the tournament to an end and claimed the NCAA District III championship. The final game was not much of a contest as Russell Johnson pitched a 3-hitter and the Rebel bats produced 14 hits and 13 runs. Every player in the Rebel lineup got at least 1 hit while Don Kessinger, Jimmy Keyes, and Fred Roberts got 2 and Chet Bergalowski got 3. Keyes and Glenn Lusk hit homers. Ironically Bergalowski was the only Rebel who did not score a run. Final score Rebels 13, Tar Heels 1. Known to be soft spoken and dry witted, Coach Tom Swayze summed up the game by saying, "It was a very, very, very, very, very good game." The Rebels totaled 28 runs and 35 hits in the three games while their opponents were held to 15 hits and 4 runs. It was on to the College World Series in Omaha, Nebraska.

Tom Swayze was named SEC Baseball Coach of the Year for the third time after the 1964 season. Coach Swayze had this to say about his 1964 team before they left for Omaha:

> I think this year's team is the best balanced that I have ever had. By that I mean speed, pitching, power, defense, and just all-around balance. Also, I do believe that this team is the most dedicated one that I have ever had at Ole Miss.

The Rebels were ranked third in the nation behind Missouri and Arizona State and ahead of fourth-ranked Southern California when they went on to the College World Series. In the CWS the Rebels lost to Southern California 3-2 and to Arizona State 5-0.

What happened in the loss to Southern California was outrageous. Simply put, the NCAA decided to go against the rule that was in effect at the beginning of the game. The *Clarion-Ledger*'s Wayne Thompson explained:

> Ole Miss and USC were playing their first games of the series with the Trojans, defending champions, holding a 3-1 lead in the top of the fifth inning when the rains came. But rather than rule it a postponed game—and the rules as printed gave them no other choice—that group [the NCAA] said it was a "suspended game" and ordered play to resume at the exact point on Tuesday night.
>
> The entire tournament was put back for 24 hours and the two clubs had ample time to get in a full nine innings Tuesday without causing

> any further delay in the proceedings. So, in essence, they had no real excuse—or for that matter, any reason.

The game against Southern California began Monday night June 8, but it wasn't completed until the next day. Southern California scored 3 runs in the second inning Monday off Rebel pitcher Richie Prine. Don Kessinger scored a run in the fourth inning after walking and being moved along by singles hit by Fred Roberts and Dennis Huffman. Rain stopped the game with USC batting with one out in the fifth inning and the score standing USC 3, Ole Miss 1. When play resumed the next day the Rebels' Bill McGlathery shut out the Trojans the rest of the game. But the Rebels were only able to muster one more run over the remaining five innings. Results—a 3-2 USC win and the Rebels in the losers' bracket.

Rain caused another delay and Ole Miss and Arizona State did not play until Friday, June 12. In the 5-0 loss to the Sun Devils the Rebels garnered only 2 hits, both of which were singles, off the Sun Devils ace Skip Hancock. This was only the second time the Rebels did not score all year; they had lost to Southern Mississippi 2-0 in the third game of the season. Ole Miss starting pitcher Larry Higginbotham gave up 3 runs and struck out 7 over 5 1/3 innings.

The University of Minnesota won the 1964 CWS by defeating the University of Missouri 5-1 in the championship game.

The 1964 CWS appearance was the Rebels' second. Coach Swayze had taken his 1956 team to the CWS where they posted a 2-2 record. The Rebels finished the 1964 season ranked seventh nationally with an overall 24-7 record.

Senior Don Kessinger, who was named All-SEC, All-NCAA District III, and All-American, led the Rebels by hitting .432 and playing the shortstop position in spectacular fashion. All-SEC and All-NCAA District III Glenn Lusk hit .358 and drove in 31 runs and All-SEC and All-NCAA District III Tommy Keyes hit .330. Senior Fred Roberts hit .420 and blasted 7 home runs. Rebel pitching was not shabby as Johnson posted a 1.19 earned run average, Bill McGlathery 1.85, and

All-SEC Richie Prine 2.00. Larry Higginbotham won five games and lost only one. Kessinger and Lusk were tied for the highest batting averages in SEC games as both of them went 20 for 50 for .400 averages in conference play. By posting a 6-0 conference mark Prine was the second-winningest pitcher in the SEC.

The year 1964 was my last semester as an undergraduate. Always a big baseball fan, I attended as many home games as possible. Strangely enough only one game of this great season is seared in my memory. The previous summer, Glenda Canterbury, a friend from Jackson and an Ole Miss student, introduced me to her friend, Dorothy Douglas, who worked in Jackson. While in Jackson for spring break I asked Dorothy out and we had two dates. On the second date I told Dorothy that I was going to marry her, and she laughed. Before Dorothy I had been dating an Ole Miss student named Jeanette McGuire, who was a baseball fan too. We had gone to several baseball games together. The Rebels' first home game after spring break was an April 14 contest with Delta State, which the Rebels won 9-6. Before the game Jeanette called and asked, "Crockett, aren't you going to take me to the baseball game?" My reply was, "Yes, I am going to take you to the game." I did and that was the last time I ever dated anyone not named Dorothy Douglas!

Despite the CWS disappointment, it was a very good year for Ole Miss Rebel baseball.

How Did the Other Teams Fare?

1964 Ole Miss Basketball

Coach Eddie Crawford's second year proved to be better than his first. While playing only 22 games, which were 2 fewer than the 24 played in the previous season, the Rebs won 3 more games. Ole Miss finished 10-12 overall and 7-7 in the SEC, which placed them seventh in the conference. The break-even conference mark reflected a 3-game improvement over the 4-10 SEC record in Crawford's first year. The SEC victories came against Auburn, Tulane, Georgia, Florida, and Mississippi State.

Highlights of the season included two victories over Mississippi State, 77-75 in Oxford and 78-61 in Starkville. The win on State's home floor was the first since 1955, and the Rebels' sweep of the two games against their in-state rivals was the first since 1952.

The great Don Kessinger finished his career with a season scoring average of 23 points per game. Kessinger scored more than 500 points for the third straight season, a feat that no other Rebel had ever accomplished. The three-time All-SEC guard finished his career as the only Rebel to have scored 300 or more points three times against SEC competition. During his three varsity seasons Kessinger piled up records. He played in more games, made more field goals, and scored more points than any other Rebel ever had. At the end of the 1963–64 season he was named NCAA District 3A All-American. Today Kessinger's career 1,553 points stands eleventh on the Rebels' all-time scoring list. His career spanned only three seasons since freshmen were not allowed to play on the varsity in the early 1960s. Only one player has scored more points in as many or fewer games. Tenth-place Gerald Glass scored 1,554, which is one more than Kessinger's total, in 60 games during the 1989–90 seasons.

1964 Mississippi State Basketball

Mississippi State's string of three consecutive SEC basketball championships came to an abrupt halt with the 1963–64 season. Leland Mitchell, Joe Dan Gold, W. D. "Red" Stroud, and Bobby Shows graduated in the spring of 1963. That quartet of seniors combined to average 52 points and 27 rebounds a game for the 1963 SEC champs, who finished with a 22-6 overall record and a 12-2 SEC mark. Juniors Doug Hutton and Stan Brinker combined to average 21 points and 9 rebounds for the 1963 champions. That is, six players contributed an average 73 points and 36 rebounds. Mitchell, Gold, Stroud, and

Shows were gone after the 1963 season. The six top scorers for Coach Babe McCarthy's 1963–64 team—Doug Hutton, Stan Brinker, Richie Williams, Aubrey Nichols, Bill Anderton, and Don Posey—combined to average 62 points and 31 rebounds. Thus, on average, the 1963–64 Bulldogs top six players averaged 11 fewer points and 5 fewer rebounds than had the 1962–63 top sextet. That turned out to be a recipe for disaster. The 1963–64 team finished with a 9-17 overall record and a 4-10 SEC mark, eleventh in the conference.

MSU's four SEC victories included two against Tulane, one each against Alabama and Florida. The Bulldogs' only other win over a major college team came against George Washington. For the season State's opponents averaged 71.4 points and the Dogs averaged 69.7. Those figures make the season look better than it actually played out. State's 69.7 average is inflated by a 44-point win over Louisiana Tech and a 40-point win over Southeastern Louisiana, both non-major opponents. The future looked brighter because the Bulldogs' outstanding freshman class posted a 21-3 record.

1964 Ole Miss Football

To say that Ole Miss fans had high expectations at the beginning of the 1964 football season would be an understatement. The Rebels were coming off two straight SEC championships and were ranked number one in the country by the Associated Press in the preseason poll. I know that this fan had confidence to burn. I had graduated from Ole Miss in the spring and during my undergraduate days the Rebs had won three SEC titles. I thought the good times would last forever.

When the season kicked off in mid-September, I was a cadet at the USAF Officer Training School (OTS) at Lackland Air Force Base in San Antonio, Texas. I had proudly proclaimed to my squadron mates that I was an Ole Miss Rebel and we were number one. Things went as expected in the first game of the season as the Rebels blanked Memphis State in Oxford 30-0. The next Saturday brought the biggest shock of my young life as Ole Miss lost a 27-21 decision to Kentucky in Jackson. The Rebels were simply not expected to ever lose a football game to the Wildcats, and they dropped from number one in the AP poll to eleventh after the defeat. The Kentucky game was played on September 26, and lucky for me my class graduated from OTS two days later. I didn't have to suffer before my buddies too long. My fiancé, Dorothy Douglas, came to the September 28 graduation ceremony with my mom and dad. (As noted earlier, on our second date only six months before I told Dorothy that I was going to marry her. We were married October 16.) My mother pinned on my gold bars. Then a bunch of new second lieutenants went our separate ways to new duty stations. Thank goodness I have seen only two of my OTS classmates since then.

Ole Miss would drop completely out of the AP poll before completing a 5-5-1 season that included a 2-4 conference mark. In addition to the first-game victory over Memphis State, there were a couple of impressive wins along the way as the Rebels beat Houston 31-9 in Oxford and Tennessee 30-0 in Knoxville. The Rebels lost by 6 points to Kentucky, 1 point to LSU, 3 points to Mississippi State (in Oxford!), and by 7 points to Tulsa in the Bluebonnet Bowl. But there was a 16-point loss to Florida in Gainesville and a stinging 7-7 tie with Vanderbilt in Nashville. The 1-point loss to LSU came on a 2-point last-minute conversion in Baton Rouge. The loss to Florida was only the second in the 10 games that the two schools had played. Mississippi State's 3-point win was the first over Ole Miss in the Vaught era, which started in 1947. For the season Ole Miss scored 217 points and their opponents scored 127. The Rebels were in every contest except the Florida game to the very end. Had they scored 13 more points Ole Miss could have finished 9-1 rather than 5-4-1 in the regular season. Ole Miss's seventh-place finish in the SEC was the Rebels' first outside the top four since 1950. The Rebels had lost only four regular-season games during the six seasons before 1964. After the regular season but before the Bluebonnet Bowl loss Ole Miss was tied for twentieth in the UPI coaches poll.

What went wrong? Well, for one thing, highly regarded quarterback Jim Weatherly had injured a toe in spring practice and even though he completed 54 percent of his passes for 1,034 yards and ran for 262 yards he never was in top form. A quarterback of the caliber of a Jake Gibbs, Doug Elmore, Glynn Griffing, or Perry Lee Dunn would not start for the Rebels again until Archie Manning donned the Red and Blue in 1968. Mike Dennis was the leading rusher with 571 yards, and he was the leading receiver, catching 29 passes for 276 yards.

1964 Mississippi State Baseball

Over a 29-game season Coach Paul Gregory's Bulldogs compiled a 17-12 overall record and a 7-7 SEC mark. In SEC play State was victorious over Alabama once, LSU twice, Florida once, Tulane twice, and Ole Miss once. But the Bulldogs also lost to Ole Miss two times, Alabama three times, and to LSU two times. In nonconference play State won three games from Arkansas State, two from Nichols State, one from North Carolina, one from Northeast Louisiana, and two from Illinois Wesleyan.

In 1964 Coach Gregory's team took a big step toward being able to compete for SEC championships. Outfielder Del Unser joined the varsity. Del is the son of Al Unser, a baseball lifer who played four years in the majors, scouted for major league teams, and managed in the minor leagues. Al Unser had been a teammate of Paul Gregory in the Pacific Coast League in 1947. Del graduated from high school in Decatur, Illinois, and chose to go to Mississippi State because of his dad's friendship with Coach Gregory. Del Unser would go on to distinguish himself in both the SEC and Major League Baseball. He played for five different teams during his 14-year major league and was on the 1980 Philadelphia Phillies team that won the World Series. In the World Series Del Unser contributed two crucial late-inning pinch hits to Philadelphia victories.

1964 Mississippi State Football

After posting one of the university's best records ever by going 7-2-2 overall and 4-1-2 in the SEC during the 1963 season, MSU reverted to its losing ways in 1964. The Bulldogs sank to a 4-6 overall mark and a 2-5 conference record. Although star running back/receiver Ode Burrell was now playing in the professional ranks, returning fullback Hoyle Granger and star lineman Tommy Neville were expected to lead the team to a winning record.

The season started with a mistake-filled 21-7 loss to nonconference foe Texas Tech in Lubbock, and it ended with a rare and satisfying 20-17 victory over SEC and in-state rival Ole Miss in Oxford. The only other SEC win came against Tulane in Starkville. The five SEC losses were to Florida, Tennessee, Alabama, Auburn, and LSU. The Bulldogs were very competitive in SEC games as they scored a total of 82 while giving up 102. That is, the scoring differential was about 3 points per game. State went 2-1 against nonconference competition, losing to Texas Tech while beating Southern Mississippi and Houston.

Famed former NFL coach Bill Parcells likes to say you are what your record says you are. Well, the record says that the Mississippi State Bulldogs had a losing record in 1964. But a closer look at the Dogs' performance on the field shows that Coach Paul Davis fielded a very stout football team in his third year as the Bulldogs' head coach. Their SEC opponents averaged scoring only 15 points a game while State averaged 12 points per game. State could move the ball on the ground. Over the 10-game season 10 players combined on 406 rushing plays to gain 1,520 yards. But gaining yardage via the pass was a real problem. State passers attempted a total of 134 passes and completed 66 (49 percent) for only 773 yards. The coaches obviously had no confidence in the passing game as they ran the ball on 75 percent of their plays. Prospects for the future looked bright if the Bulldogs could develop a more balanced offensive attack.

The 1964 Ole Miss–Mississippi State Football Game

The season summaries above clearly show that 1964 was not good for Mississippi's two SEC football teams. Both Ole Miss and Mississippi

State had disappointing seasons. The regular-season-ending game played by the rivals deserves special attention. The three-point Mississippi State victory over Ole Miss had to be the low point of the season for Rebels and the highpoint for the Bulldogs.

Wayne Thompson, sports editor of the *Clarion-Ledger*, captured what happened in four short paragraphs.

> No one alive today was around when the Red Sea was parted. But, some 30,000 folks were present here and millions of others watching on television saw a miracle of like proportions. After 18 long, mournful years the Mississippi State Bulldogs defeated the Ole Miss Rebels.
>
> The final score was 20-17 and included all the drama and suspense of any TV production, including an 81-yard touchdown scamper in the fading minutes of play when it seemed the Bulldogs had it safely wrapped. In fact, a body watching a replay in the future could be easily persuaded to bet on the loser.
>
> Saturday that loser was Ole Miss, the first time a Johnny Vaught-coached team had been on the short end of the score in this classical series with his clubs accounting for 14 victories and a trio of ties in that span.
>
> Fittingly it was fullback Hoyle Granger who scored what proved to be the winning touchdown, with 1:40 remaining, to put the game on more dependable ice.

The game produced some interesting moments and statistics. Ole Miss rushed for 99 yards, State 127. The Rebels passed for 147 yards, the Bulldogs 62 (two passes accounted for 54 of those yards); Ole Miss managed 17 first downs, MSU 11. State intercepted three Ole Miss passes while the Rebels intercepted one of State's. The Bulldogs lost one fumble while the Rebels lost none. The first three scores were field goals. Billy Carl Irwin kicked one in the first quarter for the Rebels and Justin Canale countered with two for the Bulldogs in the second quarter, the last one coming on the final play of the half. Both coaches agreed that this was the key play of the game.

State's first touchdown came in the third quarter when Bland Rhoden scored on a 17-yard pass from Don Edwards, Canale kicked the point after. Most of the fireworks came in the fourth quarter. Mike Dennis scored a touchdown for the Rebels' on a 10-yard pass from Jimmy Heidel and Irwin added the extra point. MSU's Hoyle Granger scored State's last touchdown on a 1-yard run and Canale added the point after. Doug Cunningham returned the ensuing kickoff 81 yards for a touchdown and Irwin kicked the extra point. There was 1:26 left in the game when the Rebels kicked off, and MSU promptly ran out the clock with two rushes by Don Edwards.

It was a very special day for Coach Paul Davis, his players, and MSU fans. As has been noted, Mississippi State had not beaten Ole Miss in football during the Vaught era, which started in 1947. Ironically, MSU's Paul Davis was co-captain of the 1946 Ole Miss team that lost to State. After the game Coach Davis told his players, "I want to thank you for making me the happiest man in the world. Johnny Vaught was right last week when he said the team with the most desire would win—and we did."

Coach Vaught didn't have much to say after the game. He noted that he didn't expect the Ole Miss loss to affect recruiting and that it had been a hard-fought game by both teams.

In the early 1970s I was a student at Mississippi State University working on a doctor of business administration (DBA) degree. I distinctly remember one day walking into a professor's office in Bowen Hall and seeing prominently displayed a picture of the scoreboard at Scott field that showed the final score of the 1964 game: Mississippi State 20, Ole Miss 17. If I remember correctly the picture was captioned, "Do you believe your eyes?"

1965

Mississippi State Baseball Climbs the Mountain

1965 SEC Basketball Champions—Vanderbilt
1965 SEC Baseball Champions—Mississippi State
1965 SEC Football Champions—Alabama
Final score: Mississippi schools 1 SEC championship, other SEC schools 2

The Champion

1965 Mississippi State Baseball

Coach Paul Gregory had for several years fielded quality baseball teams. His Mississippi State teams had been very competitive in the SEC and had won the 1962 SEC Western Division championship by going 14-1-1 in the regular season, but the Bulldogs lost to Florida 2 games to 1 in the SEC championship series. In 1965 MSU won the SEC Western Division by posting an 11-4 regular-season conference record. The Bulldogs then proceeded to defeat Auburn 2 games to 1 in the SEC playoffs to win Coach Gregory's first overall SEC championship.

With a 7-7 conference mark Mississippi State had finished second in the SEC Western Division in 1964, and it was understood that Paul Gregory's 1965 Bulldogs had the potential to produce an even better record. However, they faced what could be a major obstacle. In 1965 MSU would not play a single game in Starkville. MSU was in the process of constructing a building on its old baseball field and preparing a new baseball facility. Meanwhile, the Bulldogs would practice on campus but play their "home games" at Redbird Park about 30 miles away in Columbus, Mississippi. Before the regular season began, the Bulldogs got in some good practice against excellent competition. They played five exhibition games in Florida against major and minor league teams winning two and losing three.

When the regular season began on March 26, the Dogs lost to Southern Mississippi 2-0 in Hattiesburg. MSU starting pitcher Frank Chambers gave up only four hits, but MSU batters managed only three hits against USM lefthander Whitey Wilson. A scheduled second game against USM that was to be played in McComb was washed out. The Bulldogs went back to Starkville to open a scheduled eight-game home stand against LSU, Illinois Wesleyan, Alabama, and Delta State.

On April 2 LSU showed up in Columbus with an unimpressive 1-4 record. The Tigers had dropped two SEC games to Tulane the previous week. Junior Ken Tatum pitched and hit the Bulldogs past the Tigers 5-2. There was no score until the bottom of the seventh inning when Tatum smacked a double to score Mike Burns. Tatum moved to third on a passed ball and scored when Bill Bacon stroked a sacrifice fly. Russ Gatlin and Frank Portera hit back-to-back home runs in the eighth inning, and Tatum came to the plate with Burns on second base. The pitcher helped his own cause with another RBI as he drove in Burns again with a single. LSU scored its two runs in the ninth inning, too little too late. The game scheduled for April 3 was rained out.

Illinois Wesleyan won the first game of a doubleheader April 8 as they blasted the Bulldogs 7-3. State turned the tables in the second game by pounding out 16 hits and beating the Titans 11-2. Five Bulldogs got 2 hits and shortstop Gatlin Speed got 3.

Ken Tatum was back on the mound April 9, and the Crimson Tide of Alabama had no answer for him. Tatum hurled a 4-hit shutout while his teammates backed him with 15 hits and 11 runs. Eight Bulldogs, including Tatum, registered hits while Del Unser got 3 and Mike Burns got 4. The very next day Alabama pitcher Dickie Towers silenced MSU's bats and shut out the Bulldogs 1-0. Frank Chambers pitched a brilliant game but lost. Alabama left town 8-4 overall and 4-1 in the SEC while MSU stood 3-3 overall and 2-1 in the SEC.

On April 12 the Dogs were shut out again 1-0, this time by Delta State's Joe DiFabio, who threw a two-hitter and struck out 10 batters. State's bats had gone stone cold but pitcher Claude Passeau gave up only one run on six hits. The next day James Carroll made his first start of the season and struck out 16 batters while giving up only four hits as MSU defeated Delta State 6-1. The Bulldogs' bats came back to life with Burns and Speed each getting three hits as the team totaled 14 safeties including two home runs. After the split with Delta State, MSU stood 4-4 overall and 2-1 in the conference.

State batters continued to hit well as they pounded out 16 hits and beat Ole Miss 17-13 in an 11-inning game in Oxford April 16. State's outfielders Burns, Unser, and Gatlin collected a total of 8 hits, 2 of them doubles by All-SEC center fielder Dell Unser. In this three-hour-plus marathon Ole Miss sent four pitchers to the mound and MSU three. The Rebels scored all 13 of their runs in the first five innings. After that, Paul Gregory Jr. did not give up a run over the final six innings to claim the victory for his dad and MSU. In the second game of the series played the next day, the Bulldogs held off a late Rebel rally to post an 8-6 victory. MSU's hitters continued their hot streak by stroking 14 base hits. Winning pitcher Frank Chambers blanked the Rebels for seven innings but was chased with 5 runs, 4 of which were earned, in the eighth inning. Claude Passeau pitched the last two innings and gave up 3 hits and 1 run, but he got out of a one-out-bases-loaded jam in the ninth inning. State was now 6-4 overall and 4-1 in the SEC.

Tulane came to Columbus April 19 leading the SEC Western Division with a 6-1 record. The Green Wave's Tom Adams cooled off the Bulldogs' bats by pitching a 4-hitter. Tulane mustered 11 hits off of three MSU pitchers and prevailed 7-2. State's starting pitcher James Carroll gave up 5 runs over 4 1/3 innings and suffered his first loss. The next day State's bats were still cool. Tulane ace John Olagues blanked the Dogs for eight innings. Bobby Bragan started the bottom of the ninth for State with a single to center field. Gary Washington's in-field single pushed Bragan to second base, and Olagues was replaced by Dan Stevenson. Russ Gatlin sacrificed the runners to second and third, and Stevenson intentionally walked the next batter to load the bases. With a clutch squeeze bunt, Don Bell drove home pinch runner Ron Donaldson from third with the winning run. State's Frank Chambers struck out 10 and walked none while pitching a complete game 5-hit shutout to even his record at 2-2. State was now 5-2 in the SEC while Tulane slipped to 7-2. Tulane's coach Ben Abadie was tossed from the ballpark for raging at an umpire for calling a ball hit down the left-field line foul. The next day a United Press International piece in the *Clarion-Ledger* noted how angry Abadie was.

> Tulane baseball coach Ben Abadie said Tuesday his life had been threatened twice in Mississippi and vowed to never bring another team to Mississippi or Alabama. Abadie, evicted from a Tulane–Mississippi State baseball game after furiously protesting an umpire's decision, could not immediately be reached for further comment. After the game the coach came back on the field and shouted up to the press box, asking if any reporters were present.
>
> He shouted, "I want to say this: I will never bring a team back into Alabama or Mississippi. Since I've been here my life has been threatened twice." Abadie was evicted in the seventh inning of the ball game after he shouted at umpires protesting a ruling on a foul ball.

It appears that Mississippians and maybe Alabamians did not cotton to coaches abusing umpires. Tulane departed the SEC in 1966 and Abadie retired as the Green Wave's baseball coach the same year.

In Baton Rouge against the LSU tigers on April 23, MSU's bats didn't exactly go silent but the eight hits the Bulldogs accumulated were not timely. LSU's pitcher Van Quigley scattered eight hits and had at least one runner on base in every inning but State could not get clutch hits to drive in a run. The Bulldogs did not score and losing pitcher Ken Tatum gave up 6 runs over seven innings. The next day Claude Passeau gave up three hits, walked three, and struck out eight as MSU evened the series with a 5-0 victory over LSU. Passeau helped his own cause with his bat. In the third inning Don Bell, Passeau, and Ron Donaldson hit back-to-back-to-back triples and Del Unser hit a single as the Dogs scored 3 of their 5 runs. After the game MSU stood 8-6 overall and 6-3 in the conference while LSU was 4-9 overall and 2-7 in the SEC.

State moved on down the Big River to play Tulane a two-game series in New Orleans April 26 and 27. The Greenies were 9-2 in the conference and could wrap up the Western Division title with a sweep of the Bulldogs. That was not to be. Del Unser's big bat produced two home runs and four RBIs in the first game as MSU defeated the Green Wave 5-4. Winning pitcher Frank Chambers gave up seven hits and four runs over eight innings. Ken Tatum shut out Tulane in the ninth inning to save the victory. Tatum then pitched the Bulldogs to a 2-0 win in the second game. A home run by Bill Bacon accounted for one of MSU's runs. The series sweep pushed MSU into the lead in the Western Division of the SEC. State stood 10-6 overall and 8-3 in the SEC while Tulane slipped to 15-8 overall and 9-4 in the SEC.

The race for the SEC Western Division title was set to go down to the wire. Tulane had two games left to play, both with LSU. Mississippi State had four games left, two with Alabama and two with Ole Miss. If State and Tulane were tied at the end of the regular season, there would be a two-game playoff and Tulane's coach Ben Abadie would have to decide whether or not he would keep his vow never to take a team back to Mississippi.

On May 3 MSU defeated Alabama 3-2 in Tuscaloosa to bring its conference mark to 9-3 and clinch at least a tie for the SEC Western Division title. In the third inning Del Unser hit his third home run in three games to put the Dogs up 1-0. Two errors allowed Alabama to go ahead 2-1 in the fifth inning. Unser led off the eighth inning with a single and Mike Burns tripled scoring Unser to tie the game. Bill Bacon grounded to third baseman John Mosley, who made a wild throw to first base, allowing Burns to score the game-winning run. Both teams managed seven hits, but Claude Passeau outdueled Alabama's Fred Glass to bring his record to 3-0 for the season. The bad news was that State's center fielder Ron Donaldson broke his ankle sliding into second base and would be out for the rest of the season. With three games to play, State was one win away from a playoff against the SEC Eastern Division champion. The next day Ken Tatum spun a four-hitter as MSU won division laurels outright by whipping the Tide 1-0. Tatum struck out eight, walked two, and did not give up more than one hit in any inning. This was his second straight shutout and it couldn't have come at a better time because Alabama pitcher Dickie Towers threw a six-hitter and shut out the Dogs after the first inning. The only run of the game came in the bottom of the first inning when Del Unser doubled and scampered home on Mike Burns's triple.

MSU stood 12-6 overall and 10-3 in the SEC when the Western Division champs faced 1964 SEC champion Ole Miss in the final two games of the regular season at Redbird Park in Columbus. Nothing would have been sweeter for the Bulldogs than to end the campaign with a sweep of the Rebels. Ole Miss had already lost two games to the Dogs in Oxford, and they certainly did not want to end the season without a single victory over their archrival. On Friday May 7 State jumped all over the Rebels 9-3 by getting out to an early lead and relying on the strong pitching of Frank Chambers. Mike Burns hit a three-run home run in the first inning, and the Dogs never looked back. MSU added four more runs in the second inning off a two-run double by Bobby Bragan and a two-run single by Bill Hamilton. In the fifth inning Don Bell singled, stole second, and came around to score on Mike Burns's single. Del Unser capped off State scoring with a solo home run in the seventh. Ole Miss scored one run in the third, seventh, and ninth innings. The Rebels were never really in the game.

The Rebels bounced back on Saturday to win 10-7 despite Del Unser's 3 home runs and 5 RBIs. Future major leaguer Unser hit 7 home runs during the entire season and all of them came in the last six games. Russell Johnson took over from starter Richie Prine in the fourth inning and pitched five innings of two-hit relief to preserve the Rebel victory. Both hits off Johnson were home runs by Unser. State's reliable pitcher Claude Passeau left the game leading 3-1 after he pulled a muscle in the third inning. State relievers walked in 3 runs in the fourth as the Rebels tied the score at 4. Four MSU relievers gave up 9 runs as the Rebels avoided a season sweep by the Bulldogs. MSU finished the regular season 13-7 overall and 11-4 in the SEC.

Coach Paul Gregory's team would face the Eastern Division champions Auburn Tigers with an opportunity to present their coach with his first overall SEC baseball championship. This would make the third straight appearance in the playoffs for the Tigers, who had been defeated by Ole Miss in 1964. State had won SEC playoffs in 1949 and 1953 under Coach R. P. Patty, and Auburn had won two SEC playoffs. The winner of the 1965 playoff would tie Ole Miss for the most SEC playoff series wins ever.

Ken Tatum was State's key contributor in the playoff as he pitched the Bulldogs to their two victories. Tatum pitched all 9 innings as the Dogs won the first game, and three days later, he pitched all 10 innings as the Dogs took the rubber game. In the first game played May 12 the Dogs jumped on Auburn pitching for 10 hits and Tatum pitched a 5-hitter as MSU prevailed 10-1. Auburn's ace Monte Sharpe cruised through the first 4 innings and the Tigers led 1-0 going into the fifth. But in the bottom of the fifth Charlie Smith led off with a single, Don Bell and Del Unser walked to load the bases, and Burns followed with a grand slam. Portera followed that with a home run to left field and, not to be outdone, Bragan promptly hit a home run to right. The back-to-back-to-back homers put State up 6-1, and Sharpe was well on his way to his second loss of the season. Portera would drive in two more of the four runs State scored over the last few innings. The Tigers were through scoring as Tatum allowed only 1 hit after the fourth inning. Despite the game being played off campus in Columbus, it was a sellout. Reported attendance was 3,200.

The series moved to Auburn for the second game. Despite experiencing tightness in his pitching arm when he warmed up, Frank Chambers started the second game. He gave up three hits and no runs over five innings but left the game leading 2-0 with his arm "aching like a sore tooth." Claude Passeau was tagged with the loss as he came in and pitched the final four innings giving up six hits and three runs. Monte Sharpe came in relief of Auburn starter Jerry Lawter with one out and a runner on base in the top of the ninth. He pitched 2/3 of an inning and gave up no hits and no runs. Sharpe walked with two outs in the bottom of the inning and then came around to score the winning run of a single by Dink Haire. So, the pitcher who lost the first game became the winner of the second game as he scored the winning run. The reported attendance was 2,200.

The third and deciding game was the Ken Tatum vs. Monte Sharpe show again as both pitched all 10 innings. Tatum gave up one run, 9 hits, two walks, and struck out seven batters. Sharpe gave up two runs, 13 hits, no walks, and struck out nine batters. Tatum had 3 hits when he came to bat with the bases loaded in the tenth inning. He hit a liner to Auburn shortstop Scotty Long, who dropped the ball but picked it up and threw to third base forcing out Portera. Meanwhile, Burns ran home from third carrying what proved to be the winning run as Tatum shut out the Tigers in the bottom of the inning. Attendance was reported to be 3,500.

State had won its first SEC baseball championship since 1949 and was on its way to the NCAA District III playoff in Gastonia, North Carolina. MSU was joined by Florida State, Furman, and Maryland in the district playoff and drew Florida State as its first opponent. On the way to Gastonia, Coach Paul Gregory stopped off at the Southeastern Conference office in Birmingham to pick up the SEC Coach of the Year Award that he had more than earned.

In State's first game the Seminoles jumped out to a 3-0 lead in the first inning before Ken Tatum settled down and shut them out for the rest of the game. Still trailing 3-0 in the sixth inning Del Unser managed a bunt single, stole second, and came home on Tatum's triple. State scored three more runs in the seventh when Charlie Smith and Bill Bacon singled, Don Bell beat out a bunt to load the bases, and Del Unser drove all three home with a double. In the eighth inning Smith singled to drive in Tatum and Russ Gatlin, both of whom had walked. In the ninth Mike Burns walked and Frank Portera doubled him home to end the scoring. Final score—MSU 6, FSU 3. Tatum improved his record to 7-1 by giving up four hits, four walks, and three runs while pitching a complete game. Unser, Tatum, and Smith each collected two hits to lead State's nine-hit attack.

Sore-armed Frank Chambers started for MSU in the first winners' bracket game against the Furman Paladins. Chambers struck out the first six batters he faced and didn't give up a hit as he shut out the Paladins for the first five innings. MSU scored a run in the first inning on a home run by Burns and added another in the second as Smith drove in a run with a single. The Dogs would not score again. In the sixth Chambers gave up a walk, two singles, and a double as Furman scored three runs. The Paladins scored two unearned runs in the seventh as MSU committed two errors. Chambers pitched eight innings, gave up five runs, five hits, walked six, and struck out 11. The 5-2 loss pushed MSU into the loser's bracket.

On May 28, Del Unser made his pitching debut and he held Florida State scoreless for five innings, got a hit, and scored one of State's two runs. MSU's scored one run in the third inning and another one in the fourth as Justin Bell and Del Unser each drove in a run. But the Seminoles got to Unser in the sixth, scoring three runs. Unser's final pitching line—six innings, six hits, three runs (two earned), two walks, and seven strikeouts—was not bad for a first-time starter. Frank Chambers relieved Unser in the seventh inning and gave up another three runs. Florida State eliminated State by a 6-2 score and then went on to win a double header over Furman 2-1 and 7-5 to win the NCAA District III title and advance to the College World Series.

Nevertheless, the Mississippi State Bulldogs put together an SEC championship year. A closer look at some of the team members and their coach is appropriate. Coach Paul Gregory had pitched for the Chicago White Sox in 1932 and 1933 compiling a 7-12 record. His 1965 Mississippi State team had more than a little major league flavor. Paul Gregory Jr. and Claude Passeau Jr. pitched for the Bulldogs. Claude Passeau Jr. was the son of Claude Passeau Sr., who pitched for the Pittsburgh Pirates, Philadelphia Phillies, and the Chicago Cubs over a 13-year major league career posting an overall 162-150 record. Bobby Bragan was actually Bobby Bragan Jr. His dad, Bobby Bragan Sr., played for the Philadelphia Phillies and Brooklyn Dodgers during his 7-year big-league career. Bragan also managed the Pittsburgh Pirates and the Cleveland Indians and in 1965 he was the manager of the Milwaukee Braves. The most outstanding player on the team was Del Unser, who would go on to play for six major league teams over a 15-year career.

There were only three seniors on this championship team, catcher Charlie Smith, third baseman Bobby Bragan, and second baseman Bill Bacon. The future looked bright indeed for Coach Gregory's Bulldogs. When I interviewed Doug Hutton about his time at MSU, he noted that he could have been on the 1965 championship baseball team. Hutton used up his eligibility in basketball in the spring of 1964, but he had played varsity baseball only two seasons. He had chosen not to play baseball one year and make that a "red shirt" season. He could have played a third season of baseball in 1965. But things got complicated. He graduated in 1964, got married, coached the MSU freshman basketball team in 1964–65, and took a job teaching and coaching at Hazlehurst High School in 1965. Hutton was a great athlete, and it is interesting but not productive to speculate on what MSU's baseball record would have been had he pitched for the Dogs in 1965. The author's opinion is that he would have been good for several more victories and a trip to the College World Series.

Five members of MSU's SEC baseball championship team hailed from Jackson: pitchers Junior Fields, Claude Reeder, and Frank Chambers, catcher Charlie Smith, and outfielder Sid Craft. All of them had played either high school or legion ball for the great coach Robert "Cooter" Berry. I was especially interested in the success of this team because pitcher Claude Reeder and catcher Charlie Smith were a year behind me at Jackson Central High School. Frank Chambers was a sophomore when I was a senior. Reeder was an excellent high school pitcher. Smith excelled at both baseball and basketball at Central while Chambers played baseball, basketball, and football in high school. In 1978 Frank Chambers was inducted into the MSU M Club Alumni Association and Sports Hall of Fame.

How Did the Other Teams Fare?

1965 Mississippi State Basketball

The 1965 Mississippi State yearbook *Reveille* summed up the season this way:

> For the second straight year Mississippi State's basketball team had a losing season compiling a 10-16 record, but valuable experience was accumulated and prospects for the 1965–66 season are considerably brighter. The Bulldogs were a sophomore studded team, with the entire starting team composed of first-year men at times. Only two seniors are on the squad and with a season under their belt the team should improve.

The 1964–65 basketball season was the last for Coach Babe McCarthy at Mississippi State. It was not pleasant to watch. The MSU freshman team that had posted a 21-3 record the previous year joined the varsity for the 1964–65 season. Unfortunately, the infusion of young talent didn't help much as the Bulldogs, who had finished 9-17 overall and 4-10 in the SEC the year before, posted a 10-16 overall record that included a 6-10 SEC mark. Opponents averaged outscoring the Dogs five points a game and averaged outrebounding them by two.

There were few bright spots in a season that began with the Bulldogs losing 7 of their first 8 games. There were two 2-game win streaks which came against Georgia and Ole Miss and Tulane and Ole Miss. The three top scorers—Bill Chumbler, Gary Washington, and Richie Williams—combined to average 34 points a game, while the three top rebounders—Richie Williams, Buddy Walden, and Charlie Crews—combined to average 16 a game. These numbers do not compare to those posted by the top three scorers and rebounders during the glory years recently experienced. The team's inconsistency is illustrated by its contrasting performances against Alabama and Ole Miss. State won the first game against Alabama by 28 points, 96-68 but lost the second by 12 points, 95-83, a 40-point swing. Against the Rebels, MSU won the first game by 29 points, 101-72, but in the second game the margin was reduced to 1 point, 78-77.

But, as the *Reveille* indicated, there was reason to hope for a better future.

1965 Mississippi State Football

Coach Paul Davis seemed to have his Bulldogs on track in 1963 when they went 7-2-2 overall and 4-1-2 in the SEC. That team advanced to the Liberty Bowl where they beat North Carolina State 16-12. But in 1964 the Dogs slipped to 4-6 overall and 2-5 in the conference. The 1965 season began in encouraging fashion with the Bulldogs ripping off four straight wins over Houston, Florida, Tampa, and Southern Mississippi. During the win streak the Dogs scored 129 points and gave up only 29. In the fifth game against Memphis States things took a turn for the worse; State lost 33-13. The Bulldogs would go on to lose their last six games. During that debacle the Dogs scored only 70 points and gave up 143. While the Bulldogs finished 4-6 for the second straight year, they dropped to 1-6 in SEC games. That 18-13 victory came against Florida in the second game of the season.

Here are a couple of statistics that indicate State should have won more games. The Bulldogs outscored their opponents 202 to 172 and averaged scoring 20 points per game while giving up only 17. However, those figures are misleading because one of the Bulldogs' wins was over non-major Tampa 48-7 and another win came against Houston 36-0.

The fact that MSU gave up only 172 points over 10 games shows that the Bulldogs again fielded a strong defense. Unfortunately, offense was lacking. MSU was a rushing team, the Bulldogs ran the ball 401 times and passed only 94 times. Hoyle Granger was the leading rusher gaining 449 yards on 108 carries. He was also the second-leading receiver, gaining 147 yards on 7 receptions. Marcus Rhoden was the second-leading rusher, gaining 242 yards on 67 carries and he was the leading receiver with 19 catches for 158 yards. Ashby Cook was the leading passer, completing 78 of 162 passes for 1,032 yards. MSU simply could not score many points against strong competition.

Coach Paul Davis would be on the hot seat in 1966.

1965 Ole Miss Baseball

Coach Tom Swayze fielded his fifteenth Ole Miss baseball team in 1965. The previous season was one of Swayze's best as his Rebs won a third SEC championship and advanced to the College World Series. Things took a distinct downturn in 1965 as Ole Miss posted an overall 10-13 slate, only the third losing record of the Swayze era. But maybe things were not as bad as they appeared to be. The Rebels won 7 of their last 10 games and ended the season with a winning conference record, 8-7. Three of the SEC wins came against Alabama and another 3 were against LSU. The Rebs went 1-3 against SEC champion Mississippi State and 1-2 against Tulane, which had not won the yearly competition with the Rebels since 1952.

In a very unusual twist, the Rebels won only three of eight nonconference games. Two of those wins came against Nicholls State and the other one against Kansas State. The Rebels also lost one game to Kansas State, two to Memphis State, one to Southern Mississippi, and one to Nicholls State. A winning effort against nonconference opponents would have made the season record look much better.

Pitchers Richie Prine and Russ Johnson, who had contributed greatly to 1964 championship, were back in 1965, but both were plagued by arm trouble. Prine's earned run average jumped from 1.10 to 3.65 and his record dropped from 7-0 to 3-2. Johnson's earned run average rose from 1.5 to 5.64 and his record dropped to 3-3.

1965 Ole Miss Basketball

The 1964–65 season was Eddie Crawford's third as Ole Miss's head basketball coach. Crawford's first team had gone 7-17 overall and 4-10 in the SEC. His second team improved to 10-12 overall and broke even in the SEC by posting a 7-7 mark. Were the Rebels ready to make a move in basketball? No. Unfortunately, some outstanding talent from his first two teams had graduated, including Mel Edmonds and Don Kessinger. The Rebels won only 4 games and lost 21 during the 1964–65 season, and it was becoming evident that Crawford was simply not a good basketball coach.

The season included a nine-game and an eight-game losing streak against major college opponents. The only SEC win came against Tulane 62-60 in Oxford, and one of the other wins was a 68-67 heart-stopper in an away game against Centenary.

1965 Ole Miss Football

The Ole Miss football team showed much improvement during the 1965 season. The great Johnny Vaught faced three big challenges: the lack of an established quarterback, a squad loaded with 26 sophomores, and a rule change that transitioned college football from limited substitution to unlimited substitution. Vaught and his outstanding staff of assistant coaches were up to the task. The Rebels went 6-4 in the regular season and won the Liberty Bowl to finish 7-4 overall.

In the regular season Ole Miss faced only two nonconference teams, Memphis State and Houston. In the first game the Rebels defeated the Memphis State Tigers 34-14 in the Bluff City's new Memphis Memorial Stadium. Doug Cunningham returned a punt 75 yards for a touchdown, and Jimmy Keyes kicked two field goals and three extra points. But, in a shocker, the Rebels lost in the new Astrodome to the Houston Cougars 17-3 in the eighth game of the season. The offense seemed to have taken a day off in the Houston game as they suffered numerous tackles behind the line of scrimmage and ended with a net of only 59 yards rushing. The defense gave up two huge plays as Cougar quarterback Bo Burris passed to Warren McVea for touchdowns of 80 and 84 yards. As the 1966 Ole Miss yearbook says, "It was a long night in Houston."

Ole Miss floundered but grew in games two, three, and four as the Rebels lost to SEC schools, Kentucky, Alabama, and Florida. During the three-game losing streak the defense played fairly well but the offense sputtered. Things changed quickly as the young Rebs grew up. Ole Miss went on to win six straight games against SEC foes. The Rebels prevailed over Tulane 24-7, Vanderbilt, LSU, Tennessee, and Mississippi State during the regular season and Auburn in the Liberty Bowl. The 5-3 regular-season SEC mark put the Rebels in fourth place in the conference behind Alabama 6-1-1, Tennessee 5-1-2, and Florida 4-2. With their win over Auburn in the Liberty Bowl, Ole Miss actually won as many games against SEC teams during the season (6) as conference champion Alabama.

The victories over LSU October 30 and Mississippi State November 27 were especially satisfying for Rebel fans. The 1964 Rebels had suffered bitter defeats by these two rivals as LSU won 11-10 in Baton Rouge and MSU won 20-17 in Oxford.

By 1965 things were different. LSU fell to Ole Miss 23-0 in Jackson on Halloween night. The Rebels still remembered 1959! With a 5-1 record LSU came into the game ranked sixth in the country and favored by 5 points. By averaging 334 yards per game the Tigers sported the top offense in the SEC. Alas, they were no match for the Rebels. Ole Miss led in first downs 11-4 and total yards 227-52. Mike Dennis scored two touchdowns for the Rebs. The LSU Tigers, who would finish the season 8-3, had not been shut out since the Rebels turned the trick in the 1960 Sugar Bowl. It was Dizzy Dean day at Mississippi Memorial Stadium and the famous pitcher and television announcer accepted an over and under shotgun from Governor Paul Johnson and rooted for his favorite college team. The stadium was filled with 46,500 fans. Ole Miss no longer had to play most of its home games against LSU in the Tigers' huge stadium.

Coach Vaught had this to say about one of the most impressive and important victories of his illustrious career:

> I've been saying all along that the Southeastern Conference is the toughest in the nation and that on any given Saturday any team can beat any other team in the league. This was our day. Morale was the thing that made it our day.
>
> People don't realize how good of a ball player (Billy) Clay is. We lost him in the Memphis State game and he didn't play any more until last week. Our two sophomores in the defensive secondary (Jimmy James and Bruce Newell) have also come along real well.

Rocky Fleming contributed mightily on defense and offense, recovering a Joe Labruzzo fumble and making a spectacular catch on LSU's one-yard line that led to a touchdown. Coach Vaught said of him: "This Fleming is the damndest kid you've ever seen. He just keeps on scrapping. He's a good ball player and he will keep working until he succeeds."

LSU's coach Charlie McClendon had suffered through a bad day. Accepting the loss, he said:

> It was just a bad day. We had the worst breaks I've ever seen in a football game. First, we lose our quarterback [Nelson Stokley] on the third

> play of the game. Then we get a touchdown on a kickoff return called back. That one really broke our back.
>
> I want to give credit to Ole Miss. I'm not surprised by what happened here. I've said all season they're just as good as any Ole Miss team we have ever faced, but are playing a tougher schedule. They just happened to run into a couple of buzz saws earlier in the season, just like we did this afternoon.

Mississippi State succumbed 21-0 in Starkville in the last game of the regular season for both teams. The victory over the Bulldogs included a touchdown scored on a 50-yard interception return by Billy Clay and a 96-yard drive capped off by a 1-yard plunge into the end zone by quarterback Jimmy Heidel. The other Ole Miss score came after a fumble at MSU's 6-yard line and a 1-yard dive over the goal line by Mike Dennis.

Coach Vaught summed up the game this way, "Our kids really got ready for this game and played a fine tough football game, and it was rugged all the way, don't forget that."

MSU's coach Paul Davis said, "I felt like our boys gave a 100-percent performance all year, and that includes today." He went on to say Ole Miss had a great ball club and he heaped praise on their defensive secondary, saying it was probably the best in the SEC. Davis also noted the quality of the Rebel sophomores, saying, "They should be really tough for the next two years."

The 14-13 win over Tennessee in Memphis was also encouraging and it was the Rebels' seventh straight victory over the team from north of the border. The Volunteers came into the game unbeaten and ranked eighth in the country. The game was also important because it proved to be the coming-out party for sophomore quarterback Jody Graves. The young quarterback led both of the Rebel scoring drives.

My wife, Dorothy, and I watched the Tennessee game on TV from Eglin AFB, Florida. That is a great memory because we watched it with our friends John and Pat Crockett (no kin), both of whom were Tennessee graduates. John Crockett and I were both second lieutenants in the US Air Force. The air force later sent both John and me to Germany where the Crockett families maintained our friendship and traveled together. John passed away a couple of years ago, but we still are friends with Pat Crockett, who lives in Knoxville.

Over the season the Rebels scored 179 points and allowed 115. Ole Miss attempted only 135 passes and completed 67 for 726 yards all season. Starting quarterback Jimmy Heidel, who improved markedly during the season, completed 52 of 95 passes for 586 yards and rushed for 202 yards. Mike Dennis again led the team in rushing with 525 yards and also in receiving with 246 yards. Things looked better for Rebel fans as they began to contemplate the 1966 season.

1966

Another SEC Championship and the End of an Era

1966 SEC Basketball Champion—Kentucky

1966 SEC Baseball Champion—Mississippi State

1966 Football Champion—Alabama

Final score: Mississippi schools 1 SEC championship, other SEC schools 2

The Champion

1966 MSU Baseball SEC Champion

Mississippi State's defending SEC champion baseball team began its 1966 season in early March playing Florida State and Auburn in the FSU Invitational. The Bulldogs lost to FSU and to Auburn but bounced back to beat the Tigers in the third game. The Bulldogs left the Sunshine State 1-2. Next up on March 25 and 26 was a two-game series against Arkansas State at Redbird Park in Columbus, Mississippi. MSU's new campus baseball facility was not ready so, as in 1965, the Bulldogs would play all of their home games at Redbird Park. MSU won both of the Arkansas State games. The Dogs and

Delta State College played a two-game series March 28 and 29. MSU won the first game that was played in Columbus, but the Statesmen turned the tables a day later in Cleveland. Both games were won in come-from-behind fashion in the bottom of the ninth inning as the winners scored two runs. Coach Gregory's Dogs now stood 4-3 on the season and were about to wade into SEC competition.

On the first of April MSU opened SEC play with a two-game series against Alabama in Columbus. Ken Tatum pitched masterfully and his teammates fielded and hit well to defeat the visitors 5-1 in the first game. The next day it took MSU 14 innings to eke out a 2-1 victory over the Tide. Pitcher James Carroll went the distance for MSU striking out 10 and giving up 4 hits, 5 walks, and 1 run. Ken Stabler (yes, that Ken Stabler) pitched 11 outstanding innings for Alabama. He struck out 8, walked 5, and gave up 10 hits and 1 run. In this titanic pitching duel, the Tide did not get a hit until the sixth inning, and the first run was not scored until the bottom of the eighth when State's Frank Portera hit a solo home run. In the ninth, Alabama's Joe McCorquedale singled, stole second, and was driven home by pinch-hitter Bill Lippeatt's single. Binky Powers replaced Stabler in the twelfth inning and surrendered the winning run in the fourteenth when Frank Portera drove in Del Unser, who had reached first base on a throwing error by Powers. State stood 6-3 overall and 2-0 in the conference.

Paul Gregory Jr. pitched MSU to a 9-2 victory over LSU on April 4 in Columbus. Gregory pitched all nine innings and gave up only three hits while striking out eight and walking six. LSU scored its first run off two hits in the first inning. The Tigers' second run came in the sixth and was manufactured by a walk, a stolen base, and a single. Gregory doubled and scored MSU's first run in a two-run third inning. State added four more runs in the fourth inning as Ken Beasley and Del Unser both hit two-run homers. MSU tacked on three more runs in the eighth inning off LSU reliefer John Chadwick, who gave up one hit and walked seven in the inning. The Bulldogs collected eight hits off two LSU pitchers. LSU's Chadwick's line in the box score is telling, 4 1/2 innings, one hit, 11 walks, and two strikeouts. The next day Ken

Tatum threw a two-hitter and shut out LSU as MSU prevailed 3-0. The Bulldogs' ace struck out eight and walked none while his teammates committed no errors and produced six timely hits. After the sweep of the two-game series with the Tigers, MSU was 8-3 overall and tied with Ole Miss at 4-0 in the conference.

Moving on to Tuscaloosa on April 8, the Dogs dropped a game to Alabama. The Tide jumped off to an 8-0 lead in the first five innings and State could never catch up. Bama's Joe McCorquodale did most of the damage, hitting two 2-run home runs. State gradually chipped away at the Tide's lead by scoring single runs in the sixth and seventh innings and adding four more in the eighth, three of them coming on a Del Unser home run. State added another run in the ninth inning, but it was too little too late. Frank Chambers, who started and pitched 2 1/3 innings for the Dogs, gave up four hits and six runs and was charged with the loss. The next day MSU gained a measure of revenge as James Carroll gave up only one hit to the Tide and the Dogs won 4-1. McCorquodale got Bama's only hit, a single that drove in John Holley, who had walked and reached second on an error by Carroll. State batters managed seven hits that included a triple and three doubles, all of which were timely. After the series State stood 9-4 overall and 5-1 in the conference.

On April 11 MSU welcomed Southwest Conference foe Arkansas to Columbus for a two-game series. The Bulldogs prevailed in the first game 9-3. Claude Passeau started for the Dogs and won his first game of the season. Passeau left the game in the fifth inning after being injured by a hard-hit ground ball. It turned out to be a dangerous day for Bulldog pitchers as Ken Kairt, who had relieved Passeau, had to leave the game after pitching 1 1/3 innings after being hit in the mouth by a batted ball. The next day the Hogs had a really bad game as State won 18-0. Paul Gregory Jr. gave up three hits over the first six innings, and Frank Chambers gave up one hit over the final three innings to preserve the shutout. Chambers, Gary Washington, and George Paton hit home runs for the Dogs. MSU pushed its record to 11-4 overall and 5-1 in the SEC.

Reliable Ken Tatum took the mound against Tulane in New Orleans April 15. Tatum was his usual self while pitching a complete game. He struck out 5, walked 5, and gave up 4 hits and 3 runs, only one of which was earned. The Bulldogs won 7-3. Tatum improved his record to 4-1. He had given up only 1 earned run in his last 27 innings against SEC competition. Jump started by Del Unser's two-run homer in the third, State scored four more in the fifth inning and one in the seventh. The next day Tulane's Ron Scott drove in 5 runs as the Greenies got back in the Western Division title hunt by defeating the Dogs 9-6. Scott's three-run homer in the third inning was the key blow as it put Tulane up 4-0. The Green Wave scored 5 more runs over the last six innings to keep the charging Dogs at bay. The Bulldogs scored their 6 runs as Portera went 3 for 5 at the plate, Beasley hit a two-run homer, and Don Bell went 3 for 4. Bell now had 14 hits in his last 18 plate appearances. MSU now stood 11-5 overall and 6-2 in the SEC, which tied them for first in the league with Ole Miss. Tulane was still in the hunt for the divisional title with a 4-2 conference mark.

After being rained out on Monday, State had to play LSU a pair of seven-inning games in Baton Rouge Tuesday, April 19. The Bulldogs swept LSU in the doubleheader. Ken Tatum won the first game 9-1, helped along by Gary Washington and Russ Gatlin's three-run homers. Washington collected four hits while both Del Unser and Mike Burns each got two. The game was never a contest as State scored six runs in the first inning. In the second game Passeau gave up four hits and walked a batter while winning his fifth game of the season, 1-0. State scored its only run in the second inning as Gatlin walked and Junior Field drove him in with a single. LSU's losing pitcher Bruce Baudier gave up only two hits in the game with the second hit being a triple by Mike Burns in the seventh inning. State's record improved to 13-5 overall and 8-2 in the SEC.

On April 22 MSU played Ole Miss at the Bulldogs' home away from home Redbird Field. The Bulldogs got shut out 2-0 as the Rebels' Scotty Hasler threw a four-hitter. Hasler, a junior righthander, had five strikeouts and did not walk a batter. He retired 22 Dogs in a row between the first and ninth innings. Ken Tatum pitched a brilliant game for State, giving up six hits and only two runs but suffered his first SEC loss. Glenn Lusk led off for the Rebels in the seventh inning by singling to right field. Tatum retired the next two hitters, but then Mickey Williams got a Texas-League single that pushed Lusk to second. Hasler then hit a soft grounder back to Tatum, who overthrew first base, allowing Lusk to score. With two out in the Rebels' ninth, Hasler added insult to injury by hitting a solo home run to close out the scoring. After the game State and Ole Miss were virtually tied for the division lead as the Bulldogs had an 8-3 (.727) mark and Ole Miss was 7-2 (.777). The table was turned the next day as MSU posted a 2-1 victory. In the bottom of the ninth inning with the score tied 1-1 Rebel relief pitcher Russ Johnson faced MSU's George Paton, who had hit a homer to tie the score in the fifth inning. The bases were loaded and on a 3-1 count Johnson threw a ball that resulted in a walk and what today would be called a walk-off win for the Bulldogs. State claimed the outright lead in the division with a 9-3 record while Ole Miss dropped to 7-3. The Bulldogs had four conference games left on their schedule and the Rebels had six. The two teams would meet again in the last series of the season in Oxford.

MSU had a two-game series with Memphis State scheduled for Redbird Field April 25 and 26. The game slated for April 25 was washed out and the teams were scheduled to play a doubleheader the next day. Wet grounds prevented play on the twenty-sixth, too, and the series was canceled.

On April 29 State moved closer to a division title by beating Tulane 10-3 in Columbus. Ken Tatum went the distance, giving up 7 hits and 3 runs. The victory brought Tatum's record to 6-2. State's batsmen banged out 18 hits as Portera led the way with 3 followed by Unser with 2 and Bell with 2. The game scheduled for the next day was canceled because of rain. MSU stood 10-3 in the conference, which gave them a two-game lead in the Western Division over Ole Miss, who lost to Alabama and stood 7-4 in the conference.

Mississippi State lost a two-game series to Memphis State beginning May 2 in Memphis. The Tigers prevailed in both games by the score of 3-2. The series would end MSU's competition against nonconference teams for the remainder of the regular season. The Bullies stood 14-5 overall and 10-3 in the conference.

On May 6 with Ken Tatum hurling a five-hitter, striking out 9, and walking 3, MSU dashed Ole Miss's hopes for SEC honors by defeating the Rebels 6-1 in Oxford. The victory clinched State's second consecutive SEC Western Division title. State banged out 12 hits including home runs by Del Unser and Gary Washington. Both homers came off Rebel starter Scotty Hasler, who had shut the Dogs on April 22. Tatum retired 18 straight Rebel hitters from the second to the eighth inning. The next day an entirely different story unfolded. The Rebels shut out the Bulldogs 5-0 as Russ Johnson threw a no-hitter. Rebels pitchers didn't throw another no-hitter until 2019 when four pitchers combined to turn the trick against Arkansas Pine Bluff in a game won by the Rebels 25-0. State's starting pitcher James Carroll went seven innings and gave up 7 hits, 5 runs, struck out 10, and issued 5 walks. The Rebels' Chet Bergalowski went 2 for 4 at the plate, hit a home run, and drove in 2 runs. Glenn Lusk also hit a homer and drove in 2 runs. The win pushed the Rebels' record to 10-6 in the SEC, which was good for second place in the Western Division. MSU finished the regular season 17-9 overall and 11-4 in the conference. MSU would next face Tennessee, which had won the Eastern Division for the overall SEC championship.

On May 11 the Bulldogs took on the Volunteers in Knoxville in the first game of the SEC championship series. Tennessee went into the series with six regulars hitting above .300 and a .316 team batting average. Senior pitcher Ken Tatum picked up his eighth victory against only 2 losses as the Bulldogs defeated the Vols 7-4. Tatum, who had won both of State's games in the 1965 playoffs against Auburn, gave up 8 hits, 3 of them in the ninth inning, in earning his third playoff victory. State batters produced 10 hits with leading hitters Del Unser, Don Bell, Gary Washington, and Mike Burns each registering 2. Singles by Washington and Unser and a wild pitch put a run on the board in the first inning. One hit and two Tennessee errors allowed State to score 3 unearned runs in the second inning. By the ninth inning Tennessee had cut the lead to 1 by scoring 2 runs in the fourth inning and 1 in the eighth. In the top of the ninth, State got some insurance. Del Unser drove in a run with a single, and Gary Washington doubled to drive in 2 more runs. Tennessee scored a run in the ninth so the run Unser drove in at the top of the inning was the winner.

Rain washed out the game scheduled for May 13 in Redbird Park. It was a good thing it did rain, for it gave Ken Tatum two days to rest. Tatum took the mound May 14 and over nine innings gave up 6 hits, 3 runs (2 earned), struck out 8, and walked 3 as MSU pounded Tennessee 9-3. The Volunteers contributed greatly to their defeat by committing five errors. Although the Bulldogs got 16 hits, **none** of their 9 runs were earned. Coach Paul Gregory did not make a single substitution in the game. That's understandable because he had Tatum on the hill and other players were fielding their positions well (one error) and knocking the cover off the ball. Seven MSU players got multiple hits including Tatum, who got 2.

Mississippi State University was the 1966 SEC baseball champion. This was the fourth time MSU had won the SEC baseball playoff, more than any other school. Redbird Park had been good to the Bulldogs; they had won two SEC championships, playing all their home games in Columbus.

It was on to Gastonia, North Carolina, where MSU would be joined by Florida State, North Carolina, and East Carolina in the NCAA Regional III Tournament June 2. In first-round play MSU defeated FSU 4-3. Winning pitcher Ken Tatum (who else?) gave up 10 hits and 3 runs over six innings. Del Unser (who else?) got the key hit as his home run with Don Bell on base in the third inning put the Dogs up 2-0. State scored single runs in the fourth and fifth innings and, although FSU scored 3 runs in the sixth, the Bulldogs never trailed. Claude Passeau took over for Tatum in the seventh inning with runners on second and third. Passeau politely shut out the Seminoles the rest of the game. In a sterling relief performance, Passeau struck out 1, walked 1, and gave up 1 hit over the last three innings.

The Bulldogs advanced to the winners' bracket where they played a North Carolina team that had defeated East Carolina 7-1. The Tar Heels eked out a victory over MSU by outhitting the Dogs 11-5 and outscoring them 5-4. Frank Chambers took the loss as he pitched 5 1/3 innings, giving up 7 hits and 3 runs (only one earned) while striking out 4. Chambers also hit a solo home run and State scored single runs in the third, fourth, fifth, and eighth innings. The loss set up another matchup with FSU, who had beaten East Carolina. Both teams were fighting to get out of the losers' bracket to get a shot at North Carolina in the finals. State's bats fell almost completely silent and the Seminoles defeated and eliminated the Dogs. State managed only 3 singles while FSU pounded out 10 hits and scored 7 runs. Claude Passeau was the loser, going 7 innings giving up 9 hits, 6 runs, walking 2, and striking out 7. Moving on to the finals FSU won the first game against North Carolina 6-5, forcing a second game, which the Tar Heels won 6-4 to claim the championship and move on the College World Series.

The Bulldogs finished the season 20-11. It had been an outstanding year for MSU baseball as the postseason awards show. Paul Gregory was again named SEC Baseball Coach of the Year. Del Unser was named All-SEC and All-American; Ken Tatum and Don Bell were named All-SEC. Frank Portera and Gary Washington were All-SEC, Western Division.

Ken Tatum should have been an All-American in 1966. He was the Bulldogs ace, posting key win after key win and finishing with a 10-2 record. Like Del Unser, Tatum would go on to have a productive major league career. Tatum was used almost exclusively in the majors as a relief pitcher. Over a six-season career (which was shortened by a line-drive hitting him in the face), he pitched for the California Angels, Boston Red Sox, and Chicago White Sox. He won 16 games, lost 12, had 52 saves, and posted a career earned run average of 2.93.

Three members of the 1966 team have been inducted into the Mississippi State M Club Alumni Hall of Fame: Frank Chambers,

Ken Tatum, and Del Unser. Unser has also been inducted into the Mississippi Sports Hall of Fame. Ken Tatum should be in the Mississippi Sports Hall of Fame. Without Tatum, MSU would have two fewer SEC baseball championships.

How Did the Other Teams Fare?

1966 Mississippi State Basketball

The hope for a better 1965–66 basketball season that existed at the end of the 1964–65 season actually materialized. The inexperienced sophomores had become experienced juniors. Putting an end to a streak of two straight losing seasons, first-year coach Joe Dan Gold posted a respectable 14-11 overall record that included a 10-6 SEC mark. Considering the disarray of the program during Babe McCarthy's final season in which the Dogs went 10-16 overall and 6-10 in the conference, Gold's first season was a resounding success. MSU went from a losing record to a winning record both overall and in the conference. In total the Bulldogs went from six games under .500 overall to three games over, and in SEC play from four games under .500 to four games over, quite an achievement.

The top eight players on Gold's squad were senior Paul Smith; juniors Gary Washington, John Sapen, Herb Biggs, Buddy Walden, and Charlie Crews; and sophomores Dave Williams and Tom Payne. The juniors, who had been through the fire as sophomores, were greatly improved. They combined to average 41 points and 26 rebounds a game. But MSU's star was sophomore center Dave Williams, who averaged 20 points and 10 rebounds a game. Opponents had outscored and outrebounded MSU the year before. This season the Dogs in total outscored their foes 1,866 points to 1,828, an average of fewer than 2 points a game. But they outrebounded them 1,170 to 1,028, an average of nearly six rebounds a game. Eleven of MSU's 25 games were decided by 5 or fewer points. The Bulldogs' rebounding played a huge part in their success. Perhaps the success off the boards was a reflection of their coach. Joe Dan Gold had been a super rebounder for his size.

In SEC play State defeated Auburn, LSU (twice), Tennessee, Georgia, Florida, Tulane, Ole Miss (twice), and Vanderbilt. The Bullies came up short in SEC games against Tulane, Alabama (twice), Georgia, Florida, and Kentucky. The Bulldogs' 10-6 SEC mark placed them third in the 12-team SEC. Coach Joe Dan Gold was off to a good start.

1966 Mississippi State Football

Paul Davis's Mississippi State football team compiled a very disappointing 2-8 record in the fall of 1966. The Bulldogs did not win a conference game as their two victories came against Southern Mississippi and Richmond. MSU simply could not generate much offense. The Bulldogs average 87 yards per game rushing and 99 yards passing. How bad was the offense? The Dogs scored only 75 points in 10 games, which placed them 113th out of 116 teams in major college football. The competition scored a total of 176 points, averaged 161 yards rushing and 118 yards passing, and scored 18 points per game. The defense was much better than the offense; it ranked 68th out of 119 in the country. There were no impressive numbers associated with this team's offensive performance. Andy Rhodes was the leading rusher; he gained 295 yards on 75 carries. The leading passer was Don Saget, who completed 69 of 166 passes for 753 yards and 2 touchdowns.

The 1966 Bulldog football team posted MSU's worst record since the 1949 team went 0-8-1. It would prove to be the last State team coached by Paul Davis. It is easy to understand why Davis was fired. Over five years Paul Davis's SEC record was 9-22-2, and six of his SEC wins came in the first two years of his tenure. He would be replaced in 1967 by Charles (Charlie) Shire, who promptly posted a 1-9 record and did not win a single conference game.

1966 Ole Miss Basketball

Coach Eddie Crawford's 1965–66 Rebels won one more basketball game than they had in 1964–65 while playing two fewer games. So, there was some improvement in Ole Miss's dismal basketball program, but not much. The 1964–65 Rebels had gone 4-21 while the 1965–66 squad improved to 5-18, 2-14 in the SEC, which put the Rebels in the cellar. The Rebs' only SEC wins came against Tulane and LSU (which ended up sharing the SEC cellar with Ole Miss). The three other wins came against non-major competition: Arkansas A&M, Louisiana Tech, and Southern Mississippi. The team's three leading scorers, Mickey Williams, Chuck Burhorn, and Ronnie Aldy, combined to average 33 points a game. The three leading rebounders, Mickey Williams, Chuck Burhorn, and Fred Stanley, combined to average 23 rebounds a game. These numbers were not competitive in the SEC. Simply put, Coach Crawford's fourth season at the helm of Ole Miss basketball was a disaster.

1966 Ole Miss Baseball

Ole Miss played 32 baseball games in 1966, the most the Rebels had ever played in a single season. Coach Swayze had suffered only his third losing season the year before, going 10-13 overall and 8-7 in the conference. This year would be different as the Rebs went 18-14 overall and 10-6 in the SEC, which was good for second place behind Mississippi State in the Western Division. The 10 SEC victories came against Auburn, Alabama (2), Tulane (3), Mississippi State (2), and LSU (2). Four of the Rebels 14 losses came against powerhouse Florida State, the same team that eliminated SEC champion Mississippi State from the NCAA District III Tournament.

The Rebs had their share of season highlights and outstanding performances. All-SEC Scott Hasler was the Reb's leading pitcher, posting a 7-1 record and a brilliant 1.50 era. Senior Russ Johnson ended his distinguished career by no-hitting Mississippi State and finishing with a career 12-1 record. Johnson's no-hit gem was the fourth Rebel no-hitter in history. All-SEC, All-NCAA District III, and All-American shortstop Jimmy Yawn broke several team records while hitting .409. Chet Bergalowski joined Hasler and Yawn on the 1966 All-SEC team.

Coach Swayze would continue to produce excellent teams and would climb back to the SEC championship in 1969.

1966 Ole Miss Football

The 1966 Ole Miss football season holds especially delightful memories for me. I graduated from Ole Miss in May 1964 but returned in 1966 to work on an MBA under the USAF Bootstrap program. During my undergraduate days, which included the football seasons 1960–1963, the Rebels won 36 games, lost 3, and tied 3. The Rebels' SEC record was 16-2-1 and Johnny Vaught's chargers won three SEC championships. Ole Miss went to the Sugar Bowl three times winning against Rice and Arkansas and losing to Alabama. The Rebs also went to the Cotton Bowl once, where they lost to Texas. Two of the 3 losses Ole Miss experienced during my undergraduate days were in major bowls.

I was not at Ole Miss for the 1964 and 1965 football seasons. During those seasons the Rebels' football fortunes took a dip as they went 12-5-1 overall and 8-7-1 in the conference. I was hoping for a resurgence in Ole Miss football upon my return to campus. Although the Rebels did not dominate like they did in my undergraduate years, they bounded back strong with an overall 8-3 record, a 5-2 conference mark, and an appearance in the Bluebonnet Bowl, where they lost to Texas. During my time as an Ole Miss student the Rebels won 88 percent of their games by going 43-6-2. May such times return.

Before a capacity crowd of 50,160 at Memphis Memorial Stadium on September 17, 1966, Johnny Vaught began his twentieth year as the head football coach of the Ole Miss Rebels. Memphis State had never beaten Ole Miss in 20 tries, and Vaught's team saw that the streak was extended to 21 with 13-0 win over the Tigers. The Rebels' junior quarterback Jody Graves sneaked over the goal line from the one-yard line early in the second quarter and Jimmy Keyes added the extra point. The Rebels scored twice more against a stubborn Tiger defense as Jimmy Keyes kicked two field goals. The Rebel defense was even more stubborn than the Tigers' as Memphis managed only two first downs in the first half. The Tigers tacked on five more first downs in the second half but the third one didn't come until there were only 10 minutes left in the game. Late in the game the Tigers got their passing game going and made four consecutive first downs while moving to the Rebels' 27-yard line where they were stopped cold. The Rebels won the numbers game with a 14-7 advantage in first downs, a 205-87 advantage in rushing yardage, and 51-31margin in passing yardage. Rebel fullback Bobby Wade was the offensive star as he gained 111 yards on 21 carries.

The *Jackson Daily News*'s Lee Baker captured the real story of the game by writing: "Johnny Vaught's big strong boys up front—Jim Urbanek, Jimmy Keyes, and Dan Sartin flanked by Marvin McQueen and Johnny Richardson and backed by Lee Garner and Mac McClue—simply kept the pressure on all the way until the victory was certain."

Riding a two-game win streak against the Rebels, Kentucky showed up at Mississippi Memorial Stadium in Jackson to play Ole Miss September 24. Two years earlier, on September 26, 1964, the Wildcats had defeated the number-one-ranked Rebels 27-21 in the same stadium. The Rebels were still smarting from that most unexpected defeat on Mississippi turf and showed it as they shut out the visitors 17-0. The two touchdowns were scored in the first half, one by Jody Graves on a 7-yard run and the other by Don Street on a 3-yard run. Jimmy Keyes booted two extra points and a field goal in the third quarter that hit the crossbar but bounded over. Doug Cunningham was the offensive star, rushing from his tailback position for 111 yards on 17 carries. The defense led by the same players who had stymied Memphis State the week before simply overpowered the Wildcats. The only real threat that the Kentucky offense produced came on their first drive and that was halted when Bruce Dillingham intercepted a pass at the Rebel 14. Dillingham returned the ball 42 yards and with Cunningham doing the heavy lifting Graves was soon in the end zone with the game's first score. Thirty-seven thousand fans watched the Rebels gain their second shutout win and their first SEC victory of the season.

Paul "Bear" Bryant brought his Crimson Tide team to Mississippi Memorial Stadium October 1 to face Johnny Vaught's Rebels, and 46,500 fans filled the stadium. The Ole Miss defense held the Tide scoreless the first 29 minutes and 20 seconds of the game, but the Rebel offense sputtered the whole first half. Over the course of the game Alabama's Ken "Snake" Stabler completed 16 of 19 passes for 144 yards, with 9 of those aerials going to Mississippian Ray Perkins of Petal, who gained 94 yards and scored a touchdown. The Rebels outgained the Tide on the ground 126 yards to 81 and managed 13 first downs to the Tide's 10. But the Rebels lost the passing statistics by 47 yards and by giving up 3 interceptions. Rebel starter Jody Graves completed only 1 of 5 passes and had 2 of his throws picked off. Bruce Newell replaced Graves and completed 12 of 23 passes and suffered 1 interception. Down 14-7 with 6 minutes to play the Rebels started a drive for a tying touchdown from their 8-yard line. The drive was snuffed out when Dicky Thompson intercepted a Newell pass at the Rebels' 33 and returned it to the 8. Three plays later Bama kicked a field goal: final score Alabama 17, Ole Miss 7. Rebel miscues, penalties, interceptions, and a lost fumble doomed their chances and led to their first SEC loss of the season.

This was the third straight time an Ole Miss team coached by Johnny Vaught lost to an Alabama team coached by Paul Bryant. Vaught's Rebels lost the 1964 Sugar Bowl 12-7, the 1965 regular-season game 17-16 in Birmingham, and now the 1966 game 17-7. Those three games were brutal defensive struggles as Alabama outscored the Rebels a total of only 16 points.

Things didn't get any better the next week as Ole Miss traveled to Sanford Stadium in Athens, Georgia. The Rebel offense struggled mightily as the Rebels lost to the Georgia Bulldogs 9-3. Ole Miss led early when they scored first after defensive end Steve McQueen recovered a fumble at the Bulldogs' 28-yard line. After three plays gained 6 yards, Jimmy Keyes kicked a 39-yard field goal. However, Ole Miss made only one first down in the entire first half and could never manage another point. The *Clarion-Ledger*'s Wayne Thompson summed up the Rebels' performance as only a Mississippi writer could:

> To put it too plain, the Rebel offense was as shiny and polished as a gob of Mississippi mud with only partial streaks of brilliance breaking through in some surprising and inconsistent moments.
>
> That Rebel defense so highly touted and talented in most cases, did break down for one brief period in the second period as the Bulldogs drove in a sputtering sort of fashion—for the lone touchdown of the game with fullback Ronnie Jenkins barely getting over from the one.

It is a wonder the score was as close as it was. Georgia picked off four of Bruce Newell's passes and one of Jody Graves's. The Rebel defense did not intercept a single Georgia pass. Here's how badly the five interceptions hurt the Rebels: Ole Miss punted only three times while Georgia was forced to punt nine times. With a 2-2 record and both losses coming against SEC teams, the Rebels faced a real challenge over their last six games, four of which would be against SEC foes. But Johnny Vaught and his coaching staff of mighty men were still coaching the Rebs and things could change.

A nonconference battle against Southern Mississippi in Oxford October 15 produced a hard-fought 14-7 homecoming victory. With 7:22 left in the game the Rebels trailed the visitors 7-0. Three minutes and 21 seconds later the Rebels led 14-7. Doug Cunningham returned a punt 58 yards for the first 6 points, and Jimmy Keyes added the extra point. On the Rebels' next possession Cunningham finished a 54-yard drive with a 1-yard plunge into the end zone; Keyes again added the extra point. The Rebel defense stood tall the whole game. USM's only touchdown came in the first quarter after a bad snap resulted in a blocked punt, which the Southerners recovered on Ole Miss's 4-yard line. Quarterback Gary Bourgeios subsequently scored from the 1-yard line on a sweep around right end. Twenty-five thousand fans witnessed the homecoming victory in Hemingway Stadium on a perfect fall day.

The game was an anomaly in that seven quarterbacks participated, three for Ole Miss and four for USM! Each team made one first down in the first half. USM made only one first down in the second half, but the Rebel offense perked up a bit and recorded 7. Total yardage for the game—Ole Miss 244, USM 98. Union University once punted 18 times against Ole Miss in a game played before WWII. Southern Miss nearly matched that total as the Southerners punted 17 times. What a game! Sporting a struggling offense and a sterling defense the Rebels now stood 3-2 on the year. Always-dangerous Southern Miss should never have been scheduled as a homecoming foe; ask Alabama.

Wayne Thompson, who had a Mississippi way with words, wrote: "To be perfectly truthful, for the first three periods both offensives had shown the most nothing since West Texas and the next time such futility will be approached will be when someone attempts to swim the Pacific with a gin fan."

On October 22, Ole Miss trekked to Memphis Memorial Stadium to play their last scheduled nonconference game of the season against Houston. Relatively speaking, this encounter proved to be a breeze. The Rebels posted their highest point total to that point in the season and defeated the outmanned Cougars 27-6.

It was back to SEC play October 29 and a 17-0 victory against LSU in Tiger Stadium at Baton Rouge. This shutout of the Tigers was almost as sweet to me as the 15-7 victory over LSU in the same stadium in 1962. The Rebels were on a three-game win streak and stood 5-2 on the season. The Tigers, who stood 3-2-1 at the time, were never really in the game. In the first quarter Bruce Newell connected with fullback Bobby Wade for a 75-yard pass-run touchdown, and Jimmy Keyes kicked the extra point. In the same quarter Keyes booted a 35-yard field goal. The Rebels' final score came with 2:47 left in the game as Newell threw a 32-yard touchdown pass to end Hank Shows. The Tigers' only real scoring threat came in the fourth quarter, and it was snuffed out at the Rebels' 6-yard line where Jerry Richardson recovered Frank Matte's fumble. The Tigers made 13 first downs, the Rebels 6, and LSU gained 213 total yards to Ole Miss's 206. Again, the Rebel defense stood tall when it needed to and the offense scored when it had the opportunity. The most important statistic of the game was fumble recoveries—Ole Miss 3, LSU 1.

SEC play continued November 12 against the Tennessee Volunteers in Knoxville. The year before Ole Miss had defeated the Vols 14-13 in Memphis. I was still relishing the Rebs' 1965 game that my wife, Dorothy, and I had watched on television from Eglin AFB, Florida, with Tennessee graduates John and Pat Crockett. That had been quite a win for Ole Miss and I was hoping for another one, this time on the Vols' home field by a more comfortable margin.

Tenth-ranked Tennessee sported a 5-2 record and was favored over the Rebels. The matchup in Neyland Stadium packed with 55,206 fans produced another victory for the Rebels as Ole Miss extended its win streak to four games with a 14-7 victory. This was the eighth straight time Vaught's Rebels had beaten Tennessee. Victories over the Vols at Knoxville once so rare for the Rebels were becoming commonplace.

The statistics would indicate that Tennessee should have won the game going away. The Vols led in first downs 24-9 and nearly doubled the Rebels' yardage from scrimmage 311-160. Tennessee's outstanding quarterback Dewey Warren threw 37 passes and completed 21 while the Rebels' Bruce Newell completed only 4 of 7. But one of Newell's completions was the key to the Rebs' only touchdown drive. With 24 seconds left in the half Newell finished an 11-play 64-yard drive by connecting with Bill Matthews for a 22-yard touchdown. The Rebels' second touchdown came when Bobo Uzzle and Jerry Richardson hit Warren, who was attempting to pass. The ball squirted out, Richardson caught it and proceeded 60 yards for a touchdown. The Vols' only touchdown came on a 98-yard drive that ended with 5 seconds left in the game.

Tennessee's head coach Doug Dickey had this to say:

> Ole Miss played defense when it was supposed to play it—inside its own 20-yard line. We got in scoring position as many times as I thought we would, but we just couldn't score . . . Our team played well but we made a few mistakes . . . Ole Miss is an outstanding football team just as we expected.

It was back to Mississippi Memorial Stadium in Jackson November 19 as the Commodores of Vanderbilt ventured into the Magnolia State for their annual drubbing by the Rebels. Ole Miss did not disappoint as they defeated Vandy in a 34-0 blowout. Vanderbilt gained a total of 136 yards to Ole Miss's 363. Thirty-four was the most points the Rebs had scored all year, and the shutout was the fourth that the Rebel defense had mustered in nine games. Just over 10,000 fans showed up for this game that started in a pouring rain. With his usual wonderful way with words the *Clarion-Ledger*'s Wayne Thompson captured the whole occasion:

> In a game that wasn't decided until the band had finished its damp rendition of the National Anthem, the Ole Miss Rebels rolled at will to completely overwhelm the Vanderbilt Commodores by a 34-0 count at Memorial Stadium Saturday afternoon.

The Egg Bowl, played November 26 at Hemingway Stadium on the Ole Miss campus, was witnessed by about 30,000 fans. The Ole Miss defense posted its fifth shutout of the season as the Rebels prevailed over Mississippi State 24-0. The Rebels' victory capped a six-game winning streak and boosted Ole Miss's regular-season record to 8-2 that included a 5-2 SEC slate. Speaking of the Rebels recovery from a 2-2 start, Coach Vaught said, "This team staged the best 'comeback' of any I have ever coached."

The game was simply no contest as the Rebel defense limited the Bullies to 2 net yards rushing and 42 total yards for the game. The

Rebels accumulated a total of 341 yards and led State in first downs 23-6. The Rebel victory was tarnished by the loss of tackle Dan Sartin, a bright star in Ole Miss's outstanding defense. Sartin went down in the third quarter with a broken foot. Jimmy Keyes pushed his SEC record for consecutive extra points to 35 as the reliable Rebel kicked three to move the bar higher. Keyes also broke Robert Khayat's Ole Miss record for total points scored kicking by booting two field goals to bring his two-year total to 85. Khayat had scored 82 over a three-year period.

There was one impressive statistic about Mississippi State's performance. Marcus Rhoden returned four punts for 62 yards, 20 more than the Bulldogs gained by rushing and passing combined. Rhoden's total return yardage for the season increased to 572, which set a new SEC record for return yardage in a season.

The Bluebonnet Bowl played in Houston on December 17 didn't go well for the Rebels, who were favored by 6 ½ points, but lost 19-0. The offense completely malfunctioned, and the defense gave up a whopping 19 points, the most scored against the Rebs all year. Three Rebel drives, to the Longhorns' 16-, 25-, and 27-yard lines, were stopped by the Texas defense with pass interceptions. Another Rebel drive came to a halt at the Longhorn 7-yard line when Don Street was stopped inches short of a first down. Meanwhile, Texas was breaking Bluebonnet Bowl records. The Longhorns' Chris Gilbert rushed for 156 yards on 26 carries, both bowl records, and scored two touchdowns. Gilbert's fellow sophomore Bill Bradley added 107 yards on 20 carries. (Sartin was sorely missed.) Game statistics tell the sad story well: Texas led in first downs 17-7 and total yardage 378-208. Both teams suffered four interceptions and Texas lost three fumbles. The Rebels had ample chances to score but the offense was unable to capitalize.

Here are a few gems from Wayne Thompson's account of the game in the *Clarion-Ledger*:

> Chris Gilbert and Bill Bradley, a pair of dazzling sophomores, made Ole Miss's vaunted defense look as valuable as a treaty with the Russians . . .

> Ole Miss, which had fewer moments of glory than a calf born dead with two heads, . . .
>
> Then came one of the most-costly penalties since original man and his mate were banned from Paradise for attempting to add fresh fruit to their diet.

Despite the bowl loss the Rebels ended the season with an 8-3 record and exciting days lay ahead—a redhead from Drew, Mississippi, would show up on the Ole Miss campus the next fall.

THE JIMMIES AND JOES

Chapters 1–9 documented how Ole Miss and Mississippi State athletes won 12 SEC championships during the period 1959–1966 under the tutelage of outstanding coaches. But even outstanding coaches do not win championships without outstanding players—Jimmies and Joes. During that era there were many, and I do mean many, outstanding athletes who wore red and blue and maroon and white on the basketball court, baseball diamond, and football field. This chapter features three of the superstars as representatives of all of the Jimmies and Joes who contributed to the championship years 1959–1966. The three men chosen, one representing each of the big three sports, were not only great players they were and are great men also, loved and respected by their coaches, teammates, and Mississippians.

Basketball—Bailey Howell

The most important recruit of Mississippi State's legendary coach Babe McCarthy's career and in the history of Mississippi State basketball was Bailey Howell. The Middleton, Tennessee, High School All-American who graduated from MSU in 1959 is still recognized as perhaps the greatest basketball player in school history. In his three varsity seasons Howell scored a record 2,030 points, set records for the most points scored in a game (47), and the most rebounds collected (34). He led the SEC twice in points per game. During his sophomore year the 6'7" forward averaged 26 points and 20 rebounds as the Maroons finished with a 17-8 record. Howell's junior year saw the Maroons win 20 games and lose only 5. Howell's individual numbers reflected his greatness that season as he averaged 28 points and 16 rebounds. Howell's senior year topped off the most remarkable basketball career in MSU history. He averaged 28 points and 20 rebounds as the Bulldogs went 13-1 in the SEC and 24-1 overall.

Howell was All-SEC in each of his three varsity seasons. He was named SEC Sophomore of the Year in 1957 and SEC Most Valuable Player in 1958 and 1959. He was INS All-American in 1958 and AP All-American in 1959. Although Howell played only three seasons, he still holds numerous MSU records. In addition to the number of points and rebounds in a single game (47 and 34, respectively), he holds the record for career scoring (27) and rebound (17) averages, single season and career rebounds, single season free throws attempted and made, and single game free-throw percentage. Howell did all his scoring before the college game included the 3-point field goal or the shot clock. He was excellent close to the basket with a picture-perfect hook shot but he could also drain long-range jumpers. Howell's sophomore year field-goal percentage (57) led the country in that extremely important metric. Nevertheless, the quality of Howell's college performance is probably best reflected in MSU's won-loss record during his career, 64-14.

A great coach, Babe McCarthy, and a great player, Bailey Howell, led Mississippi State to the school's first SEC basketball championship in 1959. As explained in chapter 2, MSU declined the SEC champion's automatic bid to the NCAA Basketball Tournament because integrated teams participated in the tournament. Thus, the great Bailey Howell and his teammates were denied the opportunity to test their skills against the country's best.

The Detroit Pistons made Howell the second player chosen in the 1959 National Basketball Association draft. Over his remarkable 12-year NBA career Howell played for the Pistons, the Baltimore Bullets, the Boston Celtics, and the Philadelphia 76ers. He played in 950 NBA games, averaged scoring 19 points and 10 rebounds per game, and was selected as an All-Star six times. His teams made the NBA playoffs 10 times. He played in 86 playoff games and averaged 16 points and 11 rebounds in those games. Dick Vitale, the famed ESPN basketball analyst, has called Howell the greatest offensive rebounder ever. At the end of his career Bailey Howell was ranked in the top 10 in 9 out of the NBA's 10 statistical categories.

Howell was an integral part of the Boston Celtics when they defeated the Los Angeles Lakers for the1968 and 1969 NBA titles. In the 1968 championship series, which the Celtics won 4 games to 2, Howell averaged 21 points and 8 rebounds. He averaged 11 points and 5 rebounds in the 1969 championship series, which the Celtics won 4-3.

Bailey Howell was inducted into the Mississippi State University Sports Hall of Fame in 1971, the Mississippi Sports Hall of Fame in 1977, the Tennessee Sports Hall of Fame in 1981, the Naismith Basketball Hall of Fame in 1997, and the College Basketball Hall of Fame in 2006. Since 2005 the best high school basketball player in Mississippi has been awarded the C-Spire Howell Trophy.

As noted above, the Mississippi State University 1959 SEC basketball champions did not participate in the NCAA Basketball Tournament. An unwritten agreement between the state legislature and state-sponsored schools prevented those schools' athletic teams from playing integrated teams. Later events would show that Bailey Howell had no trouble playing with or against African Americans. Howell excelled in the NBA where black players had been welcomed since 1950. When Howell joined the Detroit Pistons in 1959, Earl Lloyd, the first black man to play in the NBA, was finishing up his nine-year professional career as a member of the Pistons. Lloyd became Howell's mentor and they became lifelong friends.

Howell married Mary Lou Jackson in 1964 and they have two grown daughters, Beth Hansen and Anne Strickland. Beth is the CEO of the Mississippi Association of Realtors, and Anne is married to Scott Strickland, the University of Florida's athletic director and former MSU athletic director. When Howell retired from the NBA, he returned to MSU and completed his master's degree in physical education. He soon went to work for Converse Shoe Company, where he has enjoyed a successful business career. Howell still lives in Starkville and is very much involved in Mississippi State athletics as a mainstay of the Bulldog Club, which raises money to support MSU sports.

Basketball seemed to come easy for Bailey Howell. He had exceptional natural athletic ability and was very coachable. One writer seems to have captured what were his most important characteristics as a player and person: "He is probably most known for his hook shot, rebounding ability, and work ethic as a player and person."

Baseball—Don Kessinger

Don Kessinger is the best athlete these old eyes have ever seen up close and personal. I got a real opportunity to appreciate his athletic ability when we played against each other in intermural flag football at Ole Miss; nobody could even touch him. Donald (Donnie) Eulon Kessinger was a classmate of mine during our undergraduate years at Ole Miss (1960–1964). We had a few classes together, but he has no reason to remember me. On the other hand, I remember him vividly because of the almost unbelievable athletic skills he displayed when he played both basketball and baseball for Ole Miss.

When I was an 18-year-old freshman, my two roommates and I liked to talk about high school sports. Early in the fall semester I was bragging about Larry Smith and Doug Hutton. They were the best high school athletes I had ever seen. Smith graduated from Jackson Central one year before me. Standing 6'4" and weighing about 200 pounds, Larry Smith was simply a great high school athlete as he starred in football, basketball, baseball, and track. Central was in the old Big 8 Conference and simply put Smith had dominated in four sports at the highest level of Mississippi high school athletics. He was something else. Upon graduating from Central, Smith signed with Ole Miss to play football and he was beginning the first of his three varsity years as a halfback for some of Coach Johnny Vaught's best teams. Another great athlete I had followed in high school was Doug Hutton, who was a freshman basketball player at Mississippi State in the fall of 1960. Hutton was a baseball and basketball player at Clinton High School and he had won a state basketball championship there in 1960. I attended the state championship game in the old Jackson City Auditorium, and it is something I will always remember. Hutton scored 54 points and completely dominated the game.

After I had waxed eloquent about the excellence of these two athletes, roommate Hulon Lowe chimed in about Jim Dunaway, who was beginning his outstanding varsity career as a tackle for Ole Miss. Dunaway was from Columbia, Mississippi, not far from Lowe's home in Foxworth. Hulon knew Dunaway personally and assured us that he was a super athlete—a judgment that proved to be accurate.

Then Ralph Abraham chimed in, and for the first time I heard the name Donnie Kessinger, who was from Forrest City, Arkansas. Abraham, who had played football against Kessinger in Arkansas, basically told us that Kessinger was a much better athlete than Smith, Hutton, and Dunaway. According to Abraham, Donnie was a tall skinny kid but he was close to being Superman. Abraham reported accurately that Kessinger came to Ole Miss to play basketball and baseball, but he had been named a high school All-American as a football quarterback. Describing several of Donnie's high school exploits Abraham tried to convince us that this Arkansas boy we had never heard of was superior to our Mississippi high school favorites. We weren't buying, but Abraham turned out to be right.

Both Larry Smith and Doug Hutton had good college careers but neither played professionally. Dunaway was an All-American at Ole

Miss and had a long professional career with the Buffalo Bills and the Miami Dolphins. While he was with the Bills, he went to four Pro Bowls and was once named All-Pro. He also earned a Super Bowl championship with the undefeated 1972 Dolphins. Dunaway was indeed an outstanding athlete, but he was simply no match for Kessinger in overall athletic ability.

In the fall of 1960, the NCAA prohibited freshmen from playing varsity sports, but many schools fielded freshman teams that played limited schedules in football, baseball, and basketball. When basketball season arrived, Donnie Kessinger suited up for the Rebels' freshman team. I was fortunate enough to witness most of the home games played by that team. To me the most remarkable part of the freshman phenom's game was his unconventional jump shot. He was the first player I ever saw jump high and kick his legs while in the air to launch jump shots. The kick gave this skinny kid the power to shoot accurately anytime he was within 25 feet of the basket. I thought that jump shot was a thing of beauty.

Donnie led the Rebels in scoring averaging 24, 22, and 21 points per game during his three varsity years, which ended with the 1963–64 season. His career average of 22 points per game over 70 games still ranks fourth on the Rebels' all-time scoring list. Kessinger scored in double figures in 33 consecutive games. Donnie is only seventh on the field-goals attempted list with 1,411. Although he often cut that amazing jump shot loose from long range, he shot 43 percent from the field. He also made 82 percent of his free shots. There was no three-point field goal in those days and had there been Kessinger's average would no doubt have been significantly higher because he often shot and connected from downtown. He made 612 field goals over 70 games and in my opinion at least a fourth of those (153) would have been three pointers. Adding 153 to the 1,553 points he is credited with yields 1,706 or a 24 average. He would have no doubt averaged three 3-pointers a game and I think his average would have actually been north of 25 points. During his varsity years Kessinger set 18 Ole Miss basketball records. He was named All-SEC three times and All-American in 1964.

Although he would no doubt have excelled in the NBA, Kessinger's heart and future lay in baseball. This Arkansas boy came to Ole Miss to play baseball for Coach Tom Swayze. During his varsity years 1962 through 1964, Kessinger played shortstop in spectacular fashion. In 82 games he hit .400, stole 44 bases, and drove in 55 runs. The Rebels posted an overall record of 58-24, including a 31-16 SEC slate. The 1964 Ole Miss team won the Western Division of the SEC, the overall SEC championship, the NCAA District III playoffs, and advanced to the College World Series, where they lost to Southern California and Arizona State. Kessinger was All-SEC each of his varsity seasons and he was All-American in 1964. He was also All-NCAA District III in 1962 and 1964.

Known as Don rather than Donnie in his professional baseball career, Kessinger spent 16 years in the major leagues playing for the Chicago Cubs, the St. Louis Cardinals, and the Chicago White Sox. He ended his major league career in 1979 serving as player-manager for the White Sox. Playing shortstop, the most important defensive position, Don once held the National League record for the most consecutive errorless games, 54. Kessinger led the league in double plays four times and was a career .965 fielder. He made the National League All-Star Team six times and started four All-Star Games. He was the National League Gold Glover winner at shortstop twice.

In his second full year as a Cub, Kessinger became a switch hitter under the tutelage of the famed manager Leo Durocher and batting coach Alvin Dark. Never a power hitter, he posted a respectable career .252 lifetime batting average while hitting 16 home runs. In 7,651 at bats he struck out only 759 times. While usually hitting at the top of the order he scored 899 runs and drove in 527. Don averaged 8 stolen bases a year and finished his career with 100 stolen bases. The stolen base numbers are intriguing because of his quickness and foot speed but I think there is a simple explanation. He was a singles hitter followed in the batting order by power hitters that could drive him in from first base. Also, his managers liked to play "big ball," which produces high-scoring innings, rather than "small ball," which is more likely to produce low-scoring innings. There is always a risk of being thrown out stealing and when that occurs, a low-scoring inning is likely.

Although I had a few classes with Donnie and have admired him as an athlete and person since 1960, I remember having only one conversation with him before interviewing him for this book. That conversation, which I'm sure he doesn't remember, took place in a hotel lobby in Chicago in the late 1970s when he was playing for the St. Louis Cardinals. I was in the city to present a continuing education program for the National Association of Accountants. To my surprise I saw Kessinger in the hotel lobby and as he was walking in the other direction I called out "Donnie." He turned around smiling and walked toward me. When he heard a southern accent calling him Donnie, he probably thought that whoever had that voice was from Arkansas or Mississippi. The first thing he asked me was what I was doing in Chicago and why I recognized him. I told him why I was there and that we were classmates at Ole Miss. He was delighted to see another Rebel. We had a short chat about old times.

Upon retiring from baseball Don returned to Oxford and his family has been in the real-estate business there ever since. He was head baseball coach for Ole Miss from 1991 to 1996 compiling a 185-183 record. His 1995 squad was the first Rebel team to record 40 victories in a season, and it advanced to the finals of the NCAA Regional Tournament held at Florida State. Two of Don and Carolyn Kessinger's sons, Keith and Kevin, played baseball at Ole Miss and Keith played basketball for the Rebels. Both sons signed to play professionally and Keith "had a cup of coffee" in the majors, playing in 11 games for the Cincinnati Reds in 1993. Kevin suffered an injury that limited his professional career to two games in the minors.

Don graciously agreed to allow me to interview him in early 2018. As one would well imagine, he has some great stories to tell. I asked Don why he went to Ole Miss rather than Arkansas out of high school. He said that Arkansas did not field a varsity baseball team at that time and that Ole Miss's Tom Swayze was known to be an outstanding coach and Oxford was fairly close to his home in Forrest City, Arkansas. Wise choice. He went on to say that Coach Swayze was great at teaching fundamentals and that during his professional career coaches told him he was the best player fundamentally that they had ever coached.

We talked about the Cubs' 1969 season that saw them leading the league most of the summer but ending up losing the divisional championship of the National League East by 8 games to the Miracle Mets. The Mets trailed the Cubs by 10 games on August 14. Don pointed out that the Mets had played really great baseball down the stretch to win the race. The New Yorkers played .776 ball, winning 38 of 49 games from August 14 to the end of the regular season. During that same period the Cubs won only 18 of 45 games for a .400 winning percentage. During September the Cubs suffered through a horrendous 8-game losing streak.

The Kessinger name is still very much associated with Ole Miss baseball. Keith Kessinger is an outstanding color commentator teamed with David Kellum on the radio broadcast of Rebel games. In 2019 Grae Kessinger, Kevin's son, was a junior at Ole Miss and the Rebels' starting shortstop. Patriarch Don Kessinger was honored at the 2017 SEC baseball tournament as an SEC Baseball Legend. Don still holds the Ole Miss records for season and career batting averages, .436 and .400. Kessinger has been inducted into numerous halls of fame including the Mississippi Sports Hall of Fame. In 2000 Kessinger was named an SEC Basketball Legend and in 2017 he was named and SEC Baseball Legend. Has any other person been honored by the SEC in basketball and baseball as legends?

Football—Jeremiah Dean (Jake) Gibbs

Jake Gibbs came to Ole Miss in the fall of 1957 from Grenada, Mississippi. Jake had been an outstanding high school quarterback and baseball player. As a freshman he stood in line behind two other outstanding quarterbacks, senior Raymond Brown and junior Bobby Franklin. Brown led the SEC in passing in 1956 and in total offense in 1957. Bobby Franklin was the starter on the outstanding 1958 and 1959 Ole Miss teams. Franklin was named MVP of the Gator Bowl in 1959 and the Sugar Bowl in 1960. It is easy to see why Gibbs had to wait his turn to be the starter, but he soon made his own very large mark.

It seemed that the Rebels stockpiled excellent quarterbacks in those heady days. The 1957 freshman team boasted 13 members who had played quarterback in high school. Jake Gibbs wasn't the starting quarterback on the freshman team. He started his climb to the top with a good performance during spring practice of 1958. On the varsity that fall Gibbs mostly watched as Bobby Franklin led the Rebels to an 8-2 record. Franklin was injured in the second game of the 1959 season against Kentucky. Gibbs became the starting quarterback and the rest is history. The Rebels finished the 1959 regular season with a 9-1 record, the only blemish being the 7-3 loss to LSU on Billy Cannon's 89-yard run-back of a Gibbs punt. Led by a recovered Bobby Franklin (two touchdown passes) and Gibbs (one touchdown pass), Ole Miss went on to defeat LSU 21-0 in the January 1, 1960, Sugar Bowl rematch to revenge the dreadful loss to LSU.

Like most Rebel fans of my generation I vividly remember the 1959 Halloween loss to LSU. I was planning to be a freshman at Ole Miss the next fall and I was already a dedicated Rebel fan. There was no TV coverage and my dad and I listened to the game on the radio while hanging on every word. My heart sank to the depths twice during the game, when Gibbs punted to Cannon on third down and when LSU stopped Doug Elmore on fourth and goal from the one-yard line on the Rebels' next possession. The Rebels dominated the game statistically but were too conservative on offense. As a boy of 17 I thought that Johnny Vaught trusted his defense too much in that game. Well, maybe he did and maybe he didn't. How good were Gibbs and the 1959 Ole Miss Rebels? The defense gave up only 21 points in 11 games while the offense scored 350 points.

While sharing the load with Bobby Franklin and Doug Elmore, Gibbs finished the 1959 season as the SEC's total offense leader accounting for 983 yards, 755 passing and 228 rushing. He was also responsible for 13 touchdowns, more than anyone else in the conference. The Associated Press rightfully named the 1959 Ole Miss Rebels the SEC Team of the Decade. An interesting factoid about this team is that of the 39 players that suited up for the 1960 Sugar Bowl, 33 were Mississippians.

Jake Gibbs was the undisputed number-one quarterback during the 1960 season in which the Rebels compiled a 10-0-1 record. The tie came in the October 29 televised game against LSU in Oxford. Gibbs had incurred leg injuries the previous week in a 10-7 game against Arkansas. With LSU leading 6-3 and 1:25 remaining in the game, Jake limped onto the field. Starting at the Rebels' 21-yard line, Gibbs methodically led the Rebs down the field by completing two passes to Bobby Crespino, one to Jerry Daniels and one to Ralph "Catfish" Smith. Gibbs called timeout with time expiring and the ball resting on LSU's 25-yard line. Coach Vaught sent in center Richard Ross and place kicker Allen Green. Ross snapped the ball to Gibbs, who held as Green kicked a 44-yard field goal that tied the game and preserved the Rebels' undefeated season and the SEC championship. The Rebels defeated Rice 14-6 in the 1961 Sugar Bowl and Gibbs was named the game's outstanding player. At the end of the regular season the Rebels were ranked number two in the nation behind the number-one Minnesota Gophers by the wire services. Minnesota went on to lose 17-7 to Washington in the Rose Bowl. After the bowls, the Football Writers of America voted Ole Miss the number-one team in the country and named the Rebels winners of the Grantland Rice Award.

Jake Gibbs was named first-team quarterback on nine All-American teams after the 1960 season and he was named SEC Back and Player of the Year. Gibbs was the first Ole Miss Rebel quarterback to be named All-American. He finished third in the Heisman voting. He is now a member of both the Mississippi Sports Hall of Fame and the College Football Hall of Fame. Jake was later named by *Sports*

Illustrated as the eighth-best collegiate quarterback of the modern-day era. In 2006 Gibbs was one of 12 Southeastern Conference Football Legends honored before Arkansas played Florida for the SEC football championship.

Tom Siler, sports editor of the *Knoxville-Sentinel*, captured Jake's greatness after the Rebels defeated Tennessee 24-3 on November 12, 1960. Siler wrote:

> It is doubtful if Tennessee fans ever saw a more competent triple-threater on Shields-Watkins Field. Go as far as you like . . . name one better . . . George Cefego? Dixie Howell? Charles Trippi? Frank Sinkwich? Hank Lauricella? John Majors? Babe Parilli?
>
> Leaf through the bright pages of football history, Southern style, and tell me a better package—passer, runner, kicker, defensive agent—than Jeremiah Dean Gibbs.

I doubt that Siler had many takers.

Jake also played and coached a little baseball. Playing third base for the Rebels during the 1959, '60, and '61 seasons, he compiled a career .384 batting average and flashed great arm strength. Gibbs was named All-SEC in baseball all three years. The 1959 and 1960 Ole Miss teams won SEC championships but did not advance to the NCAA playoffs because of the state's segregation policy. Gibbs was named All-American in baseball in 1960 and 1961. Signed as a "Bonus Baby" by the New York Yankees in 1961, he spent 10 years with the Yankees organization as a catcher, thanks to that great arm. Over a 10-year period, Jake played in 538 major league games. His best year was 1970 when he hit .301. He finished his career with seven broken bones and a .233 batting average.

With the retirement of Coach Tom Swayze, Gibbs returned to Ole Miss in 1971 as head baseball coach. In 1972 Jake's first team advanced to the College World Series. During Gibbs's 19-year coaching career, the Rebels won two SEC titles (1972 and 1977) and three SEC Western Division titles (1972, 1977, and 1982). When he retired from coaching in 1990, Gibbs had compiled a 486-389-9 record and was the winningest baseball coach in Ole Miss history. Gibbs returned to the major leagues for the 1993 season serving as the Yankees' bullpen catching coach. He also managed the Yankees' Class A league Florida State League team during the 1994 and 1995 seasons.

Jake was a senior when I was a freshman and I never got to know him personally or to talk to him. I knew him only by reputation and that reputation was that Jake Gibbs is not only a great athlete, he is also a great person. Since first hearing his name I have only heard good things about Jake Gibbs. My son Clint played baseball with Jake's son Monte Gibbs when I was a faculty member at Ole Miss 1977–1979. I remember talking baseball briefly with Jake at one of our sons' baseball games. The only thing I remember about that conversation is that Jake was very pleased that major league players had won free agency. Free agency gave the players financial leverage they had lacked since the beginning of Major League Baseball. That is why all major-leaguers are extremely well paid today.

In 2012 the SEC started honoring former baseball players who had excelled on the diamond by naming a small group of SEC Baseball Legends. Jake Gibbs was a member of the group so honored in 2014. I believe that Jake Gibbs is the only athlete that has been honored as both an SEC Football Legend and an SEC Baseball Legend.

Note that both Don Kessinger and Jake Gibbs have been named SEC Legends in two sports. I doubt that any other SEC university can boast that they have had two graduates so honored.

Jake was a member of the Ole Miss Seniors Golf Group, and I joined the group in 2014. We have played as members of the same foursome twice. I found Jake very personable and fun to play with. Once when we were about to tee off on the par-3 sixteenth hole on the Ole Miss golf course, I told Jake, "If you will hit your tee shot within 2 feet of the hole, I'll go up there and knock it in." Jake promptly hit his first shot within 18 inches of the hole, and I walked to the green and tapped it in despite the fact that it was a "gimme." I also remember a conversation about Ole Miss football with Jake that took place at the golf course. We were discussing the Rebels' chances of winning an upcoming game, and both of us thought those chances were not really good. I said something to the effect that while I was an Ole Miss student fans always expected to win. Jake said that the players always expected to win too (they usually did). Jake hedged a little about LSU, saying they were always the toughest team the Rebels played. Jake finished 1-2-1 (includes the 1960 Sugar Bowl) against the Tigers (3 of those games were played in Louisiana). I finished 3-1-1 against LSU over my four years as an undergraduate and my one year in graduate school.

The Teams

This chapter has featured great individual players as representatives of all of the Jimmies and Joes who played for Mississippi State and Ole Miss when the two schools ruled the SEC. But championships in basketball, baseball, and football are won by teams, not individuals. It seemed appropriate to feature a specific team to honor all of the teams that won SEC titles during that period. Choosing a single team to feature proved too difficult. I soon realized that I could not choose from all of the 12 championship teams. All of the championships were team efforts. The exploits of all of them are chronicled extensively in chapters 2 through 9. Nevertheless, it still seemed to be appropriate to write about the importance of team play in winning championships.

The solution was to feature the only group of athletes who won all three SEC championships they had an opportunity to win. Those players started their varsity careers during the 1960–61 basketball season and played on the 1961, 1962, and 1963 Mississippi State SEC championship teams. Their coach, Babe McCarthy, stressed teamwork. As has been shown in the narratives about those years the championships were unquestionably the results of superb teamwork. It should also be noted that the athletes who played varsity baseball for Ole Miss from 1959 to 1961 won two of three possible SEC championships.

The same is true for the athletes who played varsity football for the Rebels from 1961 to 1963. The Mississippi State baseball players, who represented the Bulldogs on the diamond from 1964 to 1966, also won two of three possible championships.

Thanks to Babe McCarthy's recruiting, Joe Dan Gold, Leland Mitchell, Bobby Shows, and W. D. "Red" Stroud joined Mississippi State's varsity basketball team in the fall of 1960. None of these players was a superstar like the great Bailey Howell, who led State to its first SEC basketball championship in 1959. Yet, by winning back-to-back-to-back SEC championships, their teams achieved something no other Mississippi State (or Ole Miss) team has ever accomplished. The 1961 team finished 19-6 overall and 11-3 in the SEC and claimed the conference title. In 1962 the Bulldogs finished 24-1 overall and 13-1 in the SEC and copped MSU's second consecutive conference championship. In 1963 MSU won its third consecutive SEC title. The 1963 team is remembered for more than its 22-6 overall record and its 12-2 conference mark. That team broke the color barrier and went to the Mid-East NCAA Regional Basketball Tournament where they finished third.

Sophomores Joe Dan Gold, Leland Mitchell, Bobby Shows, W. D. Stroud, and Mack Whyte had a lot of experienced help when MSU won the SEC championship in 1961. Nurturing the pups along were their senior captain Jerry Graves and junior guard Jack Berkshire, both of whom were starters along with Gold, Mitchell, and Stroud. Graves averaged 21 points and 10 rebounds, while Berkshire, a highly skilled guard and defensive player, averaged 7 points a game. During the 1959–60 season, without Gold, Mitchell, Shows, Stroud, and Whyte, the Maroons finished 12-13 overall and 5-9 in the conference. It was the incoming sophomores who provided the boost that resulted in a 19-6 overall record and an 11-3 SEC mark that won a conference championship the very next year. The three sophomore starters—Gold, Mitchell, and Stroud—combined to average 36 points and 20 rebounds a game.

Jerry Graves graduated in 1961, but the valuable Jack Berkshire was still around to provide senior leadership as captain of the 1961–62

Maroons. Berkshire started alongside Gold, Mitchell, Stroud, and either Bobby Shows or Gene Chatham at center. This SEC championship team would finish 24-1 overall and 13-1 in SEC play. Those marks would match Coach McCarthy's 1958–59 great team for MSU's best basketball record ever. Two newcomers—sophomores Doug Hutton, who averaged 10 points per game, and Stan Brinker, who contributed 6 points per game—also made significant contributions during that great season. Again, Gold, Mitchell, and Stroud led the way combining to average 46 points and 18 rebounds a game.

Mack Whyte did not play his senior year, but Gold, Mitchell, Shows, and Stroud were still around to lead the Bulldogs to their third consecutive SEC championship. The 1962–63 contingent finished 22-6 overall and 12-2 in the SEC. As described in chapters 1 and 6 this team not only won the SEC title, they destroyed the color barrier for college teams supported by the State of Mississippi. Mitchell, Stroud, Gold, Hutton, and either Shows or Stan Brinker usually started for that team. The big three—Mitchell, Gold, and Stroud—showed out all season, combining to average 47 points and 21 rebounds per game.

Doug Hutton contributed a great deal during two of the three seasons that teams led by Gold, Mitchell, Stroud, and Shows dominated the SEC. In an August 2019 interview with Hutton I said that it appeared to me that those championship teams won big because the players worked so well as a team. That is, there were no superstars, but good players, great coaching, and real teamwork produced the championships. Hutton agreed. He said that Babe McCarthy was a great coach who never got the recognition he deserved and that all the players understood and readily accepted their roles as team players. Doug used an experience he had as a sophomore on the 1961–62 team to illustrate what he meant. Senior Jack Berkshire was the team captain and a starting guard. Berkshire sustained an injury that sidelined him for a couple of games and Hutton was thrust into the starting lineup. Doug had two outstanding games scoring more than 30 points. When Berkshire was well again, Coach McCarthy inserted him back in the starting role and Hutton went back to coming off the bench. Doug said he felt no resentment and in fact thought that was the way it should have been handled. Berkshire was a senior, he was a sophomore, and Berkshire had more than earned the privilege of starting. That type of thinking makes for good teammates and good teamwork, which combine to win ball games and championships.

It also seems appropriate to take a closer look at the four individual players who played on the three consecutive SEC championship teams.

W. D. "Red" Stroud" is the most decorated. The Forest, Mississippi, native who stood 6'1" scored 1,116 points and averaged 15 points per game over his MSU career. He also made 83 percent of his free throws. By one or more organizations he was named All-Conference in each of his varsity years, third team in 1961, and first team in 1962 and 1963. He was also named the Sugar Bowl Basketball Tournament Most Valuable Player and SEC Most Valuable Player in 1962. In 1962 he was named All-American by three organizations, first team by Coach & Athlete, second team by Converse, and third team by the Helms Foundation. In 1963 he was named second-team All-American by Converse. Stroud was remembered by his teammates as a quite unassuming country boy. He was drafted by both the US Army and the Boston Celtics in 1963. Stroud served in the army but returned to basketball in 1966. He played semi-pro basketball for the Florida Sportsmen, for which the former MSU star scored 77 points in one game. He also played for the American Basketball Association's New Orleans Buccaneers during the 1967–68 season. After his playing days were over Stroud coached high school basketball in Scott County and Morton High School. He was inducted into the MSU Sports Hall for Fame in 1989 and the Mississippi Sports Hall of Fame in 1990. Stroud was named an SEC Basketball Legend in 2001. The Redhead beloved by all MSU fans was 66 years old when he died of leukemia on March 22, 2008.

Leland Mitchell from Kiln, Mississippi, was a 6'4" power forward who combined great scoring and rebounding skills. Over his 78-game MSU career he scored 1,219 points and averaged 16 points per game. He also secured 705 rebounds, averaging 9 boards a game. During his sophomore year Mitchell was MSU's second-leading scorer and rebounder behind the great Jerry Graves. Mitchell led the team in both scoring and rebounding during his junior and senior years. After his basketball career, which included a short stint in the American Basketball Association, Mitchell became a real-estate developer and eventually held properties in Mississippi, Alabama, and Tennessee. Mitchell lived in Starkville where he died at the age of 72 on July 6, 2013. He was inducted into the MSU Sports Hall of Fame in 1986. The writer can't understand why he has never been inducted into the Mississippi Sports Hall of Fame or named as an SEC Basketball Legend. Without Leland Mitchell, Mississippi State University would have three fewer SEC basketball championships.

Joe Dan Gold, who stood 6'5", scored 947 points and pulled down 616 rebounds during his varsity years at MSU, averaging 12 points and 8 rebounds per game. The Bulldogs posted a 65-12 overall record and a 36-6 SEC mark during his time on the varsity. He was named third-team All-SEC in 1963. The respect that his coaches and teammates had for this native of Benton, Kentucky, is reflected by the fact that he was named team captain his senior year. Gold also coached MSU basketball from 1965 to 1970, compiling a 51-74 record. He later coached at Paducah Community College and Mercer University before finishing his career as a high school administrator. Joe Dan Gold died April 14, 2011, at age 68. He was inducted into Mississippi State's Sports Hall of Fame in 1996 and was recognized as an SEC Legend in 2003. For his invaluable contributions to MSU's three consecutive SEC basketball championships, Joe Dan Gold should be, but is not, in the Mississippi Sports Hall of Fame.

Bobby Shows, a 6'7" center/forward, was a fourth member of the class that Babe McCarthy signed in 1959. The Brookhaven product scored 276 points and pulled down 325 rebounds in the 57 games that he played. Shows did not play much as a sophomore mainly because the great Jerry Graves was still the Bulldogs' center as well as their leading scorer and rebounder. That season he averaged only 3 points and 3 rebounds a game. During his junior and senior years Shows got much more playing time and he shared the rebounding load with

Leland Mitchell, Joe Dan Gold, and Stan Brinker. He pulled down an average of 7 rebounds a game his junior year and 6 his senior year. Although he was never a great scorer, he averaged 6 points a game as a junior and 5 points his senior year. As chapters 4–6 show, Bobby Shows made significant contributions in several key games that were instrumental in securing victories for MSU basketball as the team marched to three consecutive SEC championships. Shows earned both a baccalaureate and master's degree from MSU and then became an ordained minister. He served as director of athletics in Southern Baptist churches in Mississippi, Louisiana, and Missouri and held a staff position with the Missouri Baptist Convention. Shows was the founder and director of Sports Crusaders Ministry. He also continued his involvement with basketball as a coach and a referee. Robert Carroll (Bobby) Shows died September 12, 2017, and his funeral was held in the First Baptist Church of Brookhaven.

AFTERWORD

This book documents how Ole Miss and Mississippi State dominated the Southeastern Conference in basketball, baseball, and football for an eight-year period, 1959–1966. Since 1966 there has been no eight consecutive-year period during which Ole Miss or Mississippi State won at least one SEC championship in basketball, baseball, or football.

During the 53 years since 1966, the Rebels and Bulldogs have been more successful in baseball than any other sport. Ole Miss has won SEC baseball championships four times, 1969, 1972, 1977, and 2009 (tie with LSU). Mississippi State has won baseball championships seven times, 1970, 1972, 1979, 1985, 1987, 1989, and 2016. The Rebels and the Bulldogs did combine to win four consecutive SEC baseball titles from 1969 to 1972, Ole Miss 1969 and 1972, and MSU 1970 and 1971. Since the SEC Baseball Tournament was instituted in 1977, Ole Miss has won three tournament championships, 1972, 2006, and 2018, while Mississippi State has won seven, 1979, 1985, 1987, 1990, 2001, 2005, and 2012. Over the years only LSU, which has won 9 overall and 11 SEC Baseball Tournament titles, has been more successful than Mississippi State in baseball.

Since 1966 Mississippi State has won two SEC basketball championships, 1991 (tie with LSU) and 2004. Ole Miss still has not won an SEC regular-season basketball title. Since the SEC Basketball Tournament was revived in 1979, Ole Miss has won it twice and MSU has won it three times. From 1992 through 2011 the SEC was divided into an Eastern Division and a Western Division for basketball. The Western Division was made up of Alabama, Auburn, Ole Miss, Mississippi

State, LSU, and Arkansas. During divisional play, Ole Miss won the Western Division three times, 1997, 1998, 2001, and tied Mississippi State for the title twice, 2007 and 2010. In addition to the two ties with Ole Miss, Mississippi State won Western Division titles outright four times, 1996, 2003, 2004, and 2008. The Bulldogs also tied Arkansas for the title in 1995. During the twenty years the divisions existed, Ole Miss and Mississippi State won or shared the title nine times. Arkansas won the title three times and tied MSU once. LSU won the title three times and tied Alabama once. In addition to tying LSU once, Alabama won the title twice. Auburn won the title once. It is fair to say that during divisional play the Mississippi schools, Ole Miss and Mississippi State, excelled in SEC Western Division basketball.

Neither Ole Miss nor Mississippi State has won an SEC football championship since the Rebels won the title in 1963. In 1998 Mississippi State won the Western Division title but fell to Tennessee 24-14 in the SEC championship game. In 2003 Ole Miss tied LSU for the Western Division championship, but LSU held the tiebreaker because the Tigers defeated the Rebels 17-14 during the regular season.

During the 53 years since 1966 Ole Miss and Mississippi State have won the following: baseball championships: Ole Miss 4, Mississippi State 7; basketball championships: Ole Miss 0, Mississippi State 2; football championships: Ole Miss 0, Mississippi State 0.

Total number of outright SEC championships in the big three sports in 53 years: 13. This is only one more championship than Ole Miss and MSU combined to win during the 8-year period focused on in this book, 1959–1966.

It should be noted that over the same 53-year period, Ole Miss and Mississippi State did combine to win 10 SEC baseball tournaments. They also won the SEC basketball tournament championship 5 times. The Bulldogs and Rebels also won or tied for the SEC Western Division basketball title 10 times. In football MSU tied for one Western Division championship and Ole Miss tied for one.

While researching this book I noted that there has been another eight-year period during which two schools from the same state won

12 SEC championships. From 1971 to 1978, Alabama won 7 football titles and 3 basketball titles (2 ties), and Auburn won 2 baseball championships. The Mississippi championships between 1959 and 1966 were better distributed.

SOURCES

Foreword

Websites

Associated Press
courier-journal.com
lib.msstate.edu
meridianstar.com
misstate.edu
olemisssports.com
nola.com
theundefeated.com
upress.state.ms.us
wtva.com

Chapter 1. The Coaches

Books

Midnight Train. Jim Weatherly and Jeff Roberson. Yoknapatawpha Press (2018).
The Mississippi Encyclopedia. University Press of Mississippi (2017).
Mississippi State Yearbooks—*Reveille* (1959–1967).
Ole Miss Rebels, Mississippi Football. William W. Sorrels and Charles Cavagnaro. Strode Publishers (1976).
Rebel Coach. John Vaught. Memphis State University.
University of Mississippi Yearbooks—*Ole Miss* (1959–1967).

Websites

baseball.almanac.com
baseballhall.org/hall-of-famers
cfbhall.com
clarionledger.com/archives

collegebasketballexperience.com/hall-of-fame
egrove.olemiss.edu/yearbooks
hailstate.com (Media Guides)
hottytotty.com
kingfish1935.blogspot.com (Jackson Jambalaya)
laprogressive.com
loyolaramblers.com
lib.msstate.edu/specialcollections/collections/archives/studentpubs/
magnoliastatelive.com
mississippitoday.org
msfame.com
olemisssports.com (Media Guides)
remembertheaba.com/Kentucky-Colonels
secsports.com

Interviews

Warner Alford
Doug Hutton
Don Kessinger
Frank Montgomery

Newspapers

Daily Mississippian (Ole Miss Student Newspaper Archives Ole Miss Library)
The Reflector (Mississippi State University Student Newspaper Archives MSU Library)

Chapter 2. 1959: The Beginning of Great Things

Books

Mississippi State Yearbooks—*Reveille* (1959–1967).
Ole Miss Rebels, Mississippi Football. William W. Sorrels and Charles Cavagnaro. Strode Publishers (1976).
Rebel Coach. John Vaught. Memphis State University.
University of Mississippi Yearbooks—*Ole Miss.*

Websites

clarionledger.com/archives
collegebasketballexperience.com/hall-of-fame
egrove.olemiss.edu/yearbooks

hailstate.com (Media Guides)
hottytotty.com
lib.msstate.edu/specialcollections/collections/archives/studentpublications
mississippitoday.org
msfame.com
olehottytoddy.com
olemisssports.com (Media Guides)
secsports.com
secsportsfan.com
sports-reference.com

Newspapers

Daily Mississippian (Ole Miss Student Newspaper Archives Ole Miss Library)
The Reflector (Mississippi State University Student Newspaper Archives MSU Library)

Chapter 3. 1960: Another Banner Year

Books

Mississippi State Yearbooks—*Reveille* (1959–1967).
Ole Miss Rebels, Mississippi Football. William W. Sorrels and Charles Cavagnaro. Strode Publishers (1976).
Rebel Coach. John Vaught. Memphis State University.
University of Mississippi Yearbooks—*Ole Miss.*

Websites

clarionledger.com/archives
egrove.olemiss.edu/yearbooks
hailstate.com (Media Guides)
hottytotty.com
lib.msstate.edu/specialcollections/collections/archives/studentpublications
msfame.com
olemisssports.com (Media Guides)
secsports.com
secsportsfan.com
sports-reference.com

Newspapers

Daily Mississippian (Ole Miss Student Newspaper Archives Ole Miss Library)
The Reflector (Mississippi State University Student Newspaper Archives MSU Library)

Chapter 4. 1961: Another Championship, Basketball Rising

Books

Mississippi State Yearbooks—*Reveille* (1959–1967).
Ole Miss Rebels, Mississippi Football. William W. Sorrels and Charles Cavagnaro. Strode Publishers (1976).
Rebel Coach. John Vaught. Memphis State University.
University of Mississippi Yearbooks—*Ole Miss*.
Wizard of Odds. Charley Rosen. Seven Stories Press (2001).

Websites

clarionledger.com/archives
egrove.olemiss.edu/yearbooks
hailstate.com (Media Guides)
hoopshall.com/hall-of-fame/jack-waters
lib.msstate.edu/specialcollections/collections/archives/studentpublications
msfame.com
olemisssports.com (Media Guides)
rebeljackwaters.blogspot.com
secsports.com
secsportsfan.com
sports-reference.com

Interviews

Doug Hutton
Don Kessinger
Frank Montgomery
Larry Wagster

Newspapers

Daily Mississippian (Ole Miss Student Newspaper Archives Ole Miss Library)
Nashville Banner (December 1960)
The Reflector (Mississippi State University Student Newspaper Archives MSU Library)

Chapter 5. 1962: Maybe the Best Year in Mississippi Sports History

Books

Mississippi State Yearbooks—*Reveille* (1959–1967).
Ole Miss Rebels, Mississippi Football. William W. Sorrels and Charles Cavagnaro. Strode Publishers (1976).
Rebel Coach. John Vaught. Memphis State University.
University of Mississippi Yearbooks—*Ole Miss.*

Websites

clarionledger.com/archives
egrove.olemiss.edu/yearbooks
hailstate.com (Media Guides)
hoopshall.com/hall-of-fame/jack-waters
lib.msstate.edu/specialcollections/collections/archives/studentpublications
msfame.com
olemisssports.com (Media Guides)
secsports.com
secsportsfan.com
sports-reference.com

Magazine

Sports Illustrated, October 2, 1961

Interviews

Doug Hutton
Don Kessinger
Frank Montgomery

Newspapers

Daily Mississippian (Ole Miss Student Newspaper Archives Ole Miss Library)
Nashville Banner (December 1960)
The Reflector (Mississippi State University Student Newspaper Archives MSU Library)

Chapter 6. 1963: Two out of Three Again and History Made in the NCAA Basketball Tournament

Books

Mississippi State Yearbooks—*Reveille* (1959–1967).
Ole Miss Rebels, Mississippi Football. William W. Sorrels and Charles Cavagnaro. Strode Publishers (1976).
Rebel Coach. John Vaught. Memphis State University.
University of Mississippi Yearbooks—*Ole Miss* (1959–1967).

Websites

clarionledger.com/archives
content.time.com/time/magazine/article/0,9171,865147,00.html
egrove.olemiss.edu/yearbooks
hailstate.com (Media Guides)
lib.msstate.edu/specialcollections/collections/archives/studentpublications
olemisssports.com (Media Guides)
saturdaydownsouth.com
secsports.com
secsportsfan.com
sports-reference.com

Interviews

Doug Hutton
Don Kessinger
Frank Montgomery

Newspapers

Daily Mississippian (Ole Miss Student Newspaper Archives Ole Miss Library)
Jackson Daily News (on clarionledger.com archives)
Nashville Banner (December 1960)
The Reflector (Mississippi State University Student Newspaper Archives MSU Library)
Times-Picayune (November 1963)

Chapter 7. 1964: A Baseball Championship and Freedom to Play in the College World Series

Books

Midnight Train. Jim Weatherly and Jeff Roberson. Yoknapatawpha Press (2018).
Mississippi State Yearbooks—*Reveille* (1959–1967).
Ole Miss Rebels, Mississippi Football. William W. Sorrels and Charles Cavagnaro. Strode Publishers (1976).
Rebel Coach. John Vaught. Memphis State University.
University of Mississippi Yearbooks—*Ole Miss.*

Websites

clarionledger.com/archives
egrove.olemiss.edu/yearbooks
hailstate.com (Media Guides)
lib.msstate.edu/specialcollections/collections/archives/studentpublications
msfame.com
olemisssports.com (Media Guides)
saturdaysdownsouth.com
secsports.com
secsportsfan.com
sports-reference.com

Interviews

Doug Hutton
Don Kessinger

Newspapers

Daily Mississippian (Ole Miss Student Newspaper Archives Ole Miss Library)
The Reflector (Mississippi State University Student Newspaper Archives MSU Library)

Chapter 8. 1965: Mississippi State Baseball Climbs the Mountain

Books

Mississippi State Yearbooks—*Reveille* (1959–1967).
Ole Miss Rebels, Mississippi Football. William W. Sorrels and Charles Cavagnaro. Strode Publishers (1976).

Rebel Coach. John Vaught. Memphis State University.
University of Mississippi Yearbooks—*Ole Miss*.

Websites

baseball-reference.com/players
clarionledger.com/archives
egrove.olemiss.edu/yearbooks
hailstate.com (Media Guides)
lib.msstate.edu/specialcollections/collections/archives/studentpublications
msfame.com
olemisssports.com (Media Guides)
secsports.com
secsportsfan.com
sports-reference.com

Interview

Doug Hutton

Newspapers

Daily Mississippian (Ole Miss Student Newspaper Archives Ole Miss Library)
The Reflector (Mississippi State University Student Newspaper Archives MSU Library)

Chapter 9. Another SEC Championship and the End of an Era

Books

Mississippi State Yearbooks—*Reveille* (1959–1967).
Ole Miss Rebels, Mississippi Football. William W. Sorrels and Charles Cavagnaro. Strode Publishers (1976).
Rebel Coach. John Vaught. Memphis State University.
University of Mississippi Yearbooks—*Ole Miss*.

Websites

baseball-reference.com/players
clarionledger.com/archives
egrove.olemiss.edu/yearbooks
hailstate.com (Media Guides)

lib.msstate.edu/specialcollections/collections/archives/studentpublications
msfame.com
olemisssports.com (Media Guides)
secsports.com
secsportsfan.com
sports-reference.com

Newspapers

Daily Mississippian (Ole Miss Student Newspaper Archives Ole Miss Library)
The Reflector (Mississippi State University Student Newspaper Archives MSU Library)

Chapter 10. The Jimmies and Joes

Books

The Mississippi Encyclopedia. University Press of Mississippi (2017).
Mississippi State Yearbooks—*Reveille* (1959–1967).
University of Mississippi Yearbooks—*Ole Miss*.

Websites

baseball-reference.com/players basketball-reference.com/players
clarionledger.com/archives
egrove.olemiss.edu/yearbooks
hailstate.com (Media Guides)
hoophall.com/hall-of-famers/bailey-howell
lib.msstate.edu/specialcollections/collections/archives/studentpublications
mlb.com/player/don-kessinger
msfame.com
olemisssports.com (Media Guides)
secsports.com
secsportsfan.com
sports-reference.com

Newspapers

Daily Mississippian (Ole Miss Student Newspaper Archives Ole Miss Library)
The Reflector (Mississippi State University Student Newspaper Archives MSU Library)

Afterword

Websites

hailstate.com (Media Guides)
olemisssports.com (Media Guides)
secsports.com
sports-reference.com

INDEX

Adams, Billy Ray, 62, 67, 91, 92
Ainsworth, Sterling, 70, 77, 81, 84, 98, 103
Aldy, Ronnie, 195
Alworth, Lance, 46, 63
Anderson, Hoss, 45, 59, 61, 63, 66

Bacon, Bill, 168, 171, 172, 175, 176
Ball, Coolidge, xiv
Bell, Matty, 23
Bergalowski, Chet, 154–57, 190, 196
Berkshire, Jack, 68, 73–81, 95, 100, 101, 104
Berry, Robert, 17, 177
Bianco, Mike, 56
Blackwell, Bubba, 22
Blair, George, 45, 49, 59–62
Bluebonnet Bowl, 162, 196, 203
Bolin, Treva, 61, 65, 91
Bomquist, Denny, 57
Bragan, Bobby, 170, 173–74, 176
Brewer, Billy, 46
Brewer, Johnny, 46, 59, 62, 66
Brown, Allen, 105, 108, 115, 140, 145
Brown, Raymond, 26, 214
Brumbelow, Mark, 22
Bryant, Paul, 25, 27, 147, 148, 198
Bullock, Al, 41
Burhorn, Chuck, 195
Burkett, Roy, 17
Burns, Mike, 168–69, 172–75, 188, 190
Burrell, Ode, 112, 118, 145–46, 149–50, 164

Canale, Justin, 145, 150, 166
Cannon, Billy, 47–50
Carroll, James, 170, 186–87, 190
Chambers, Frank, 17, 170–77, 192
Chumbler, Bill, 178
Clay, Billy, 141, 182–83
Cleveland, Rick, 17, 51, 78
Coleman, Roy, xv
Colvard, Dean, 11
Conerly, Charlie, 25–27
Cothren, Paige, 58
Crawford, Eddie, 134, 150–51, 160, 180, 195–96
Crespino, Bobby, 44–45, 60–69, 215
Crews, Charlie, 178, 193
Cristil, Jack, 31
Cunningham, Doug, 166, 181, 197–99

Dabbs, Willis, 60
Dabbs, Woody, 108–9, 114
Daniels, Jerry, 68, 215
Dantone, Sammy, 66–67
Davidson, J. W. "Wobble," 59, 87–88
Davis, Paul, 113, 117, 139, 149, 164, 166
Davis, Reed, 109, 145
Day, Eagle, 26
Dennis, Mike, 140–45
Dicky, Doug, 202
Dietzel, Paul, 48, 65, 137
DiLiberto, Buddy, 143
Dill, Kenny, 144–45
Dillard, Godfrey, xiv
Dillard, Steve, 21

Donaldson, Don, 170–72
Doty, Art, 61, 63
Dowsing, Frank, xvi
Drew, Harold, 25
Drew, Red, 25
Dunn, Perry Lee, 26, 92, 105, 109, 112, 114, 127, 138–42

Edmonds, El, 76, 84, 103, 118
Edmonds, Mel, 76, 84, 101, 103–4, 118, 120, 134, 151, 180
Edwards, Don, 150, 166
Ellis, Sammy, 83
Elmore, Doug, 88, 90–92

Fisher, Sonny, 112, 150
Floyd, Lee, 128
Ford, Cecil, 140, 145
Franklin, Bobby, 26, 44, 47, 214–15
Fulton, Robert (Steamboat), 34, 75, 96, 100, 102, 128, 133
Furlow, Charlie, 112

Garner, Lee, 197
Gatlin, Russ, 168–69, 170, 175, 188
Gibbon, Joe, 19
Gibbs, Jake, 19–21, 27, 41, 44–51, 57, 60–68, 88, 91, 104, 114, 137–38, 163, 213–17
Glass, Gerald, 160
Gold, Joe Dan, 69, 74–78, 80–81, 94, 97–103, 124–26, 129–37, 160
Goodrich, Bill, 63
Graham, Bonnie, 19, 38, 42, 80, 84–87, 118
Grantham, Larry, 49–50, 52
Graves, Jerry, 38, 69, 72, 74–83, 95, 219
Graves, Jody, 183, 197, 108
Greene, Allen, 60–66
Gregory, Paul, 7–8, 14–16, 83, 149, 163, 166, 175–76, 187
Gregory, Paul, Jr., 169, 176, 186–87
Griffin, Louis, 43
Griffing, Glynn, 59, 62, 91, 92, 105, 107–8, 110, 112–15, 137–38, 163
Guy, Louis, 108–13, 115

Halbert, Frank, 88
Hall, Whaley, 88, 114, 140, 146
Hatch, Garnie, 33
Heidel, Jimmy, 105, 141, 144–45, 166, 183–84
Higginbotham, Larry, 116, 121
Hilbun, Ben, 39
Hill, Billy "Tootie," 67
Holloway, A. J., 105, 110
Howell, Bailey, 30–39, 57, 69, 205–8, 219
Howell, Jamie, 57
Hull, Charles, 31, 35–37
Hutton, Doug, 124, 127, 129–32, 135–36, 152, 160–61, 176, 209, 220

Inman, Tommy, 146, 150
Irvin, Billy Carl, 113, 165–66, 140–41, 145, 146

James, Jimmy, 182
Jenkins, Jerry, xv
Jennings, Dave, 21, 112, 152
Jobe, Don, 41
Johnson, Russell, 154–58, 173, 180, 189–90
Jones, Billy Ray, 57, 88
Jones, Jimmy, 154

Kairt, Ken, 187
Keeton, Jerry, 31–32, 36–37
Kessinger, Don, 103, 116, 118, 120–21, 127, 134, 151–52, 154–60, 180, 208–13, 217
Keyes, Bill, 152
Keyes, Tommy, 152, 154, 156, 158
Kilpatrick, Bobby, 57
Kinard, Bruiser, 51, 145
Kinard, Frank, 145
Knight, Wesley I. (Doc), 24–25, 110

Labruzzo, Joe, 143, 182
Lamb, Billy, 121
Lambert, Frank, 146
Lawson, B. W., 12
Lea, Billy Ray, 17, 105, 110, 118–19, 134, 151
Leissner, Rube, 23

Manning, Archie, xv, 163
Mattina, Rodney, 21, 140, 145
McCarthy, Babe, 4, 7–15, 29–31, 35–39, 69, 75–78, 81, 95–97, 100–103, 122, 124–27, 129–30, 134–37, 177, 206, 218, 220, 222
McClendon, Charlie, 182
McClue, Mac, 197
McGlathery, Bill, 158
McGuire, Bill, 158
Mississippi Board of Trustees of the Institutions of Higher Education, 39
Mississippi Southern College, 5, 8, 16, 21, 115, 127
Mississippi Sports Hall of Fame, 51–52, 83, 85, 92, 151, 193, 207, 213, 215, 221–22
Mitchell, Leland, 69, 74–75, 77–81, 94–95, 97–102, 124–37, 160, 219–23
Mitts, Billy, 12
Montgomery, Frank, 16–17, 116, 152
Moore, Bernie, 39
Morris, Chuck, 88, 111–12, 114
Myles, Harold, xv

Namath, Joe, 147–48
Nash, Cotton, 100, 130, 150
Netherland, Ken, 58
Newell, Bruce, 182, 198, 201
Neyland, Robert, 27, 111, 201
Nichols, Aubrey, 161
Noble, Dudy, 9, 15
Northington, Nathaniel "Nate," xiv

Page, Gene, xiv
Parker, Guy, 16, 70, 116
Partridge, Dewey, 44–45
Passeau, Claude, 169, 171–76, 187–88, 191–92
Paton, George, 58
Payne, George, xiv
Perkins, Ray, 198
Perkins, Richie, 154
Poole, Buster, 25
Porter, Don, 57
Portera, Frank, 168, 174–75, 186, 188–89, 192
Posey, Don, 161
Price, Richard, 68–69, 148
Prine, Richie, 153–56, 158–59, 173, 180

Randall, George "Buck," 107, 109, 113–14, 138–39
Reed, Jack, 19
Reed, James, xv
Reeder, Claude, 17, 120, 177
Rhoden, Bland, 166
Rhoden, Marcus, 179
Richardson, Jerry, 201
Richardson, Johnny, 197, 203
Richmann, Ivan, 33, 70
Roberts, Freddie, 21, 109, 112, 121, 138, 140, 142, 144, 145–46, 154, 156–58
Rupp, Adolph, 9, 10, 78, 130
Russell, Fred, 91, 104

Saget, Don, 194
Sartin, Dan, 197, 203
Schmidt, Francis, 23
Schreiber, Bernie, 19
Shire, Charles (Charlie), 194
Shows, Bobby, 69, 74, 94, 99–100, 103, 119, 126, 132, 160, 219–20, 222–23
Shows, Hank, 201
Siedell, Robert, 116, 121
Sloan, Steve, 148
Smith, Charlie, 173, 175–77

Smith, Ralph "Catfish," 62–63
Smith, Tad, 25
Stabler, Ken, 186, 198
Stoll, Gary, 34, 38
Street, Don, 197, 203
Stroud, W. D. (Red), 13, 74–82, 94–104, 124–33, 136–37, 160, 219, 221
Sullivan, Wes, 59, 67, 105, 110
Sumrall, Billy, 140, 154
Swayze, Tom, 17–21, 40–41, 122, 153, 155, 157–58, 179, 196–97, 211–13, 216

Tatum, Ken, 168–69, 171–75, 186–93
Terrell, Marvin, 46, 50–51, 57, 165, 199–200, 202
Thompson, Wayne, 63, 111, 139
Tuohey, Chuck, 57

University of Southern Mississippi, 4–5, 15, 127, 154
Upchurch, Robert, 145
Urbanek, Jim, 197
Usher, Ted, 31, 37
Uzzle, Bobo, 201

Vann, Thad "Pie," 115–16
Vaught, Johnny, 4, 7–8, 16–27, 43–46, 51–52, 59, 64–66, 104, 108, 110–17, 137, 139–40, 143–47, 151, 162, 166, 180–83, 196–99, 202, 204, 215

Wade, Bobby, 197
Wagster, Larry, 84–88
Walden, Buddy, 179, 193
Walker, Wade, 52, 67, 71, 83, 117
Wallace, Perry, xvi
Walters, Carl, 46–47, 97, 106, 113
Washington, Gary, 178, 187–88, 190–93
Waters, Jack, 33, 43, 76, 81, 84–86, 118
Weatherly, Jim, 26, 108–9, 112, 139–45, 148
Weaver, Mackie, 112
Weese, Norris, 26
White, Bill, 84, 87, 98
Wilkinson, Bud, 25
Williams, Ben, xv
Williams, Larry, 41, 57
Williams, Mickey, 189, 195
Williams, Richie, 129, 136, 161, 178
Wise, Jimmy, 10
Woodruff, Cowboy, 36, 44, 49
Wyatt, Bowden, 66

Yawn, Jimmy, 19, 196
Young, Glen, xv

ABOUT THE AUTHOR

Courtesy of the author

James R. Crockett is professor emeritus at the University of Southern Mississippi and adjunct professor of accountancy at the University of Mississippi. He is author of Hands in the Till: Embezzlement of Public Monies in Mississippi and Operation Pretense: The FBI's Sting on County Corruption in Mississippi, both published by the University Press of Mississippi.